ENGLAND

NIGEL BLUNDELL

PRC

This edition published in 2002 by,
PRC Publishing Ltd,
64 Brewery Road, London, N7 9NT
A member of the Chrysalis Group plc

British Library Cataloguing in Publication Data:
A catalogue record for this book is available from the British Library.

ISBN 1 856486 27 3

Printed and bound in China

Contents

INTRODUCTION 8

PART 1: THE LAND

1 GEOLOGY AND GEOGRAPHY 20
2 LONDON 32

PART 2: THE HISTORY

3 THE MYSTERY OF STONEHENGE 38
4 AGES OF BRONZE AND IRON 42
5 VENI, VIDI, VICI 48
6 THE LEGEND OF CAMELOT 62
7 THE DARK AGES 68
8 THE VIKING SCOURGE 72
9 THE DANELAW: A COUNTRY DIVIDED 78
10 THE NORMAN CONQUEST 82
11 THE PLANTAGENETS 90
12 THE MEDIEVAL PERIOD 98
13 REBELLION AND CIVIL WAR 122
14 THE TUDOR AGE 134
15 GOOD QUEEN BESS 148
16 REGICIDE AND RESTORATION 152
17 THE GEORGIAN PERIOD 158
18 VICTORIA 168
19 THE TWENTIETH CENTURY 174

PART 3: THE ARTS

20 ARCHITECTURE AND DESIGN 188
21 LITERATURE 194
22 FINE ART AND PAINTERS 230
23 MUSIC 234

PART 4: A TASTE OF ENGLAND

24 BEERS 240

PART 5: AN ENGLISH CHRONOLOGY

25 CHRONOLOGY 248
INDEX 256

Boats bobbing at anchor in Penzance harbour, Cornwall. England's most westerly big town, there is a sea link between Penzance and the Scilly Isles.

INTRODUCTION

Introduction

The creation of England's physical and social landscape as we know it today is a diverse and dramatic story. As in every history it is people and their lives over thousands of years who shape their environment and leave their mark on every fibre of their country for generations of their ancestors to discover and marvel upon.

A series of transient presences — from the time primitive humans (*homo erectus*) made their first appearance about two million years ago, through the ensuing waves of their migrating successors until the 20th century — cannot be its mystery and magic. Ancient sites still survive, ancient stones still stand and ancient signs still exist of those who walked these shores and thus designed the land and culture. We can sometimes only surmise the purpose of these treasures unintentionally bequeathed to us.

Yet much of England's intriguing canvas of changing colours, contours and scenes was determined millions of years before man's intervention. The band of limestone running from Devonshire, Dorset and Somerset through the Cotswolds, Oxfordshire and on to the North Yorkshire moors, for example, was formed 200 million years ago beneath the waters of tropical seas. The downlands of southern England are all that remain of the Great Chalk Sea which covered most of Europe 100 million years later. Countless layers of tiny, single-cell creatures collected on the sea-bed at the rate of one metre every 100,000 years. The carpet of white chalk is 500 metres (approximately 1,500 ft) thick in places.

Some 18,000 years ago all of 'Britain' down to South Wales and the Wash lay under an ice sheet, which was up to a mile thick in places. This was the Fourth Ice Age, the last in a series of glaciations which peaked every 100,000 years. South of the ice line lay a vast area of Arctic tundra, extending down as far as Bordeaux in south-west France. Beneath the ice, valleys were gouged out in the mountains of Snowdonia, whilst the hills of North England were ground smooth where the rocks were soft, or carved into jagged peaks if they were hard. Between these four Ice Ages, a new species crept across the harsh landscape — *homo sapiens*.

Palaeolithic (Old Stone Age) Man had arrived across the land-bridge which linked 'Britain' with the rest of the continent. Little is known of those very early peoples and the methods they used to forge a living from their surroundings, as most traces of them have been obscured by the effects of time and obliterated by the great glacial grindings and upheavals.

Human progress from the end of the last Ice Age presents a clearer picture. From, around 10,000 BC, man, armed with weapons fashioned from stone, stalked the migrating herds of mammoths, woolly rhinoceros and reindeer which grazed the Eurasian plains. As he became more sophisticated, he hunted many of these larger beasts to extinction. With the reduction of the plant-rich tundra, other species disappeared — leaving the two-legged human as master of the bleak lands he surveyed.

The Ages of Prehistory

Scholars divide the long span of prehistory into several ages. These dates, although only approximate, are commonly accepted divisions for the prehistory of England:

Palaeolithic or Old Stone Age:	300,000 to 8000 BC
Mesolithic or Middle Stone Age:	8000 to 2700 BC
Neolithic or New Stone Age:	2700 to 1900 BC
Bronze Age:	1900 to 500 BC
Iron Age:	500 BC to 51 BC*

It was 8,500 years ago that the remaining glaciers of the last Ice Age finally melted and swelled the grey, gloomy sea waters to an unprecedented level. Slowly, as if aware of the historic waves it was making, the sea swamped miles of marsh lands. Thus, around 6500 BC, Britain became an island.

That enforced isolation created a fresh canvas, upon which the only marks were the rudimentary settlements and tracks left by the mysterious, vanished Palaeolithic (Old Stone Age) Man. Now, with the hairy Ice Age beasts replaced by the bear, boar and wolf, the most primitive inhabitants of this land were also supplanted, by Mesolithic (Middle Stone Age) Man.

Now that the lumbering, large beasts had been eradicated, new sources of food had to be found and new ways of securing it developed. The human hunters learned to give the wild animals the chance to breed, instead of immediately slaughtering any edible creature they encountered. It made good sense for communities to have charge of their own wild herds. People discovered, too, that cereals and berries grew more plentifully on countryside cleared of dense woodland. Both newly-found ways of ensuring continued food supplies were the ancient basis for today's farming practices.

Other early inhabitants soon realised that the very sea which had cast them adrift from the rest of the world could be their friend too. Existence relied on regular fish harvests and campsites in the most prolific areas were soon set up. These included what is today the lower Bann Valley in and around Lough Neagh, in the north-east of Ireland, and the beaches of modern day Devon and Dorset, where an abundance of crab, limpet, whelks, oysters and lobsters provided a varied diet.

Up until this time, the human population of England probably numbered only a few thousand. Then came a 'population explosion'.

*51 BC was the date of publication of Julius Caesar's *Gallic Wars* and the beginning of fully recorded history in north-western Europe.

Right: *Perhaps the most potent symbol of English nationality is the country's patron saint, St George. This wall painting, at Pickering Parish Church, shows him saving a maiden from a dragon – a legend that seems to be based on adventures of the winged horse, Pegasus, in Greek mythology. The cult of St George emerged strongly in England after it was spread by Crusaders returning from the Middle East.*

From 5000 BC, Neolithic (New Stone Age) Man began arriving from the Mediterranean. These accomplished sailors and traders came in boats laden with wheat, barley and domesticated animals. They were organised farmers and undertook extensive deforestation. Their knowledge of grain growing, animal husbandry and agriculture set in motion a social revolution and their numbers grew to between 30,000 and 50,000.

This more civilised approach to living was followed in turn by greater respect of the dead — their ancestors. Neolithic man made his mark on the landscape with great ritual monuments, venerating the dead and marking the cycles of the seasons. Up to 4400 BC, bodies had been simply covered in earth. Now, following continental burial procedures, tombs which were designed to hold several bodies were built.

There were two main types of tomb: the chambered tomb, usually a rectangular box of large rock slabs (of which remains still stand at Waylands Smith in Berkshire) and a similar structure made of wood, built in areas where rock was scarce (such as at Fussell's Lodge in Wiltshire). Other larger burial sites (including Hambledon Hill in Dorset and Hazelton in Gloucestershire) were later established, the dead only being laid to rest after increasingly elaborate rituals.

Britain's landscape was now visibly changing. Two thousand years of relatively stable climate resulted in the isles being covered by broadleaf woodland. Only the highest mountains, the extreme north and the coastal dunes and marshes lacked a rich and varied range of trees.

The first trees to return after the ice were those which could survive in colder climates, such as birch, sallow and aspen. Then, over a period of several thousand years, warmer climate trees began to grow, including pine, alder, hazel and the mighty English oak. It was within these woods that settlers made bases for hunting and gathering food. These settlements had skin tents with sunken floors to give proper shelter. Sites such as those discovered at Church Hill, Findon, West Sussex, were excavated on a massive scale to gather flint for making hunting weapons and tools. Hard rock, as found at Cornwall's Lizard Peninsula, was used for making axes not only for hunting but as 'money' — exchanging the weapons for cattle and other goods. Another remote site, the Pike of Stickle summit, at the head of Langdale Valley in the Lake District, still shows indentations created by axe makers who were prepared to risk their lives for stones they believed had magical powers.

Working the land, crop growing and eating habits continued to undergo changes as the people grew more sophisticated and knowledgeable about their lands. Ploughs and draught animals were employed, taking over from simple crop cultivation using sticks. Large areas of forests were being cleared to provide greater areas for crops and herds. Farming became established as the key to prosperity and social standing, so certain cattle herders began to control neighbouring groups or tribes. These tribal leaders established ringed enclosures, such as Hambledon Hill in Dorset and Crickley Hill in Gloucestershire. Fierce rivalry broke out and settlements deemed too rich were attacked.

The diet of the native Englishman became more varied. Evidence at sites such as Runnymede, Surrey, proves that clay pots were used for storage and as cooking vessels — the latter, by 4100 BC, were used for the recently introduced continental dishes of stews and casseroles.

It was in these changing, often violent times, that perhaps England's most magical, most mystical of landmarks were created. They are what is known as 'henges', large, circular monuments developed from old enclosures, ringed with ditches. One particular site — Stonehenge in Wiltshire — is on an astonishing scale. In the following chapter we will explore its magic further. Suffice to say here that modern Britons, while marvelling at the monumental scale of the ancient site, can only guess at why and how those massive stones could have been put in place by an apparently primitive people, who at that stage had not even discovered the wheel.

It is believed that these henges were used for communal ritual. The new gods were the sun, the moon and the earth, and worship was undertaken with the accent on death being shut out from these temples. This makes sense, for by now death was no longer revered but instead feared. This fear saw communal burial places and tombs sealed off to make death, quite simply, disappear from sight. Gigantic rocks still exist at West Kennet, Avebury, in Wiltshire, 'barring' the way to tomb chambers. People no longer worshipped their ancestors in tombs filled with skulls. Similar henges were constructed at Duggleby Howe, North Yorkshire, and at Shepperton in Surrey.

Not all henges were man-made, however. Today there still exists at Castlerigg, overlooking Derwent Water in Cumbria, an imposing circle of stones left behind by the glaciers all those thousands of years ago.

What kind of people worshipped at these places? Britain was no longer home only to the ancient British migratory races who had settled there in prehistoric times. As the populations in such far-off lands as Assyria and Mesopotamia grew and land became over-farmed to feed hungry mouths, these peoples left their native surrounds. Over generations, by taking tortuous routes toward the

Above: *An aerial view of Grimes Graves showing some of the 300 collapsed flint mine-shafts; flint from here was used to meet demand for small, good-quality tools across much of southern England. Mining was one of the biggest concentrated industries of the day.*

Above Right: *Some of the shafts have been excavated and shored up, allowing them to be opened to the public. Many areas, however, remain in an unstable and dangerous state.*

Mediterranean basin, up the Danube valley and across central Europe to the shore of the Baltic and on to the North Sea, they finally found their new home in Britain.

The tiny British Isles became haven to bands of immigrant farmers whose techniques were to shape the country's agriculture. Something else was becoming vital to the life of ancient Britain around 2000 BC; a new type of metal had been discovered — bronze.

Left: *An artist's impression of a thanksgiving ceremony at Grimes Graves, a massive network of Neolithic flint mines in Norfolk.*

Above: *Arbor Low near Buxton, Derbyshire. One of the finest of northern England's henges, Arbor Low's stones lie less proudly than Avebury's but it is, nevertheless, a magnificent sanctuary set inside a bank and a ditch.*

Top Left: *A typical family group gathered beside a river at Boxgrove flint quarry, a Palaeolithic site near Chichester.*

Left: *An artist's impression of how Boxgrove Man might have looked.*

Far Left: *A reconstruction of a gathering at Avebury, one of Europe's greatest stone circles and a key religious site in the west of England. Avebury comprises two separate circles, totalling some 60 stones, with a further 100 forming a larger, irregular ring.*

Above and Right: *The stones at Avebury are thought to have been raised around 2500BC.*

Castle Rigg, northern England's most impressive stone circle, stands below the snow-capped peaks of Cumbria. Legend has it that the stones can never be properly counted.

Left: *A closer view of Castle Rigg's stones. The circle has a diameter of 34m (111ft) and contains a rectangular stone on its south-east side.*

Top: *The purpose of Silbury Hill, the largest man-made mound in Europe, is still a mystery. It is founded on a natural chalk spur and was built up to 40m (130ft) by a series of stepped layers. Carbon dating for the first phase suggests work began at around the same time as Avebury.*

Above: *The Belas Knapp long barrow in Gloucestershire; a later Neolithic style of burial, with graves set into the sides, as well as the centre, of the mound.*

Right: *An artist's impression showing the huge labour force needed for the construction of Silbury.*

PART 1: THE LAND

1 Geology and Geography

For a small country England has a very diverse landscape. From the 'backbone' of the country — the Pennines — to the soft rolling downs of the south; from the rugged coastline of the south-west to the fast eroding shores of the east, dramatic contrasts can be experienced without having to travel vast distances. Think of England's 'green and pleasant land' and what invariably comes to mind is a picture of the traditional country village with its little church, cricket ground and local pub but in truth the variations are endless. A rich geological heritage can be seen in the distinctive limestone of the Cotswolds, the flint and brick cottages of the South and the slates of Cumbria. England is bounded on the north by the Cheviot Hills and Scotland; on the south by the English Channel; on the east by the Straits of Dover (Pas de Calais) and the North Sea; and on the west by the Atlantic Ocean, Wales and the Irish Sea.

A geological study of the British Isles will reveal that the oldest rocks make the hills and mountains of the west and north with the newest forming the comparatively flat country that makes up the vast bulk of England. This relatively flat land lies south and east of a line running from Devonshire to North Yorkshire and there is a marked division between the upland and lowland areas of England. The real lowlands of England lie in the Vale of York, East Anglia and the area around the Wash with the Cambridgeshire Fens, in the valleys of the Great Ouse and the River Nene, below sea level in certain places. The low lying sand and shingle coastlands of the North Sea between the Thames and the Humber are subject to much erosion which has necessitated the construction of sea defences along many stretches.

England consists of 46 counties and shires but it is not necessary for the purposes of this book to look at them individually as they have to some extent been formed to facilitate administration. I realise this could be a provocative statement as this can be an emotive subject; try telling a Yorkshire man that his county is merely an administrative area, or a Middlesex cricket fan at Lords that his county does not exist and furthermore, at the time of writing, the powers that be have just decided that Rutland is in fact a county after all. It is far more interesting to look at specific areas of the country from a geographical and geological viewpoint to see how and why the differing landscapes and scenery were formed. To do this let us take a zig-zag journey across the country starting in the south-east which is the nearest point of the realm to continental Europe.

In the south-east corner of England the Weald covers much of Surrey, Sussex and the north of Kent. The underlying rocks of chalk, sands and clays were, in the most part, folded when the Alps were pushed up, forming a syncline under London and a dome-shaped anticline to the south. Erosion of large quantities of material in the recent geological past has created the great chalk escarpments of the North and South Downs. From vantage points on North Downs such as Box Hill the opposing scarp of the chalk forming the South Downs can be seen at a distance of approximately 40km (25 miles) away. The eastern end of the South Downs meets the English Channel at the spectacular vertical cliffs of Beachy Head whereas the North Downs constitute the famous white cliffs of Dover where they reach the coast. The soil derived from the breakdown of this calcareous stone is very fertile and is important for the many orchards and hop fields of the 'garden of England' as Kent is often called. In Canterbury stands the historic Canterbury Cathedral the site of the infamous murder of Thomas à Becket by Henry II's knights in AD 1170. The shrine to the murdered Archbishop in the cathedral was the destination of Chaucer's pilgrims as related in his famous *Canterbury Tales*.

Travelling west along the south coast we now come to the scenic county of Hampshire with its New Forest which attracts many visitors and campers in the summer months. The term forest is used here in the original meaning of hunting ground and the area contains many low lying wet areas where the peaty soil supports thick deciduous woodland with an abundance of small streams babbling through attractive glades. The pine woods of the forest to the west are on drier soils of sands and gravels. The forest also contains open heathland with gorse and heather where the famous New Forest ponies can be found grazing. The triangular shape of the Isle of Wight is responsible for the hold of high water at Southampton, the leading British deep-sea port in the Channel and one of the finest natural harbours in the world. Further west is the historic maritime city of Portsmouth occupying Portsea Island. Portsmouth is the home of the Royal Navy and Royal Marine Museums and houses Nelson's flagship HMS *Victory*, HMS *Warrior* (Britain's first 'ironclad' warship) and the recently salvaged Tudor warship the *Mary Rose*.

West of Hampshire and to the east of the river Exe lies east Devon and Dorset. The county of Dorset is beautiful and has a great variety of scenery encompassing heathlands, downland, clay vales, woodlands, limestone country and a scenic coastline. The bays at Studland and Swanage on the Isle of Purbeck with the headlands at Handfast Point — the Old Harry Rocks — and Peveril Point are spectacular examples of what happens when hard rocks (chalk and limestone) and soft rocks (sands and clays) are exposed at right angles to the coastline. Along the stretch of coastline between Durlston Head and Weymouth the progression of erosion can be seen in all its stages. The effects of tides and currents, battering away at both sides of a headland of hard rock until it breaks through, forms arches like the one seen at Durdle Door. At Lulworth Cove, one of Dorset's best loved beauty spots, we can see

Previous Page: *Kinder Reservoir, Edale, Derbyshire. In the middle of the Peak District National Park, Edale is famous for being the starting point for a 250-mile long distance path that finishes across the Scottish border at Kirk Yetholm — the Pennine Way.*

Right: *Map of England, showing major cities and geographical features.*

Holy I.
The Cheviot
CHEVIOT HILLS
Newcastle upon Tyne
Tyne
Carlisle
Durham
PENNINES
Lake District
Middlesbrough
Isle of Man
Douglas
Swale
Flamborough Head
Walney I.
Leeds
Kingston upon Hull
Preston
Spurn Head
Manchester
Sheffield
Liverpool
ENGLAND
Trent
The Wash
Derby
Norwich
Wolverhampton
Welland
Peterborough
Birmingham
Coventry
Severn
Cambridge
Ipswich
Northampton
Wye
COTSWOLD HILLS
Cheltenham
Luton
Colchester
Gloucester
Oxford
London
Thames
Canterbury
Reading
NORTH DOWNS
Dover
Bristol Channel
Bristol
Lundy
Ilfracombe
Salisbury
Folkestone
SOUTH DOWNS
Southampton
Bude
Brighton
Exeter
Bournemouth
Isle of Wight
DARTMOOR
Portland Bill
Plymouth
Lyme Bay
Penzance

what happens when the arch collapses and there is erosion of the softer rocks behind. Complete erosion of the outer hard rock forms an open bay seen in its early form at Warbarrow Bay and at a later stage in Christchurch Bay.

The New Red Sandstone of the Triassic and Permian geological periods are much in evidence in the buildings in the eastern part of Devon. The stone formed the source of local building materials for centuries and Exeter, the administrative centre of Devon, is often referred to as the 'Red City'. On the borders of Devon and Cornwall at the confluence of the Tamar and Plym rivers stands the historic city of Plymouth with its rich maritime history. The port was the home base of Sir Francis Drake and was the starting point for his circumnavigation of the world. Plymouth is also renowned as the last port of call for the *Mayflower* on its epic journey to the New World with the Pilgrim Fathers in 1620.

The south-west peninsula of Devon and Cornwall, west of the Exe valley, includes the stark beauty of the inland moors of Dartmoor and Exmoor as well as the southernmost point of the realm, the Lizard, and the westernmost tip, Land's End, both in Cornwall. Some 400 million years ago the sedimentary rocks were laid down on the sea bed and about 100 million years later volcanic activity caused a massive slab of volcanic rock to intrude through the sedimentary layer. Today the surface reveals five outcrops of this granite rock but deep down it is all one massive slab. Land's End is one of these five outcrops and the distinctive shaping of the rocks at the headland is due to fractures in the granite crust. The buildings in this part of the country reflect the geology of the area and the climate. The brown and red sandstones, shales and slates or grey granite, are not conducive to expansive architectural styles and the prevailing westerlies coming in from the sometimes wild Atlantic means that it makes practical sense to construct a plain, solid slate roofed type of building. The beauty in this part of the country lies in the magnificent coastline featuring little fishermen's cottages clustered among the sandy beaches and rocky coves bounded by rocky headlands. The heavily indented coastline of Devon and Cornwall is renowned for its natural beauty. The headlands are formed from comparatively hard rocks which have largely resisted the battering of the sea whereas the bays and coves consist of softer rocks which have succumbed. A specially adapted Long Distance Path allows the visitor to fully explore the varied, beautiful and sometimes wild coastline of the area on foot. This footpath encompasses the entire coastline but can be utilised to make a series of short section circular walks.

A feature of the desolate beauty of the moors of Dartmoor and Exmoor are the granite tors, the High Willhays on Dartmoor stands at 622m (2,038ft) and Dunkery Beacon on Exmoor at 1,704ft (520m). These rounded summits are capped by clumps of craggy outcrops which have been left exposed by the effects of erosion. During the time of the volcanic activity in the region escaping gasses, forced out through fissures in the sedimentary rock, deposited minerals in the form of lodes. The existence of these

Right: *Brittany has Finisterre, Cornwall has Land's End where rocky granite cliffs meet the Atlantic.*

minerals led to a comparatively healthy mining industry. The mining has now all but ceased and the last working tin mine in Cornwall has recently closed down. Evidence of the old workings can be seen on the edges of the moors in the derelict buildings and crumbling engine house chimneys. In the town of Helston there is a Coinagehall Street, the site of Coinage Hall where the assaying of tin ingots took place. Corners were broken off the ingots to assess their purity and these pieces were referred to as 'coins'. In Cornwall today 'tin' is a local colloquialism for money.

Moving eastwards now, away from the coast, we come to Somerset with its spectacular Cheddar Gorge, the English Grand Canyon. The gorge cuts for over a mile through the Mendip Hills flanked by breathtaking limestone cliffs rising to over 450 ft. At the Cheddar end of the gorge the water worn caves give access to an almost surreal underworld fantastically ornamented with stalagmites and stalactites. Many theories have been put forward to explain the existence of this natural phenomena from ancient earthquakes to the remnant of a gigantic cavern whose roof has subsequently collapsed. Today it is widely accepted that the limestone gorge was cut by a river whose course has long since disappeared underground. Further east and to the west of London lies Berkshire and Wiltshire, another area of chalk downlands. The express train or motorway (M4) will speed you through Wiltshire but a more leisurely appreciation of the area is afforded by the Kennet and Avon canal which provides a waterway between Reading and Bristol with the towpath providing a cycleway along most of its length. There is much evidence of the ancient civilisations of England in this area, most notably Stonehenge on Salisbury Plain, and the stone circles at Avebury. The thin soil with the white chalk underneath led to the cutting of effigies on the hillsides with the White Horse at Uffington in all probability being the oldest piece of outdoor work in existence in England.

The north-west corner of Wiltshire extends into the end of the Cotswold Hills which merit a paragraph on their own. In the hills and valleys of the Cotswolds the little villages and towns, with their honey-coloured cottages built from local stone, create a breathtaking beauty in one of England's most scenic regions. The rich 'gingerbread' stone contains a good deal of iron which accounts for its rust colour. In clement weather the views over the Vale of Severn from the highest parts of the hill ridge on the western escarpment, east of Gloucester and Cheltenham, are stunning. Geologically the Cotswolds are but one section of a limestone outcrop which stretches from south Dorset through east Somerset, Gloucestershire, Northamptonshire, Lincolnshire and on to the North Yorkshire Moors. Many little springs whose sources are along the Cotswold dip create the tributaries which form the River Thames (the longest river wholly in England) as it begins its 350km (215 miles) journey eastwards, across the country, to the North Sea.

To the north of the Cotswolds, on the western borders of England, the foothills of the Welsh mountains extend into the counties of Shropshire (the Wrekin 408m/1,334ft — Long Mynd 425m/1,694ft), Hereford and Worcester where the Worcestershire Beacon (517m/1,394ft) stands in the Malvern Hills. In clear weather the panoramic view from the Worcestershire Beacon takes in an area of some 5,000sq km (2,000sq miles), 59-65km (30-40 miles) in every direction. Hereford and Worcester are agricultural counties with a strong farming tradition and the alluvial soils of the picturesque Vale of Evesham, which runs from Tewkesbury to Stratford-upon-Avon, is noted for its market gardening, soft fruits and plum orchards. To the east of these counties lie Staffordshire, West Midlands and Warwickshire. Theatre lovers the world over make pilgrimages to the beautiful Warwickshire town of Stratford-upon-Avon to pay homage at the birthplace of England's greatest poet, William Shakespeare. At the heart of England in the West Midlands lies the heavily industrial area of the so-called Black Country. The smoke and grime from England's second city, Birmingham, used to engulf the whole region in the post Industrial Revolution. West of Birmingham is the rebuilt modern city of Coventry which as a prime industrial area was savagely bombed in the Second World War. The new cathedral, built to replace the one destroyed in the bombing, was ingeniously planned by Sir Basil Spence, in and around the ruins of the old one and attracts many visitors and tourists.

South of the West Midlands the River Thames, from its humble beginnings in the Cotswolds, continues its journey through Oxfordshire and the Berkshire — Buckinghamshire borders. As the river passes through the historic city of Oxford, the home of England's oldest university, it is called the Isis. To the north of Oxford, near Woodstock, stands the birthplace of Sir Winston Churchill, the fine Baroque dwelling Blenheim Palace given to the 1st Duke of Marlborough in the late 17th century. Where the Thames snakes out of Oxfordshire through the Goring Gap, which separates the chalk of the North Wessex Downs from the Chilterns, it passes under the fine 18th century five-arched bridge at Henley, home of the world-famous annual regatta and festival. The river now follows the Buckingham-Berkshire border through the pretty village of Cookham, once the home of the painter Sir Stanley Spencer, and on to Royal Windsor. Here the river separates the town with its famous castle on the south bank from the renowned Public School of Eton on the north bank.

Let us now leave the Thames as it continues on its way through Runnymede, where the Magna Carta was signed, and on past Hampton Court to the capital and eventually the North Sea. Moving north-east from London we come to East Anglia, the lowland area of England with a profusion of minor roads and delightful village pubs. Lowestoft in the county of Norfolk marks the easternmost point of the realm. Strictly speaking East Anglia is the area north of the River Stour but geologically the north of Essex forms part of the same rock formations. Because of isostatic movement (the movement of the continental plates on the molten magma of the earth's core) the whole area is sinking at the rate of about six inches per century. Little is left now of the mighty forests which once covered most of Essex but, on the fringes of Greater London, Epping Forest — the old hunting ground of Saxon, Norman and Tudor monarchs — still remains. To the north of the forest stands the ancient city of Colchester, one of the finest Roman settlements north of the Alps, and the site of many battles between the Icenae Queen Boudicca and the Romans.

North of Essex and over the River Stour into Suffolk stands Flatford Mill, Dedham Vale, made famous by the painter John Constable in his renowned painting *The Hay Wain*. To the north of Suffolk lies the large and mostly flat county of Norfolk which boasts one of England's longest and loveliest stretches of coastland and hinterland. The famous Norfolk Broads in the eastern part of the county provide a veritable paradise for lovers of boating and

Ullswater and Red Tarn below Helvellyn.

holidays afloat. The tranquil lakes and waterways, once thought to be natural features of the geography of the land, are in fact the remains of medieval peat diggings which have since flooded and the low hills, made up of sands and gravels, along the north coast of Norfolk attracts 'twitchers' from afar as they provide ideal nesting and hunting grounds for many varieties of birds. East of Suffolk and Norfolk is the county of Cambridgeshire whose famous university town has its own 'dreaming spires' to match that of its arch rival Oxford. East of the River Cam, King's Parade joins Trumpington Street to form one of the most beautiful thoroughfares in the world. North of Cambridge lie the Fens, areas of semi-marshland below sea-level in places, the land of Hereward the Wake, the great Saxon hero who held out against the Normans. The glorious old cathedral at Ely, with its massive oak beams, towers majestically above the surrounding fenlands.

To the north of East Anglia, in what might be termed the East Midlands, lies the county of Lincolnshire with its lovely sandy coastline behind which lie the glorious Lincolnshire Wolds with their tranquil vales dissecting the rolling chalklands. Lincolnshire and the surrounding shires of Northampton, Leicester, Nottingham and Derby provide some of the world's finest rural scenery. The Grand Union Canal runs through this part of the country and an example of British inventiveness can be seen at Foxton, Leicestershire, where the canal travels through a flight of locks creating a sort of liquid staircase where the canal traffic can negotiate the most difficult gradients. The forests of Nottinghamshire are of course world renowned as the home of the legendary Robin Hood and his band of merry outlaws. As the stories tell us Robin's main adversary was the Sheriff of Nottingham who resided in the castle at Nottingham which stands on a huge sandstone rock that is riddled with man-made caves. The jewel in the crown of the scenery of this area must be the Peak District National Park which is detailed later in the paragraphs about the Pennines.

Continuing our whistle-stop jaunt around the country we now move northwards into Yorkshire, Durham and Northumberland where the most northerly part of England lies a few miles above of the mouth of the River Tweed at Berwick. The Holderness coast in the Humberside region of South Yorkshire has for centuries been remorselessly bombarded by the sea with ever increasing loss of land beneath the waves but the eroded rock has been swept by the currents and tides to build up the spectacular Spurn Head at the southern end of the coastline. Further north up the coast is the precipitous chalk cliff, Flamborough Head, with its fine array of sea stacks and sea caves which gives an excellent example of the sea at work on a chalk headland. The erosion is similar to that seen at Durdle Door and Lulworth Cove in Dorset but here, the waves angled northwards and southwards by the changing tides and winds, have worn away the headland on both sides breaking through to form an arch. Eventually this will collapse leaving an isolated stack out to sea. Further up the coast towards Durham stands the town of Whitby on the edge of the North Yorkshire Moors, another of England's National Parks, their highest point being Urra Moor (454m/1,490ft).The fishing port and seaside resort of Whitby is renowned as the birthplace of the great navigator Captain James Cook who charted vast stretches of what is now Australasia. The North Yorkshire Moors mark the northern extremity of the belt of Oolitic Limestone which runs from the centre of England from Dorset, encompassing the Cotswolds, and in late summer the extensive tracts of blooming heather adorning the Moors creates a stunning spectacle.

Moving inland, the city of York itself has a long and varied history originally being the fine Roman city called Eboracum and later, after being captured by a Viking army in AD 866, as Jorvik it became one of the biggest and most important Viking settlements in Europe. Much of the medieval city walls and gateways remain in York and York Minster, which is one of Europe's best examples of Gothic architecture, has its own Archbishop second only to Canterbury's in the ecclesiastical hierarchy. To the east of York, the southern part of the Yorkshire Dales National Park is incredibly rich in natural beauty as exemplified by the 73m (240ft) high limestone cliff at Malham Cove where Malham Beck once tumbled down in a waterfall but today flows through the limestone, bubbling to the surface at the base of the cliff.

North of Whitby and Teeside lie the remote sandy bays, peaceful fishing villages and ancient castles of the Northumberland coast with its historic Holy Island — Lindisfarne. Near the city of Newcastle, the administrative centre of Northumbria, Wallsend marks the eastern extremity of Hadrian's wall which was built by the Romans to keep the savage Scots and Picts at bay. The city of Newcastle-upon-Tyne itself was also originally erected as a defence against the Scots and today it has nine bridges spanning the Tyne. Inland, and now moving south again, Durham Cathedral, the most massive of all British cathedrals, stands on a rock girdled by an ox-bow bend of the River Wear. This building, more a fortification than a spiritual haven, houses the coffin of St. Cuthbert who founded the Priory on Lindisfarne. To the west of Durham and in the eastern foothills of the Pennines, High Force in Upper Teesdale is one of the most spectacular waterfalls in England where the waters of the River Tees cascade over the Great Whin Sill with a drop of more than 21m (70ft). Millions of years ago a sharp ridge of tough rock was forced upwards in a molten state through the existing rocks, this solidified to form the Great Whin Sill which runs east to west from Lindisfarne right across the north of England, over the Pennines, to Cumbria.

In what is now northern Cumbria is the western end of Hadrian's Wall at Bowness-on-Solway, near Carlisle which is situated about ten miles from the Scottish border. The ruins of Carlisle castle bear testament to the city's unenviable position as the bastion and bulwark protecting England during centuries of skirmishes and battles with its ferocious northern neighbour. Carlisle is situated at the confluence of the River Caldew and the River Eden which runs through the beautiful, fertile and evocative sounding Vale of Eden. A tributary of the Eden, the Eamont, rises in the magnificent Lake Ullswater in the heart of England's best known and biggest National Park, the Lake District with its majestic hills and mountains. Here are the names familiar to all schoolchildren — Scafell Pike (979m/3,210ft) the highest peak in England, Skiddaw, Derwent, Windermere etc — a group of the highest mountains in the land separated by deep vales and valleys carved out by glacial erosion thousands of years ago and filled with the numbingly cold waters of the melted ice. The rounded rocks of the valleys contrast starkly with jagged scars and ridges offered by the rougher aspect of, for example, the Langdale Pikes. Here the outcrops were formed by resistant volcanic rocks which were thrust upwards about 450 million years ago. It is easy to appreciate the allure of the

Birker Force, Eskdale.

Wharfedale in Yorkshire runs from Grassington up through Kettlewell until it joins Langstrothdale. The Dales Way runs along the River Wharfe — named after the goddess Verbena — from Ilkley through Wharfedale on its way to Bowness-in-Windermere in the Lake District.

natural beauty of the Lake District for the great English poets Wordsworth, his sister Dorothy, Thomas de Quincy and Samuel Taylor Coleridge. Their poems extolling the miracles of nature formed one of the great watersheds in the history of English poetry.

South of Cumbria lies Lancashire with it famous coastal holiday resorts including Blackpool, with its 158m (518ft) high imitation of the Eiffel Tower, and the great industrial conurbations of Merseyside and Greater Manchester. At the peak of the industrial revolution Manchester, with its steam, coal and cotton, was the richest city in Europe but was landlocked. In 1894 the Manchester Ship Canal was opened and this engineering wonder of the day carried ocean going ships over 35 miles from Liverpool to the heart of the city with raw materials, then back out to sea with the finished products. Liverpool, with its acres of docklands, was the foremost port for the Atlantic trade in England and today boasts two cathedrals. South of Liverpool, across the Wirral in the county of Cheshire near the Welsh border, stands the historic city of Chester on the River Dee. The ancient city walls form an almost complete two mile circuit around the centre of the town.

South of Cheshire takes us back into the 'heart of England' which we have already covered so let us finish our tour by looking at the 'backbone of England', the Pennine Chain, which contains some of the most hauntingly beautiful scenery in the land. This is a range of mountains and hills which have been formed by an upfold of the underlying Carboniferous rocks. Either side of the anticline are the synclines in which the youngest rocks of the Carboniferous Period, the coal measures, are to be found, forming the Lancashire, Yorkshire and other coalfields. At the northern limit of the Pennines are the most northerly mountains of England, the Cheviots which form a natural border with Scotland, where the Cheviot mountain itself (807m/2,647ft) is the granite core of a volcano with a rounded almost featureless summit that is now a treacherous bog which has defeated many a fell walker. From the Cheviots, the Pennines continue southwards incorporating the Fells of West Northumberland and Durham. As the Pennine Chain continues southwards it runs to the west of the Yorkshire Dales where the hills are honeycombed not only with natural caves, but also with old lead workings. The Dales are a series of glaciated valleys running approximately west to east from the central watershed and are known by the names of the rivers which run through them.

As the Pennines extend south into Derbyshire the range culminates in the Peak District where Kinder Scout (637m/2,088ft) is the highest point. In a poll for the most picturesque beauty spot in England the limestone-lined Lathkill Dale and Dove Dale in Derbyshire's Peak District would surely come near the top. In the same area Chatsworth House, the ancestral home of the Dukes of Devonshire, has to be one of the most magnificent of England's great houses. The superb grounds were laid out by the famous landscape gardener 'Capability' Brown with the aid of no lesser a person than the architect Joseph Paxton, designer of the incredible but ill-fated Crystal Palace. For the hardy walker, the Pennine Way is a cross-country route which extends from the Northumberland National Park, which includes the scenic volcanic outcrop of the Cheviot Hills, southwards to the Yorkshire Dales National Park, with its sheltered valleys and exquisite limestone and sandstone landscapes, to Derbyshire's Peak District.

London, the capital and largest city of the United Kingdom, is located in south-east England at the head of the Thames estuary to the west of its mouth on the North Sea. The river is tidal, and London has been a port for seagoing vessels since the Roman period. The docks were originally located near London Bridge in the city centre but in recent years these inner docks have been replaced by larger and more modern facilities to the east. The city is noted for its museums, performing arts, exchange and commodity markets, and insurance and banking functions, as well as a host of specialised services. In popular and traditional usage, the term City of London, or the City, is applied only to a small area that was the original settlement and is now part of the business and financial district of the metropolis. Modern London is a cosmopolitan multiracial city with a large immigrant population from Britain's former colonies, especially from South Asia and the West Indies, with some quarters of the city dominated by specific ethnic groups. London attracts millions of visitors each year, and tourism, especially in the summer, is a major industry and contributor to the economy. To the west of London, economic development has been stimulated by the presence of Heathrow International Airport, and to the south, by Gatwick International Airport.

Below: *No it's not the tower that's called 'Big Ben,' but the bell inside which is named after Sir Benjamin Hall, Commissioner of Works in 1858 when it was cast. Beautifully repainted and restored, the 98m (320ft) tower stands at the north end of the Houses of Parliament.*

Moon over Loughrigg Fell.

2 London

The first settlement, the Roman Londinium, was founded in AD 43 on a terrace near the north bank of the River Thames and during the 1st century AD became a town of considerable importance, although not an administrative centre. The importance of London declined following the fifth century, during the period of Anglo-Saxon and Scandinavian invasions. Gradually, however, the significance of the city's site along the Thames reasserted itself, and it became a prosperous trade centre. In the 9th century King Alfred made London the capital of his kingdom and, in 1066 when the Normans invaded Britain, William the Conqueror granted London its charter and made the city his capital. He then began construction of the Tower of London intending it as a citadel to overawe the populace. Throughout the Middle Ages London was the political centre, largest city, and chief port of England. New palaces replaced the Tower as the royal residence, notably Westminster, Whitehall, and St. James's, and the city reached a new level of pre-eminence during the reign (1558-1603) of Queen Elizabeth I. The opening of the Royal Exchange in 1566 marked the growth of the city in world importance, William Shakespeare's plays were first performed in the Globe Theatre, book publishing began, and London became the centre of England's newly emerging foreign trade.

By the 17th century London was a crowded city of narrow and twisting streets. In 1665, during the Great Plague, nearly 70,000 Londoners succumbed to the disease within a period of a year and this dreadful epidemic was followed by the Great Fire of 1666, which, because the buildings were largely of wood, consumed much of the city. The Rebuilding Act of 1667 stipulated that only stone and brick be used in the new buildings that rose from the ruins. The rebuilding of the city was distinguished by the work of the architect Sir Christopher Wren, notably in Saint Paul's Cathedral and over 50 city churches which bore little resemblance to the quaint wooden dwellings of old London. In the 18th century the city again began to grow with the building of elegant housing to the west and north-west of the old city. The walls and gates of the city, among the last vestiges of the medieval town, were demol-

Left: *The old and the new: offices tower over the Tower of London, dwarfing the White Tower — the Norman Keep, largely the work of William the Conqueror — which today is commanded by the Constable of the Royal Palace and Fortress of London.*

Right: *London in the 19th century: capital of a huge empire, the biggest city the world had seen, and clogged — then as now — by traffic. St. Paul's, in the background, rises above it all.*

Left: *A scene in Hyde Park in summer 1869. The largest central London park, it used to be for deer hunting until 1768 and was a notorious haunt of highwaymen for centuries. In the 1860s the area was transformed by the planting of flowers and the building of formalised gardens with fountains and an Italian Water Garden.*

Right: *Nelson's Column being erected in Trafalgar Square, November 1843. The monument was designed by Edward Hodges Baily (who also carved the reliefs for Marble Arch) .*

ished in the 1760s. London became the focus not only of politics but also of literary and artistic society.

During the 19th century urban development continued, with industrial suburbs spreading to the north-east and east of the city and the docks and dock-related industries spreading down river. To the north of Oxford Street, along the Marylebone, Euston, Pentonville, and City roads, the major railroad companies located the stations of Paddington, Marylebone, Euston, Saint Pancras, King's Cross, and Liverpool Street, which today serve all of England to the west, north and east of London. In 1890 the world's first electric underground railroad was built. During this Victorian era straight, elegant streets were constructed through the congested inner city and open spaces, such as Trafalgar Square, were created. The 19th century was also a period of reform and establishment of municipal services: in 1829, Sir Robert Peel established the Metropolitan Police Force, whose world famous 'bobbies' were named after him. Many suburbs were incorporated into Greater London, all the bridges in the city were rebuilt in stone, and the streets were newly illuminated, first with gas, and later with electricity.

Today tourists are attracted to London for many reasons not least being the historical heritage of the city and its vibrant night life and 'theatre land'. The most venerable building in the city, and one of London's oldest landmarks, is the Tower of London begun by William I (the Conqueror) about 1079. Originally a centre of defence for the king, the Tower has served as a royal residence, state prison, execution ground and today is the home of the crown jewels. Adjacent to the Tower the distinctive Victorian structure, Tower Bridge, crosses the Thames. To the west lies the City, the heart of London and its financial district with Saint Paul's Cathedral, the Bank of England, Mansion House and many other landmarks. To the west of the City, where the Thames bends about ninety degrees to the south, stand the Houses of Parliament (Palace of Westminster) topped by the famous clock tower Big Ben, named after the main bell. The nearby Westminster Abbey is a splendid example of English Gothic architecture and has long been the setting of coronations, royal weddings and recently the funeral of the tragic Diana, Princess of Wales.

Trafalgar Square with its famous column and statue of Lord Nelson, commemorating his victory at the Battle of Trafalgar, lies to the north of Westminster. The Mall, a long road cutting through Saint James's Park, runs westwards from Trafalgar Square and ends at Buckingham Palace, the residence of the royal family. The Palace has been the official residence of the monarch since 1837, when Queen Victoria moved her court from Saint James's Palace, which is also located on the Mall. Soho, where many of London's restaurants and nightclubs are located, is near the main shopping district of Regent and Oxford Streets and Piccadilly. To the south lie Belgravia, Knightsbridge, Kensington, and Chelsea, all fashionable residential areas. Covent Garden, designed by the English architect Inigo Jones in the early 17th century, was London's first formal square surrounded by town houses. It eventually became an important fruit, flower, and vegetable market until 1974 when it became a centre for fine restaurants and specialist shops. Covent Garden served as a model for Bedford, Belgrave, Berkeley, Grovesnor, Russell, and a host of other squares in the now fashionable neighbouring districts of Soho, Mayfair, Belgravia, Bloomsbury, and Marylebone.

London is also noted for its abundance of park spaces particularly the Royal Parks (formerly royal estates) Saint James's Park , Green Park, Hyde Park, Regent's Park and Kensington Gardens. In the 1950s, after the Second World War, most of the war damage in London was repaired. As a result of the reconstruction, the skyline of the city began changing with the 30-story Museum Radio Tower of the General Post Office building, built in 1965, dominating the West End. Today the London skyline is one of tower blocks rather than of spires and church towers.

Above: *Designed by William Railton in 1843, the Nelson Monument — Nelson's Column — rises above the aptly named Trafalgar Square. It's a 51m (167ft 6.5in) high Corinthian column on top of which the 5.3m (17ft 4.5in) statue of Admiral Lord Nelson stands. Below him, at the base of the column, Landseer's guardian lions, added in 1867, were cast from the bronze of cannon recovered from the wreck of the* Royal George.

Left: *The Thames Barrier, down-river from Greenwich, was designed by Rendel, Palmer and Tritton and begun in 1974. It was opened in 1982, is 558m (1,830ft) wide, and the hydraulic machinery in the boat-shaped piers lift 1,300-ton gates if high tides threaten London. In the background is Canary Wharf.*

The Emperor Hadrian decided to build his eponymous wall on a visit to England in AD 122. A defence against Pictish invaders, it ran from Wallsend to the Solway Firth and was completed in c. AD 130.

PART 2:
THE HISTORY

3 The Mystery of Stonehenge

Few relics of the ancient world are as mystifying as the great standing pillars of Stonehenge. These megaliths of ancient man defy belief: how did they get there, what is their purpose, where did the technology to erect them come from?

Across the centuries, the giant, brooding stones of this awe-inspiring ruin have stood as a challenge to man's knowledge of himself and his ancient world. But despite every theory, they still keep their secrets. For they are made from rocks only found hundreds of miles from Stonehenge. How were the stones transported? How was this miracle of engineering performed? And above all, why?

Stonehenge, however, is but one cluster in a swathe of gigantic monumental rocks which stretches around Europe and the British Isles, from as far north as the Shetland Islands to Malta in the south. There are around 900 sites of standing stones in Britain alone. But Stonehenge, rising above the flat plateau of Salisbury Plain, is easily the most famous of them. Indeed, among all the great stone sites of Europe, Stonehenge remains unique because of the sophisticated way that the blocks appear to have been designed to fit one another and to form a carefully complete whole.

It is only relatively recently that archaeologists have been prepared to say that these great stones may have been the work of advanced astronomers or mathematicians rather than barbarians and savages. Astute detective work has resulted in extraordinary theories on the history of the megaliths (the word is Greek for 'great stones') which should not be dismissed lightly.

Above and Right: *Stonehenge remains one of ancient England's most enduring and intriguing mysteries. Evidence increasingly points to its use as an early astronomical observatory and the sheer extravagance of the design implies that the site was of major social and religious significance.*

The site of Stonehenge was a prehistoric sanctuary in use from circa 3100 to 1100 BC. The temple itself was built in three distinct stages, spanning a period of over 1,000 years. Each group of people who began the mammoth task did not quite finish it, leaving the legacy of completion to the succeeding generations.

The first builders were Neolithic, working on the site around 2700 BC. It was they who set up the encircling ditch and bank and the heel stone, which is aligned so that the first rays of light from the sun on midsummer's day strike both it and the central point of the two stone circles. These same people created the 56 shallow pits called the Aubrey Holes — named after the writer who discovered them — which form a ring just inside the bank, and which when excavated were found to contain bones and cremated objects.

Some 800 years on, the men and women whom we call the Beaker People moved in on the site. They, by means unknown, accomplished one of the truly great engineering feats of all time. In an age when tools were of flint and bone and the wheel had not been invented, they hewed rock from the Prescelly Hills in South Wales and carried it the 480km (300 miles) to Stonehenge. The 80 mammoth bluestones, each weighing more than 4,000kg (4 tons), were then assembled into a double circle inside the earlier enclosure.

Around 1500 BC, the builders of the third Stonehenge again brought in massive boulders, this time from the Marlborough Downs, probably dragged to the site on primitive sledges by upwards of 1,000 men. The individual boulders weighed more than 51,000kg (50 tons) each, and were hewn from sarsen rock, one of the hardest minerals found in these islands. After the arduous journey, they were fashioned into the shapes which now stand like gaunt sentinels on the bleak, windswept plain.

Finally, a people who could not read or write or fashion a wheel devised a system to put the huge stone lintels on top of the upright stones. In addition, Stonehenge man shared something with the prehistoric builders at other sites around Europe — all these monuments are constructed using the same unit of measurement, a unit archaeologists have come to call the 'megalithic yard': a distance of 0.83m (0.9yd). No one has yet been able to explain either how or why this common unit could have come to be used so widely by so many distant peoples at the time.

Although the strange cult of the modern Druids, or Celtic Priests, now lays claim to Stonehenge, experts concur that it is far too old to have been constructed by their Celtic forerunners. So which cult and which people were behind the megalithic mystery?

Theories about the structure abound, but perhaps the following bears the greatest credence. In 1934, after a hard day's sailing, Professor Alexander Thom, of Oxford University, took his boat into Loch Roag on the Isle of Lewis, off Scotland's bleak west coast. Silhouetted against the rising full moon were the standing stones of Callanish, Scotland's own 'Stonehenge'. The professor went ashore. Standing in the middle of the stone circle, he checked

the position of the Pole Star and noted that it showed the structure was aligned due north-south. Because this monument was prehistoric and was built in the days when the Pole Star's constellation had not reached its present position in the sky, Professor Thom deduced that the people who had built it must have had some other way of determining the alignment of the stones.

His discovery there launched him on a quest around 600 standing stone sites both in Britain and Europe. He proved that although the stone circles may look rough and weathered today, worn down by both time and human activities, they were originally precise works of engineering skill. Of Stonehenge, he declared that it was a Stone Age observatory, where even small irregularities on the extremities of the site were created artificially, specifically to mark the significant moments when the sun and moon rose and set.

In 1963 studies at Boston University revealed that Stonehenge was like a giant computer: a huge observatory capable of extremely complex calculations based on the sun, moon and stars. When all the data about the site was fed into a computer, the startling result was that the stones could be used to predict the occurrence of eclipses. It seemed that the highly educated astronomer priests of the time could have stood in the centre of the great circle and determined the position of the sun or moon in its orbit by using the stones as a guide.

Such sophistication among the ancients seemed at first difficult to accept; yet the men who built Stonehenge had proved by the feat itself that they were not primitive. It has even been claimed that these people had established an elite 'academy' where the most gifted priests may have lived and studied their craft. Remains found at Durrington Walls, near Stonehenge, reveal a race of people who ate a rich diet, who wore woven cloth and who enjoyed a status above that of their nearest neighbours.

If the academics are right, that Stonehenge and the other standing stone sites were indeed designed for making astronomical observations, it is likely that there was an intellectual elite within the primitive Stone Age farmers we know inhabited the earth — an elite who carried out the complex calculations necessary to chart planetary movements in an age when there was no written word.

Other theories about Stonehenge exist — that the site was a temple for human sacrifice, a place where infertile women went to be blessed by the gods, even that it was a beacon for beings from outer space. It has even been suggested that Stonehenge had a much broader purpose. Charts point to the strange geometric pattern that exists between Stonehenge, the prehistoric hill site nearby called Old Sarum, and another Neolithic settlement called Grovelly Castle. The three sites are 9.6km (0.6 miles) from each other, so that when joined on a map a near-perfect equilateral triangle emerges; was this town planning on a huge and precise scale, or merely coincidence?

Despite these diverse propositions, the observatory theory stands best the test of time. And scientists now accept the once unbelievable proposition that a phenomenally intellectual race long ago learned to operate a gigantic stone 'computer'...

Below: *A bird's eye view of Old Sarum, near Salisbury, Wiltshire, as it is today and* **(Above Right)** *as it would have appeared in the middle of the 12th century. Some of the original stonework, like that at Bishop Roger's Palace* **(Below Right)**, *is still in place.*

OLD SARUM

Old Sarum is a ghost town, probably the finest example in England of an entire city deserted at the height of its development. People lived on the site for more than 4,000 years, ever since it was first occupied by Iron Age tribesmen. They were followed in turn by Romans, Saxons and Normans, who built a castle, cathedral and two royal palaces.

However, when a new cathedral was built at New Sarum, or Salisbury, in the 13th century, the old city quickly declined. Today all that remains are 227sq m (56 acres), including the earthworks and 202sq m (50 acres) of ruins that create an eerie reminder of tribal life in England five millennia ago.

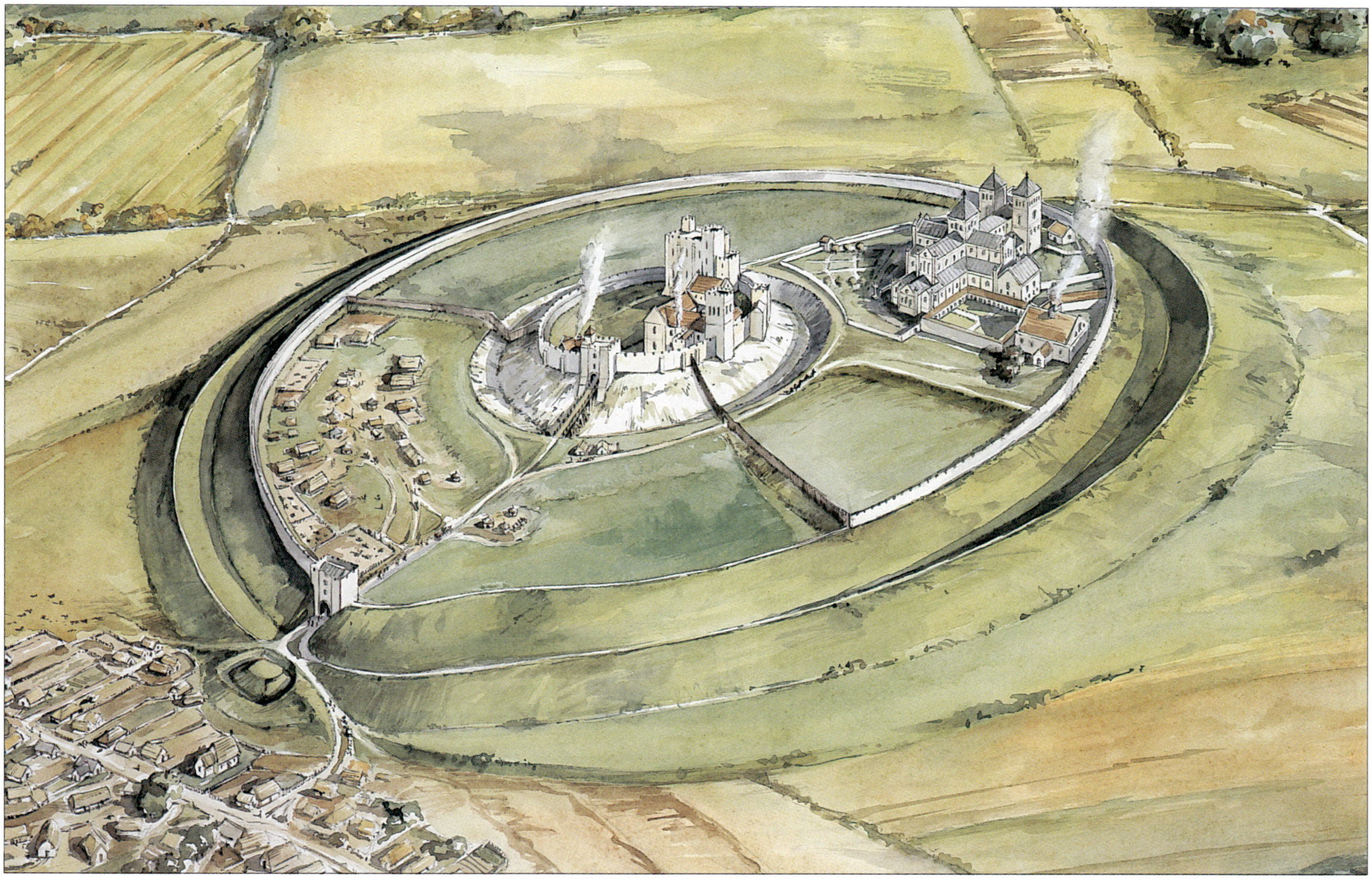

4 Ages of Bronze and Iron

The practice of burial and religious ritual flourished with the arrival of the Beaker People from their homelands on the Rhine around 2000 BC. Indeed, their name is derived from their habit of burying ornate pottery artefacts which were discovered inside their burial mounds. The Beaker People also brought with them skills in working bronze, a mixture of copper with a little tin. Their ability to work metal and make tools led to more sophisticated methods of cultivation which resulted in turn in a population explosion. Over a few hundred years, the number of people in Britain rose to about one million. Settlements flourished as did fortified hilltop villages, each linked by a network of tracks. Large systems of cultivated fields appeared, covering thousands of acres. This signified the start of the deliberate sculpting of the British landscape which would continue through four millennia.

But what sort of people were these Bronze Age Britons? How did they get here and how harsh was their existence once they had arrived? The greatest clue came only in the last decade of the 20th century — with the discovery of a single wooden boat ...

The so-called Bronze Age Boat was a history-shattering archaeological discovery made on the site of a later Roman harbour wall during road-widening work in Dover, Kent, in 1992. About 7m (20ft) down was a largely intact, plank-sewn boat, some 18m long by 3m wide (60ft by 10ft). Beautifully built, it was a sophisticated piece of marine engineering crafted 3,500 years ago.

Today crossing the 35km (22 miles) of sea between Britain and France is plain sailing. But in prehistoric times, the adventures of the motley crews who manned Dover's Bronze Age Boat touched on the miraculous. They journeyed in what was little more than tree trunks, with oxen and sheep jostling at their elbows and with water lapping at their ankles. It would have taken around eight hours for Bronze Age Man to cross the short stretch of sea at about six knots, with up to 24 paddlers stopping every so often to bail out.

There being no nails or glue in those days, the Dover Bronze Age Boat was made up of just six timbers from three giant oak trees. Saws had not been invented either but the timbers had been hewn and split with absolute precision, using bronze axes, gouges, chisels and even flint tools. They were then lashed together with 'rope' made from flexible yew stems. Moss, used to fill gaps left between rope and wood, was still growing. Pieces of French pottery were found in the boat, proving that it was, in effect, an 'international ferry'. Odd items used for plugging leaky holes were also still in place; somebody's underpants or shirt tail has been ripped off to caulk one of these holes because it has sprung a leak at sea.

With a date of 1500 BC, the Bronze Age Boat is therefore the oldest craft in Europe and the third oldest in the world — beaten only by two ancient Egyptian boats. That means that as masons were putting their finishing touches to Stonehenge, accomplished seamen were already operating the first-ever ferry between the harbours of what were to become Dover and Calais. The boat's remarkably preserved state was due to it being encased in sediment laid down during a rise in sea level after the Bronze Age. Also encased in the mud were fragments which did not come from the craft. They weren't fully worked, suggesting that the site was where boats were manufactured or repaired — in other words a boat yard.

Above: *The Cerne Abbas giant in Dorset is cut into a chalk hillside. It has been an unmistakable fertility symbol for centuries.*

Right: *An artist's impression of a couple of remote Bronze Age huts as they would have appeared in the rugged country of Brean Down, a narrow headland near Weston-super-Mare.*

Dover's Bronze Age gem has given us the most amazing insight into Britain's past since modern man first marvelled at Stonehenge. For Dover, known through recent history as the 'Key To England', is now known to have been exactly that an amazing 3,500 years ago. And Kent is now known to have been a bustling trading region ... at a time when it was believed Ancient Britons could not even build ships!

Thus we know of a sophistication hitherto undreamed of in an age of prehistory which has left us no language, no literature and, apart from the henges, few structures on the landscape. Until recent years it was thought that England at this time was submerged in a series of barbaric invasions from the continent. In fact, the Bronze Age history of England was probably a series of many native-born

developments. Not only is continental pottery found in England but English pottery is found on the continent. There was a large-scale trade in metals, the main market for British bronze being to Scandinavia. English farmers were wealthy enough to bury their dead with gold, amber and even beads from the Orient.

Having developed the ox-drawn plough, agriculture flourished to an unprecedented degree. Farms, with dwelling sites, on a large scale are still evident on the untrammelled heaths of Dartmoor and the moors of North Yorkshire. More prominent are the 'barrows', or circular burial mounds, of the Sussex Downs, Salisbury Plain, the Derbyshire Peak District and the Yorkshire Wold.

From this evidence we know that England was populated by a stable, industrious peasant population, living by agriculture and the keeping of livestock, as well as by hunting and fishing. They lived in hut villages along riverbanks or in isolated farms on the chalk downs or upland moors, largely cleared of native forest and scrub. There was little sign of fortification. Which means that Bronze Age Man was totally unprepared for the next period in the history of ancient England: the Age Of Iron.

Although bronze implements remained in use, particularly in northern Britain, until the last century before Christ, iron was a stronger material for both sword and plough share. First dug and forged on the continent, iron was brought to England in a fresh series of invasions — by a people whose origins remain mysterious.

From the styles of their weapons and drinking cups, it is surmised that the early Iron Age invaders emanated from as far afield as Austria and Switzerland. Archaeologists have no clues as to their languages or even the names they used for themselves. It was

only when Greek explorers and Roman conquerors came to these northern shores in the late Iron Age that the inhabitants of France and Britain were uniformly labelled 'Gauls' or 'Celts'. But it is a mistake to think that the Celts were a single race with a common culture. The present-day people of Scotland, Ireland, Wales, Cornwall and Brittany, who term themselves 'Celtic', are simply the independently spirited survivors who were squeezed to the edges of the known world upon the decline of Rome. But Rome's fall was still 1,000 years away as, in around 700 BC, the iron-based culture of the Celts first began to spread towards Britain.

Nearly all Iron Age people lived in villages among fields, on river gravels or light upland soils. These stable settlements came about with the establishment of a new farming procedure, repeatedly harvesting, ploughing and resowing their fields. Most villagers depended on a variety of grain as their staple diet and stored it in underground pits. Managed stock-breeding created new, healthy breeds of oxen, pigs, sheep and cattle. Houses were built of wood and wickerwork and coated in mud to weatherproof them. Food was stored, cooked and served in pottery vessels.

Iron Age Society might sound quite civilised but it was, in fact, a violent, often barbaric era. Noblemen of the time won praise for raids, duels and war. Human heads, severed in battle, were said to hold magical powers and were often used in rituals to the gods. Such places as Wookey Hole, in the Mendip Hills of Somerset, were the site of vast stashes of heads and skulls.

As the Iron Age settlements increased, so too did the fighting, sometimes provoked by scarcity of good farming land. A tribal system developed and with it tribal wars. As villages became more prosperous, everyone had more to defend. Huge hilltop forts and camps began to spring up; these consisted of a single rampart, sometimes of stone, but usually an earthwork riveted with timber and protected by a ditch. Some forts contained 50 houses or more, complete with grain stores, and could sustain around 200 people. One massive construction was at Danebury, near Andover, Hampshire.

In the latter years of the Iron Age, one tribe of immigrating Celts — the Belgae from northern Gaul — spread over Essex, Hertfordshire, and parts of Oxfordshire. Their settlements then began to cover Hampshire, Wiltshire, Dorset and part of Sussex. These new settlers preferred living in towns in valleys, and they established themselves as the elite tribes of Britain as they spread across increasing areas of the country. They built new towns on sites they claimed, including Wheathampstead, Verulamium (St. Albans), Camulodunum (Colchester), Calleva (Silchester) and Venta Belgarum (Winchester). These later Iron Age people were also the first to introduce coinage of silver and copper.

The Gallic Celts, being ferocious fighters, tore down many of the 2,000 hill forts that still existed on the British landscape and made the sites their new homes. The Belgae might have acted differently had they known what was about to descend upon them. But then, nothing and no one could have withstood the approaching legions of Rome.

Below: *How the Bronze Age village at Grimspound, on top of Dartmoor in Devon, might have looked. The cattle and sheep in the foreground would have been regarded as a measure of the settlement's prosperity.*

Above Left: *A view of the Carn Euny ancient village in Cornwall, where stone huts replaced timber in the 1st century BC. This Celtic village includes a fogou — an underground chamber for which the purpose is not known.*

Below Left: *A general view of Grimspound today. There are still the remains of 24 huts and an example of a fine granite slab entrance on the south side.*

Above: *The Ridgeway near Uffington Castle on the Berkshire Downs. Nearby the famous white horse is carved into a hillside.*

Left: *A reconstruction of a typical gathering at Danebury Hill Fort in Hampshire. Excavations suggest that by the time of the Roman invasion Danebury was a sophisticated settlement with carefully planned 'streets'.*

Above Right: *Iron age fortifications still survive at Stanwick, in Northamptonshire.*

Far Right: *An artist's impression of a battle scene at Danebury around 100 BC. Iron age forts such as this one seem to have been more-or-less continually occupied over many centuries. In times of war between Celtic chieftains they were seen as a safe refuge for families in otherwise exposed farming settlements.*

Right: *The stone cist at Drizzlecombe in the middle of Dartmoor, Devonshire.*

5 Veni, Vidi, Vici

Only now are we about to enter the period of recorded history. This is what an ambitious Roman general, one Julius Caesar, wrote about the unknown island across the water … towards which he was now turning greedy eyes.

'The interior of Britain is inhabited by people who claim, on the strength of an oral tradition, to be aboriginal; the coast by Belgic immigrants who came to plunder and make war — nearly all of them retaining the names of the tribes from which they originated — and later settled down to till the soil. The population is exceedingly large [in fact, probably a little over a million], the ground thickly studded with homesteads, closely resembling those of the Gauls, and the cattle very numerous.

'For money they use either bronze or gold coins or iron ingots of fixed weights. Tin is found inland and small quantities of iron near the coast; the copper that they use is imported. There is timber of every kind, as in Gaul, except beech and fir. Hares, fowl and geese they think it unlawful to eat, but rear them for pleasure and amusement. The climate is more temperate than in Gaul, the cold being less severe.

'By far the most civilised inhabitants are those living in Kent, a purely maritime district, whose way of life differs little from that of the Gauls. Most of the tribes in the interior do not grow corn, but live on milk and meat and wear skins. All the Britons dye their bodies with woad, which produces a blue colour and gives them a more terrifying appearance in battle. They wear their hair long and shave the whole of their bodies except the head and upper lip.

'Wives are shared between groups of ten or twelve men, especially between brothers and between fathers and sons. But the offspring of these unions are counted as the children of the man with whom a particular woman cohabited first'.

This was how Caesar saw Britain, forming his opinions from the reports of traders. He viewed them as barbarians. And indeed they were, in one particular custom: human sacrifice. The Celts of Iron Age Britain used this practice to appease the hundreds of gods whom they worshipped. The sheer numbers of gods sealed the fates of criminals and innocents alike. Caesar further noted of the Celts:

'They believe that the execution of those who have been caught in the act of theft or robbery or some crime is more pleasing to the immortal gods but when the supply of such fails they resort to the execution even of the innocent'.

Roman and Greek writers were genuinely appalled at the barbarity of the Celts even though their own cultures had bloody ceremonies. Elaborating on the ritual of Celtic sacrifices, the contemporary Greek writer and geographer Strabo wrote: 'They would strike the condemned man in the back with a sword and then divine from his death struggle'. In other words, they would 'read' the future from

the manner of his death throes — before minutely examining his entrails for further omens.

Alternatively, the Celts might shoot the victims with arrows or impale them at the chosen holy site. Most horrific, however, was the fate of those victims who were crammed dozens at a time into giant wicker cages fashioned in the form of a god and then burned to death. In attendance at such rituals were the Druids, the band of priests and soothsayers whose bloodletting swept France, Britain and Ireland at the time.

Celtic shrines have been unearthed to reveal quantities of human bones, alongside the bones of animals and of tools which have been ritually smashed, all believed to have been gifts to the gods. The Celts are known to have placed such relics in deep shafts — dug, it is believed, in an attempt to communicate with the underworld.

Yet the Celts who lived in late Iron Age England were clearly far from being mere savages, even if the nature of their society was very different from that of Rome. They lacked a developed urban civilisation, a sophisticated system of government with clearly differentiated administrative functions, a permanent army or a literary culture. And, of course, their sacrificial rituals were wholly alien to the more advanced culture of Rome.

But being different is not the same as being primitive. Agriculture was both varied and extensive; arable and pastoral farming were practised, much of the woodland had been cleared, and ploughs with 'mould-boards' were used to scrape the surface of the earth in readiness for planting crops.

A high and increasing level of settled population was supported and the surplus helped to sustain an aristocratic society. In southern Britain, Celtic 'states' had developed with monarchical patterns of government. The beginnings of towns were to be seen both in the hill forts and in low-lying centres such as Camulodunum (Colchester), capital of the Trinovantes of Essex.

But Britain was not a nation. Not even the southern part of it, which later became England, was in any sense one country. England was first united as a result of conquest – conquest by the most powerful and extensive empire in the history of Europe, that of Rome.

It was in the summer of the Roman year 699, now described as the year 55 BC, that the Proconsul of Gaul, Gaius Julius Caesar first set his sights on Britain. The island both fascinated and troubled him, for he well knew it was home to tribesmen similar to those who had confronted the Romans in campaigns in Germany, Spain and Gaul. He also knew the 'islanders' had helped the local tribes in the late campaigns along the northern coast of Gaul. British volunteers had shared the defeat of the Veneti on the coasts of Brittany in the previous year. Furthermore refugees from conquered Gaul were welcomed and sheltered on the island.

Caesar had gleaned further knowledge about this intimidating place called Britannia and was already contemplating putting the island's uneducated, uncouth inhabitants to work as his slaves. The land was green and fertile from which many farming riches could be reaped. He had even heard talk of a pearl fishery and of the presence of gold.

In short, it was time for him to see Britannia for himself. This was no small decision for Caesar to make for the Romans hated and feared the sea. But these feelings were overruled by Caesar's desire to land on such a mysterious and remote island and thereby win great acclaim from all of Roman society. His boast from earlier campaigns had already swept the empire: '*Veni, Vidi, Vici*' ('I came, I saw, I conquered').

As S. A. Handford says in *Caesar, The Conquest of Gaul*:

'Even if it was not time for a campaign that season, Caesar thought it would be of great advantage to him merely to visit the island, to see what its inhabitants were like and to make himself acquainted with the lie of the land, the harbours and the landing places. Of all this the Gauls knew next to nothing'.

Caesar withdrew his army from Germany and throughout July of 55 BC marched westwards towards the Gallic shore somewhere between what is today Calais and Boulogne. Here, Caesar's men, aboard their Roman galleys, were forced to learn rapidly about the indiosyncracies of these strange waters. The tides were unlike those in the Mediterranean. Storms were more frequent and more severe than they had ever encountered before. With no maritime forecasting available to him, the only invasion strategy Caesar could make was to pick a fine spell before setting off for the island of Britannia. August, he decided, was as good a month as any.

And so, on 25 August 55 BC, Julius Caesar landed in Britain. It is likely he came ashore at Walmer, near Deal in Kent. The Britons were there to meet him. The enemy Islanders, with their chariots and horsemen advanced into the sea to challenge the invaders. Caesar's transports and warships grounded in deeper water. The legionaries, uncertain of the depth, hesitated in a shower of javelins and stones. Eventually, Caesar brought his ships and his men firing catapults upon the British flank. Then, as the Romans leaped into the sea, there followed a short, ferocious fight. But the Romans reached the shore and forced the islanders to flee.

Caesar and his men were to spend a three-week reconnaissance on the island. It was, on reflection, a singularly unimpressive visit.

Left: *This drawing shows Maiden Castle, in Dorset, around the time of the Roman Conquest. It was arguably England's greatest southern hill fort and an important centre of government for Celtic chiefs. The Romans took it after a heavy battle.*

Above: *A general view of the amphitheatre at Corinium (now known as Cirencester), one of Roman Britain's principal towns.*

Below: *The ruins of the Roman Pharos at Dover Castle as they appear today. The site was strategically important and the fort was among the first built by the Romans in the second century and supported a squadron of the British fleet. It has been added to and embellished down the centuries.*

Left: *The great Roman fort at Richborough, in Kent, from the air and* **(Right)** *a close-up view of its earthwork fortifications.*

Below Right: *Portchester Castle, above Portsmouth Harbour, was one of the forts of the Litus Saxonicum (Saxon Shore) and was built principally to counter sea-borne landings by Germanic pirates. It was occupied for much of the fourth century.*

Below Far Right: *The remnants of Roman architecture at the town of Venta Icenorum, in Caister-by-Norwich, Norfolk.*

Caesar hardly moved from his camp at the landing place except to see off another attacking British force. When he eventually set off on his journey home to Gaul, it was without 12 of the vessels and a substantial number of men with which he had set out. He had paid dearly for his inexperience of sea storms. Caesar was later to admit:

'A number of ships were shattered and the rest, having lost their cables, anchors and the remainder of their tackle, were unusable, which naturally threw the whole army into great consternation. For they had no other vessels in which they could return, not any materials for repairing the fleet, and since it had been generally understood that they were to return to Gaul for the winter, they had not provided themselves with a stock of grain for wintering in Britain.'

Caesar was well aware his expedition had not been a great success. Nevertheless, he did get safely home, and with a few islanders as hostages. Furthermore he had decided to return to the island the following year — this time for a real invasion.

In 54 BC, Caesar was again approaching the Kent coast. His arrival was far more awesome than the last time. For now he had 800 ships and the Islanders stood no chance of holding back his invasion from landing on their shores. But again, the weather was to cause Caesar problems. Raging storms battered a great number of his ships and he had to retrace the 19km (12 miles) he and his army had marched inland, back to the shore to haul the vessels ashore. This was no mean feat and took ten days.

It also provided an excellent opportunity for the Britons. As the *War Commentaries of Caesar* reports:

'While this work was going on, one legion had been sent out as usual to bring in grain ... Since the grain in this area had all been cut except for what was in one place, the enemy guessed where our men would go and lay hidden in the woods during the night. Then when our men, their arms laid aside, were scattered and busy reaping, they suddenly burst out on them, killed a few and threw the rest into confusion before they could form up, swarming around them with cavalry and chariots ...'.

But then Caesar was on the march again, cutting down all Britons he found sheltering in forests. He crossed the Thames near Brentford. Conquering this strange island looked a simple business, but Caesar did not anticipate the intervention of a mysterious figure called Cassivellaunus.

The Britons had found a leader in this chief Cassivellaunus, a master of war in conditions which were alien to their invaders. Dismissing the rag taggle army of peasants who formed to fight Caesar, Cassivellaunus kept pace with the enemy march by march with his chariots and horsemen. Caesar gave a detailed description of the tactics:

'In chariot-fighting, the Britons begin by driving all over the field hurling javelins, and generally the terror inspired by the horses and the noise of the wheels are sufficient to throw their opponents' ranks into disorder. Then, after making their way between the squadrons of their own cavalry, they jump down from the chariots and engage on foot. In the meantime, their charioteers retire a short distance from the battle and place the chariots in such a position that their masters, if hard pressed by numbers, have an easy means of retreat to their own lines. Thus they combine the mobility of cavalry with the staying power of infantry; and by daily training and practice they attain such proficiency that even on a steep incline they are able to control the horses at full gallop and to check and turn them in a moment. They can run along the chariot pole as quick as lightning'.

Cassivellaunus's other tactic was to cut off Caesar's foraging parties. It was all a noble and brave effort, but Caesar captured his first major stronghold and attempts to destroy his shoreside base failed. The time had come for talking. Cassivellaunus negotiated the surrender of hostages and terms of submission. In turn, Caesar agreed to leave the island. He had finally triumphed — and gladly turned his face for Rome. There he was greeted as a world-conquering hero. In 45 BC Emperor Caesar attained absolute power, ushering in Rome's golden age. The following year he was assassinated.

It would take another 100 years until the Emperor Claudius was able to conquer Britain. Until then, the British Islanders had been left in peace, building up trade with Rome and happily accepting Roman traders in their midst. It was, for its time, an ideal situation. But sadly, it was this idyll which once more brought the island to the attention of the greedy empire, as reports of the wealth and possibilities of a stable government increasingly interested those back in Rome. Eventually, they began to tantalise Emperor Claudius who was determined to cast off his reputation as simple and ineffectual. Storming Britain was the ideal way to do it.

Above: *The quality and structure of Roman roads was such that many can still be found today across England. Here a typically straight example stretches out for more than a mile across Wheeldale high up in the North Yorkshire Moors, not far from Goathland.*

Above Right: *A superb example of intricate geometric patterning on a Roman mosaic as it appears on a pavement in the old town of Isurium Brigantum, now Aldborough in the vale of York.*

Right: *A Roman coin bearing the head of the Emperor Trajan (98-117 AD). Finds such as this one, which turned up during excavations at the Stanwick Iron Age site, are relatively common.*

In 43 AD Claudius's invasion fleet, under Aulus Plautius, landed at Richborough, on the Kent shores. It comprised an army of some 20,000 men — and the islanders were not expecting them. The Romans marched inland, easily winning the first of their skirmishes with the British. Then onwards towards the River Medway, where a fierce two-day battle was fought. Togodumnus, a British resistance leader, died in the fighting. His brother, Caractacus fled north-westwards with the surviving troops, believing that the Romans would try to cross the river by bridge. But Roman auxiliary troops moved upstream to ford the river and launch a pre-emptive strike, shooting down the horses of the feared British charioteers. Legionaries under Flavius Vespasianus (the future emperor Vespasian) and his brother Sabinus then crossed the river despite

strong resistance, and an offensive led by Hosidius Geta the next morning finally put the Britons to flight.

By the summer of 43 AD, the south-east of Britain and the Isle of Wight had fallen to the Romans. To mark his victories, Emperor Claudius presided at an awesome surrender ceremony at Colchester, the capital of the defeated Trinovantes tribe. There was a grand parade which included the emperor's personal bodyguard — and elephants. No one dared mention that this was the emperor's first real visit to the battle-torn island. Until now, while the fighting raged he had awaited news of his invasion from the safety of France. Only after Vespasian's victory did Claudius cross the Channel, bringing his elephants and reinforcements with him.

But the invaders were having trouble taking command of other areas. The westerly Atrebates tribe and the fierce Durotriges tribe of Dorset stood their ground. Further west still, the Dumnonii tribes of Devon and Cornwall remained outside Roman control. But the second legion of Romans under Vespasian slowly advanced across the island, cutting down their British foes.

The invaders had become particularly skilled at attacking the islanders' earthwork hill fortresses. First an artillery barrage showered the defenders with a lethal iron rain forcing them off the ramparts. A direct infantry assault would follow as the Britons scrabbled around to find cover. Forts such as Badbury Rings and Maiden Castle soon fell. By the middle of 44 AD, the Roman invasion of Britain was complete.

The brave Caractacus was still on the run, however, taking refuge in swamps and forests. He was to muster tribes and continue the resistance against the Romans for six long years. He was finally betrayed by his compatriot, Queen Cartimandua of the northerly Brigantes, who handed him over to the Romans. What happened next shows remarkable presence of mind by Caractacus. Paraded through Rome, watched by thousands to whom his name had become legend, he refused to bow his head or show fear. Instead, he boldly approached where the Emperor was sitting and made this speech:

'If to my high birth and distinguished rank I had added the virtues of moderation, Rome had beheld me rather as a friend than a captive, you would not have rejected an alliance with a prince descended from illustrious ancestors and governing many nations. The reverse of my fortune to you is glorious and to me humiliating. I had arms and men and horses. I possessed extraordinary riches and can it be any wonder that I was unwilling to lose them? Because Rome aspires to universal dominion must men therefore implicitly resign themselves to subjection? I opposed for a long time the progress of your arms and had I acted otherwise, would either you have had the glory of conquest or I of a brave resistance? I am now in your power. If you are determined to take revenge, my fate will soon be forgotten and you will derive no honour from the transaction. Preserve my life and I shall remain to the latest ages a monument of your clemency'.

Claudius granted Caractacus his liberty, saying he was free to live with his family in Rome. Meanwhile back in Britain, Queen Cartimandua was well rewarded for her loyalty to Rome and betrayal of Caractacus: in the form of Roman handouts and luxury goods.

Claudius died in 54 AD, possibly from eating poisoned mushrooms. He was succeeded by Nero, his 17-year old adopted son. Nero did not find peace easy to maintain in those early days of his furthest-flung province.

In 60 AD the southern British Iceni tribe rose up in rebellion after the humiliation of seeing their leader Boudicca (or Boadicea, as she was later known) flogged and her daughters raped. The Iceni were backed by the Trinovantes, much of whose land had been confiscated to support the colony of Roman veterans at Colchester. The major Roman settlements, Camulodunum, Londinium and Verulamium (Colchester, London and St. Albans) were stormed, and their inhabitants slaughtered with great cruelty. The governor, Suetonius Paulinus, was campaigning in North Wales when the rebellion broke out, met the rebel forces somewhere in the Midlands and crushed them. Boudicca herself died, probably by committing suicide, and the Iceni and their allies were then 'pacified' with typical Roman brutality.

After relative calm was restored in Britain, the conquerors were forced to turn their attention homewards. The Roman civil war, which began with Nero's suicide in 68 AD, was the first of a series of internal conflicts that weakened the Roman military effort and presence in Britain. Nevertheless, the pace of advance resumed in 71 AD with the subjugation of the Brigantes of northern England (71-74 AD), the subjugation of most of Wales (73-76 AD) and, during the governorship of Cnaeus Julius Agricola (77-83 AD), the completion of the conquests of Wales and northern England.

The Romans also attempted the conquest of Scotland but their hold there was always tenuous — and these northern reaches finally proved to be the furthest outpost of their empire. Agricola, having marched into southern Scotland with the Ninth Legion In 81 AD, advanced to a front-line position betwixt the estuaries of the Rivers Clyde and Forth. He built a chain of forts across the land, sustained by the Roman fleet, and in 83 AD Agricola vanquished the local Caledonians in the battle of Mons Graupius, believed to be the Hill of Moncrieffe.

We know of these events from the writings of the Roman historian Tacitus, who happened to be Agricola's son-in-law. Tacitus wrote proudly of his relation's victories, principally against the Caledonian chieftain Calgacus, but criticised subsequent Roman strategy. For in 84 AD, only months after Agricola had subdued the Lowland Scots, the general received sudden orders from Rome to withdraw. As Tacitus wrote: '*Perdomita Britannia et statim omissa*' ('Britain is conquered then is at once thrown away').

Imperial strategy became defensive rather than offensive. The Emperor Hadrian himself visited Britain in 121 AD and ordered the building of new defences along a line back into England far south of Agricola's earlier frontier. The famous Hadrian's Wall, between the estuaries of the Solway and the Tyne, was to be a deterrent to the raiding parties of the factionalised northern tribes, particularly the Picts. This most impressive of structures, eventually comprising a stone wall 113km (70 miles) long with supporting forts known as 'housesteads', still stands today for most of its length.

Less than 20 years later, however, the new Emperor Antoninus Pius ordered the restoration of Roman rule over the defiant northerners. Within months of succeeding Hadrian in 138 AD, the tough new emperor decided to abandon Hadrian's Wall, which was still being modified, and push the frontier back to Agricola's earlier positions, some 120km (75 miles) further north. The then governor of Britain, Lollius Urbisuc, was given the task of constructing the Antonine Wall during the years following 142 AD. It ran for about 60km (37 miles) across the narrow waist of Scotland formed by the Rivers Forth and Clyde.

Roman armies were now defending an empire which extended from the Clyde to the Euphrates. Who were these soldiers charged with the task of defending the province of Britain, first from behind Hadrian's Wall and then the Antonine Wall? At the start, most of them would be highly trained legionaries; not necessarily Romans but possibly mercenaries and local recruits. Most of the summer they would have spent north of the walls on patrol, chasing off raiders and supervising the local tribes. Workers for the maintenance of the walls would have been mainly local in origin. For like the Britons in the south, the Pictish-Scottish inhabitants of the north were now beginning to learn the long, slow lesson of living as neighbours with the Romans. For a while, uneasy peace reigned in the north of Britain.

It was only when the Romans tried to push their boundaries still further northwards that the remaining warlike tribes retaliated. In 208 AD the Emperor Severus, having vanquished half of the near-east, ordered the conquest of all Scotland. The Caledonian defenders had learned their military lessons, however, and rather than confronting the disciplined Roman ranks in pitched battle, fought guerrilla warfare through the Grampian mountains and forests. Severus, who had been personally supervising the invasion, returned to his northern British headquarters at Eboracum (York) and died. Encouraged, the Caledonian tribes again went on the offensive. The Romans abandoned the Antonine Wall and fell back to the older Hadrian's Wall, which for the next 100 years remained

Above: *More coins recovered from the Stanwick site.*

Below: *Looking west towards an old Roman wall at St Albans in Hertfordshire. Roman architecture must have been a revelation to any Celtic tribe which had direct contact with the invaders.*

the northern frontier of Rome. The far north of Britain was again cast into the mists of little-recorded history.

The Romans were not to persist in their attempts to unite all Britain militarily. Plans for the total subjugation of Ireland were shelved in part due to the competing demands of the vulnerable Danube frontier, which also meant a reduction in the considerable military effort devoted to Britain, just as earlier Nero had withdrawn troops in preparation for campaigning on the Asian frontier of the empire.

Despite the costly military presence that typified all frontier provinces, Roman territorial ambition gradually gave way to peaceful co-existence. It was peace not war which ensured the direct Roman impact on England for a full half-millennium — about 330 years of which (from 78-409 AD) the whole of England and Wales was ruled by imperial Rome.

This period is the real starting point of the fully recorded history of England, not only because of its political unity, but also simply because Roman remains provide us with information about what life was like. Christianity, introduced in the late second century and organised into dioceses by the early fourth century, also meant the spread of literacy and the better recording of events.

From the writings left to us by chroniclers, generals and churchmen, it is abundantly clear that the four centuries of Roman rule brought a prolific growth in culture and communications. This intensification of all the progress which had taken place in the previous 1,500 years was tempered by economic and political changes — and even an early sense of 'ecological' responsibility as the new rulers curbed the over-exploitation of the land itself.

Roman Britain displayed the characteristics of other imperial provinces. The settlement of people from elsewhere in the empire, many of them ex-soldiers, was matched by the Romanization of the British elite. The word civilisation is from the Latin '*civis*' (a city), and the Romans instituted what would now be termed a 'construction boom'. Towns appeared where there had previously only been hill forts. By the mid-second century, London, the lowest bridging point on the Thames, had become the capital and the major port of Roman Britain. York, Chester and Caerleon were the permanent bases of three legions, while Colchester, Lincoln and Gloucester were '*coloniae*': towns founded for veterans. Provincial capitals included Canterbury, Chichester, Winchester, Dorchester, Exeter, Cirencester, St Albans, Leicester and Carmarthen.

Gridded street plans developed in these towns. The streets were bordered by shops and houses, centring on communal buildings, such as baths, temples, theatres and the forum. Roman engineers diverted rivers to aid planning, as in Winchester, Chichester and Cirencester. More than 600 country villas were built (the Latin word 'villa' simply means a farm), all constructed in a Roman style and heated from under the floor by a hypocaust system. These buildings, floored with mosaics, must have appeared magnificent households, extolling the obvious virtues of Roman culture to the conquered Britons who still lived in timber and mud huts.

Around 9,600km (6,000 miles) of roads linked the Roman towns, villas and garrisons. Many of these roads are still used today — the A5, for example, follows the route of old Watling Street. Roads, remarkably straight as can be seen from any modern map, were built to a high standard, with stone foundations and gravel surfaces. They constituted a planned network, testimony to the impact of a powerful governmental structure that also organised a large-scale drainage scheme in East Anglia. Finally, and of course most importantly, there was an effective taxation system, partly to fund and supply the standing army.

As goods and money were regularly moved across greater distances, including to and from the Continent, inter-regional contact increased and new fashions and designs were disseminated, as in the pottery industry. The greater quantity of archaeological material surviving from the Roman period suggests a society producing and trading far more goods than its Iron Age predecessors.

Roman religious cults spread, though assimilation with native Celtic beliefs was important. When Christianity became the state religion further cultural links between England and the Continent were forged. The druids, whom the Romans had stamped out, and the cults of the Olympian gods, which they had originally introduced themselves, lacked doctrinal regulation and any diocesan structure. Pagan practices continued, however, and outside the lowland towns and centres of imperial authority and culture, Britain was not as thoroughly Romanised as other provinces of the empire, such as Gaul.

However, the introduction of more sophisticated farming implements — scythes, for instance, were unknown before the Romans — and the peaceful centuries which followed the settlement of England led to an unprecedented prosperity, with a consequent further growth in the population of the British Isles of about four million.

But Roman Britain suffered from one recurring flaw: the greed for power among the imperial elite. The province was weakened by the inability of the Roman empire to devise a consistently accepted system of imperial successions, and by the willingness of military units to support their commanders in bids for power. In 296 AD Britain had to be invaded in order to defeat a rebel Roman leader. These upheavals interacted cumulatively with the burden of defending Roman Britain from outside challenges, including Picts from Scotland, Scots from Ireland and Saxons from northern Germany and southern Scandinavia. Their attacks became serious in the middle of the 4th century AD, while a successful invasion in 367 AD led to widespread devastation. Order was restored by Theodosius in 368-369 AD. The construction of town defences from the 3rd century indicated an increasingly 'siege mentality'.

Civil war in the empire and barbarian invasions led to new problems in the 400s AD. In 406 AD Gaul was invaded by a vast number of barbarians. Britain, threatened with being cut off from the rest of the empire, created its own emperor who took a significant part of the island's military forces to counter the barbarian threat. They did not return. In 410 AD the Britons, disillusioned with the rebel Constantine III's activities, expelled his administrators and appealed to the true Emperor, Honorius, for the restoration of legitimate rule. He, hard pressed in Italy by Alaric, the Visigoth leader who captured Rome that year, could do no more than tell them to look to their own defence.

This was the end of the Roman empire in Britain. The history of England was about to take another, violent turn.

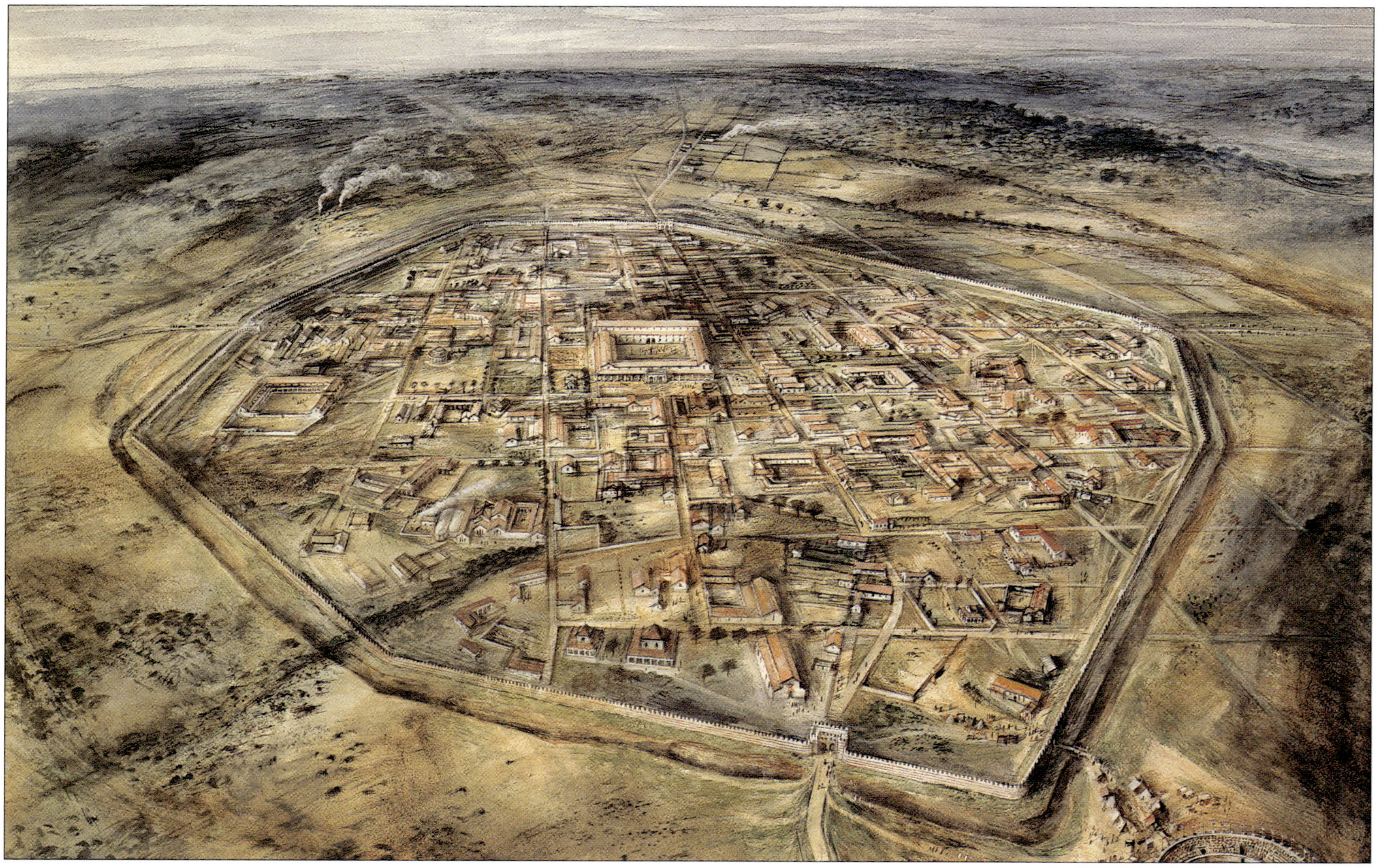

Above Left: *Roman building sites were organised, highly efficient places – and there was never a shortage of cheap labour. This drawing shows a gang constructing the city walls at Silchester, near Reading.*

Below Left: *Looking down on Silchester, one of England's most impressive Roman cities, in its heyday.*

Above: *A closer look within the city walls at Silchester which the Roman's called Calleva Atrebatum. The great square building would have served both as a barracks and the centre of local government.*

Right: *The view as it is today at Corbridge, on Hadrian's Wall. The Romans never conquered Scotland and the wall, begun in 122 AD, was designed as a first defence against marauding bands of Scottish tribes heading south.*

Above: *Hardknott Roman Fort on the Wrynose Pass, Cumbria.*

Left: *Walltown Crags, Hadrian's Wall, as it would have been seen by its Roman defenders. For many years it was thought the wall had suffered two great destruction's by northern tribes — in 197 AD and 296. Many archaeologists now believe this scenario is flawed.*

Below Left: *The impressive Chesters Fort, on Hadrian's Wall, was a vital strategic garrison on the Roman empire's north-west frontier. To the soldiers who served there however, the isolation and the long, freezing winters must have made it a posting to dread.*

Right: *Brunton Turret as it probably looked shortly after construction in the 2nd century AD. These signalling turrets were interspersed with fortlets every mile, along with 16 larger garrisons spread along the 120km (75 miles) stretch of the wall.*

Overleaf: *Chesters Fort.*

6 The Legend of Camelot

By the end of the 4th century, the last isolated Roman outposts along the Roman empire's northern boundaries were being abandoned. Troubles closer to home were presaging the collapse of the mightiest empire the world had ever known. One by one, the legions were recalled from Britain to defend their Mediterranean trade routes. By 430 AD the whole of Britain had been abandoned.

The 5th century is a particularly obscure period, but it is clear that, despite the mythology that has built up around these Dark Ages, a measure of social continuity existed. Rather than being a period simply of conquest and resistance, the collapse of one regime and the rise of another, the situation was far more complex. Romanised town and villa life, and the practice of Christianity, did not cease abruptly, and archaeological evidence of violent destruction is limited. Nevertheless, as elsewhere in western Europe, 'barbarian' mercenaries were hired and came to demand power for themselves. Alongside continuity in, for example, Kent, many other regions of Britain fell into the pre-Roman pattern of warring tribes.

In the north, the departure of the legions encouraged the ever bolder Caledonian tribes to push further and further south. But they soon encountered a mass movement of humanity that was imploding upon the British Isles in the vacuum left by the departing Romans. Teutonic invaders, the Jutes, the Angles and the Saxons, swarmed across the North Sea to plunder the countryside. They drove the native Britons westwards and northwards, back into the West Country, the Welsh borders and southern Scotland. The influx of these Germanic invaders in the fifth century was modest in terms of numbers, but their effect on the previously well-ordered, Romanised British society was cataclysmic.

The defenders of Britain could no longer call for assistance from the Continent to beat off the invaders, as they had in the fourth century. Moreover, being divided into warring kingdoms, their assailants were able to marshal their forces in ever-growing bases in lowland England. The Celtic natives, forced ever westwards, were desperately in need of a unifying leader to rally around.

Romano-British resistance was not uniformly unsuccessful, however, and in about 500 AD it achieved a major victory — supposedly at Mons Badonicus and under a warrior leader of the period called Artorius. One of the most enduring, inspiring and romantic legends in history was born …

The man was called 'The Once And Future King' — and certainly his heroic exploits survived the centuries to inspire and to intrigue. Legend has it that King Arthur battled to save his Celtic Britons from the invading Saxon armies. In a barbarous age, he ruled his people with benevolence and justice for all. His Knights of the Round Table came to epitomise everything that is chivalrous in human endeavour. His capital, Camelot, has become a byword for all that is gentle, noble, virtuous, righteous and learned.

So who was King Arthur? Did he really, as the ancient tales tell us, have a wizard called Merlin, a queen named Guinevere, a sword Excalibur, a round table, an island of Avalon and a fabulous castle called Camelot? Indeed, did this monarch and his noblest of champions truly exist — or is Arthur simply the most enduring and fascinating myth of English folklore?

The earliest reference to such a king is in the seventh century epic Welsh poem *Gododdin*, which speaks of a 'mighty warrior' in the continuing battles against the Saxons. There is little historical doubt that about 200 years before the poem was written a valiant leader did indeed live in the west of England and Welsh Borders around the year 518 AD. It is likely that the man now known as King Arthur was a Romanised military leader who united the battle-weary peasants before turning the tide of war against the Anglo-Saxons.

Some historians believe he may even have been the military mastermind behind a little-known British general, Ambrosius Aurelianus, whose armies when pushed back to the Welsh borders by the advancing Saxons, stood and fought at the Battle of Mount Badon in 518 AD. Largely thanks to the tactical genius of one of his chieftains, known only as Arthur, the English army defeated the occupiers so convincingly that peace was restored in the region for half a century.

Early Welsh scribes called Arthur 'a king of wonders and marvels' and the Arthurian legend took on a life of its own. In 1135 Geoffrey of Monmouth described Arthur in his *Historia* as the conqueror of western Europe. That is obviously far from the truth; Arthur's reign was over only a region of old England. In the 12th century another work, *Roman De Bru*, elaborated on Arthur's prowess and imbued him with the qualities of chivalry and piety that have remained interlocked with his legend ever since.

Knights were added to Arthur's court by the French poet Chrestien de Troyes. In his 13th century romance *Perceval*, these valiant knights embark on a quest for the Holy Grail, the chalice from which Christ drank at the Last Supper. *Sir Gawain And The Green Knight*, published around 1370, was the next major work to reinforce the legend. Then came *Morte d'Arthur* by Sir Thomas Mallory, the most important and certainly the most detailed mediaeval account of the Arthurian legend.

It is strange how the story of Camelot grew to reflect the aspirations of the peasantry of Britain, with its strange mixture of Christian beliefs and pagan wizardry. But how can one sift the fact from the fable — for fact there certainly is in the legend of this English warlord?

Right: *The Roman city of Viroconium (Wroxeter), Shropshire. Folklorists have speculated that this was the site of Camelot, from where Arthur, a Romanised Briton, unified the native Celtic peasantry against Anglo-Saxon invaders.*

Supposedly, Arthur was the illegitimate son of Uther Pendragon, King of Britain, and his mistress Igraine. Upon Uther's death, Arthur inherited his throne simply by publicly declaring it was rightfully his. It was at this time, too, that Arthur pulled the legendary sword Excalibur from a block of stone. Engraved on the stone were the words: 'Whosoever pulls this sword from the stone and anvil is the rightful king of England.' Folklore has it that no one claiming the throne had achieved this before. Thus Arthur, who until this point had been brought up in secret and whose existence was not even known to most, became the rightful heir. Merlin, the court wizard who was to become Arthur's mentor, bowed down before him and proclaimed him king.

However, Arthur's success was not immediate. Contrary to what legend would have us believe, there were many years of fierce fighting before Arthur's right to the kingdom was accepted. Not everyone loved and revered him but he protected himself and his realm by instituting the glorious regime of his famous Round Table Knights. And he married a beautiful bride, Guinevere (actually his second wife).

Arthur's principal enemies included his own treacherous sister, Morgan la Fay, and his nephew, Mordred. Morgan was a witch who plotted against her brother and once, while Arthur was away in battle, seized the throne. Arthur eventually killed Mordred, but not before he was fatally wounded himself. His body was buried on the holy isle of Avalon, where it was believed a miracle would one day take place and restored him to life. That burial place is still undisturbed.

So much for the legend. What of the facts that support the existence of such a man and his court? The two keys are the location of 'Camelot' and 'Avalon'. We know that a war leader who fitted the Arthurian image did indeed live in England's West Country and Welsh Borders around the year 518 AD. But the legends that embellished his brief history might have remained no more than folklore but for research into the chronicles of Glastonbury Abbey in Somerset.

Writing in about 1120, William Malmesbury had described Arthur's grave as having been discovered in the oldest part of the cemetery of the Abbey's Lady Chapel. The grave was marked by a cross inscribed (in Latin) with the words: 'Here lies the famous King Arthur with Guinevere, his second wife, buried in the Island of Avalon.'

This story conformed with the records of the Abbey. Some of the more important graves had been excavated in the tenth century as the level of the cemetery was raised. According to a Bishop Dunstan, the new surface level was protected by a wall. If the monks had gone to this trouble, it would have been logical to erect a fresh stone over the grave of Arthur and Guinevere. The abbey records also contain a report that in 1190 Abbot Henry of Sully exhumed the royal coffin from a pit about 5m (16ft) deep and removed it to the Abbey's treasury.

Glastonbury received two other royal visitors in 1275 — this time live ones. King Edward I and his Queen Eleanor made a pilgrimage to consecrate the abbey's high altar. On this auspicious occasion, the abbot broke open the treasury's ancient coffin to reveal two caskets, each decorated with coats of arms. In one was the skeleton of a tall man, in the other was that of a slightly-built woman. They were rewrapped in shrouds and presumably returned to the vaults or reburied.

In 1960 archaeologists excavated the area within Glastonbury Abbey where Arthur's grave might have been. They discovered that a deep pit had once been dug out and refilled with the indent of a headstone above it. But of the bones of King Arthur and his queen there was unfortunately no sign.

But why should the Somerset town of Glastonbury, which is well inland, ever have been called the Isle of Avalon? In Arthurian times, the place was an isolated area of high ground surrounded by marshland, effectively turning it into an island. In Welsh, it is known as Ynys Avallon, meaning the Island of Apples.

If Glastonbury was Avalon, where was Camelot? The conflict at which Arthur was reputedly killed was known as the Battle of Camlann and is believed to have taken place near Cadbury, Somerset, site of an ancient castle. Thousands of man-hours have gone into excavations there but archaeologists still have not found proof of the existence of Camelot, its knights or the most romantic king in British history.

The reason, according to fresh evidence unearthed in 1995, is that Camelot may be nowhere near Cadbury — nor even the West Country. The site of the mythical castle, it is claimed by some, may well be a marshy field about 13km (8 miles) outside Shrewsbury, Shropshire. It is possible that Arthur was in fact a king of Powys, a powerful dynasty that ruled much of Britain's western boundaries after the Romans departed. Their power base was the old city of Veraconium, now mere ruins outside the town of Wroxeter, and their burial place was known as the 'chapels of Bassa', believed to be the small village of Baschurch, outside Shrewsbury. Archaeologists have established that the site was once a Dark Ages fort surrounded by water — remarkably similar to the mythical Camelot.

Right: *Few legends have captured the imagination of English story-tellers as strongly as Camelot. Standing stones and burial chambers from an earlier age were often linked to his adventures, as with Arthur's Stone at Dorstone, near Hereford.*

Below: *Glastonbury Tor, in Somerset, was a medieval settlement thought by some to be the burial place of King Arthur.*

Far Left: *The 1193 exhumation of bodies, said to be those of Arthur and Guinevere, at Glastonbury Abbey.*

TINTAGEL CASTLE

Tintagel Castle situated high up on the Cornish cliffs remains one of the most spectacular and romantic spots in all England, destined to remain a place of mystery and romance long associated with the Arthurian legend.

The story goes that King Arthur lived in a castle here, and Merlin the magician lived in a cave on the beach. Is it the place the Romans called Durocornovium? Was it a Celtic Christian monastery? Was it the stronghold of the kings of Cornwall in the Dark Ages? Questions like these add to the magic and mystery of Tintagel, balanced perilously between a rocky promontory and the mainland.

What is clear is that the present castle was laid out in the 13th century by Richard, Earl of Cornwall, younger brother of Henry II, and that by Tudor times it had fallen into the ruins seen now. The keep on the mainland is thought to date from 1236-72, and the remains of the chapel on the summit of the promontory are thought to be 13th century as well.

But the site was obviously occupied before this. It was probably the stronghold of the Earls of Cornwall from about 1150. The numerous ruined buildings dotted around the promontory probably date from the same period. Recent excavations have uncovered traces of a Celtic monastery occupied from around 500 to 850 AD. There may even have been a Roman signal station here to warn ships, by smoke signals, that an invasion was imminent.

Right: *On a stormy day the mouth of Merlin's Cave, below Tintagel, exudes a magical atmosphere.*

Below: *The inner ward and great hall at Tintagel Castle, on Cornwall's rugged Atlantic coast. It is one of the most famous and mysterious sites of Dark Age England and is said to have been Arthur's birthplace. The ruins have yielded evidence of both a medieval castle and a monastery but there is no other known castle which bears direct comparison.*

7 The Dark Ages

According to the *Anglo-Saxon Chronicle*, the kingdom of Kent was founded in the mid-5th century AD by Jutes under the possibly mythical Hengist and Horsa. Sources for this invasion period are scant and often unreliable. Indeed, *The Anglo-Saxon Chronicle* was not written until much later, probably in King Alfred's reign, and the Germanic invaders themselves were illiterate. However, archaeological evidence does prove there was a strong Germanic invasion of Angles, Saxons and Jutes from northern Germany and Denmark, with the latter establishing themselves in Kent, the Isle of Wight and parts of Hampshire. The more dominant Saxons founded the kingdom of Wessex in the upper Thames Valley, around Dorchester-on-Thames, and expanded its power into Hampshire. And the Angles, although not the strongest presence in the conquered lands, nevertheless were to give their name to the nation we now call England.

Britain was taking on a new shape, created from conquest and tribal differences.

The 6th century saw yet more cultural and community changes, with certain of the more powerful tribes increasing their domains. The Wessex Saxons spread west and north, while the Angles established kingdoms in the Midlands (Mercia), Yorkshire (Deira), north of the Tees (Bernicia) and East Anglia. Bernicia was probably established at or near Bamburgh in the mid-6th century and Deira, to the north of the Humber, in the late 5th century.

This spread of power by the new settlers continued for over three centuries. Bernicia expanded greatly under Aethelfrith (593-616 AD), reaching as far as Lothian, and also probably pushed back the frontier of North Wales, while Deira gained the vales of York and Pickering. The British kingdoms of Elmet, centred on Leeds, and Rheged, around the Solway estuary, were absorbed by Northumbria (created from Bernicia and Deira) in the late sixth and seventh centuries, although Strathclyde survived. Elsewhere, the spread of these new kingdoms did not go so smoothly. The Saxon occupation of Dorset did not happen until the late 6th or 7th centuries, Cornwall was only conquered by Wessex in 838 AD and the kingdoms in Wales were never conquered.

In those areas that were conquered, the 'Romano-Britons' largely fled or survived as slaves and peasants. There was, however, a significant drop in the population — partly due to devastating outbreaks of plague. By now, the original British language and culture were largely lost in England.

The former Roman Empire within the country had fallen; but Anglo-Saxon civilisation, such as it was, still inevitably owed much to its predecessors. Farming techniques remained unaltered, with the Anglo-Saxons commandeering land that had already been worked. But the new custodians of England's rich soil did not enjoy wealthy, trouble-free times. With plague and violence raging, people existed on the bare minimum. Evidence of this comes from the excavation of few coins from the period and even fewer 'luxury' possessions. Only a couple of areas have yielded rich and ornate goods — many from the continent and Byzantium — to suggest some successful economic trade. Relics found in cemeteries in Kent and some parts of East Anglia indicate that, while Britain's inland population found life a struggle, coastal dwellers realised the importance and benefits of commercial links with the continent.

The numerous small kingdoms of the 6th century took a long time to merge and form friendly, larger communities. And such a state did not come about without fierce rivalry and wars. Penda of Mercia (c. 632-654 AD), for instance, was said to have had an army which included forces contributed by 30 subordinate leaders, many of whom would once have been the independent rulers of small territories. The West Midland kingdoms of the Hwicce and the Magonsaetan were absorbed by Mercia which, after the death of King Anna (654 AD), dominated the formerly independent East Anglia. Overkings, or rulers who enjoyed leadership over other kings, such as Aethelbert of Kent in the late 6th century AD, found their successes short-term.

For much of the 7th century, most of the power belonged to the rulers of Northumbria. Oswald (634-641 AD), Oswin (641-670 AD) and Egfrith (670-685 AD) ruled the lands between the Humber and the Forth on the eastern side of Britain, and between the Mersey and the Ayr on the west, and were at times treated as overlords by the rulers of Mercia, Wessex, Strathclyde and the Pict and Scottish territories. This hegemony finally ended following defeats at the hands of Mercia in 678 AD and the Picts in 685 AD, after which Northumbria lost its position as an almighty Anglo-Saxon kingdom. That accolade was now taken by Mercia, while Wessex became more dominant in southern England, conquering the Isle of Wight in 685 AD.

Though records of this period of English history are scant, it seems that settlement in the middle Saxon period — 650 to 850 AD — were widespread, if scattered. The preferred dwellings were houses and farmsteads which were gathered together within small hamlets.

Poorer peasants lived in villages with large numbers of huts with sunken floors. A surviving example of this is at Mucking in Essex. Furthermore it is to the Anglo-Saxons that we owe many of today's place names, with name endings such as 'ham', 'ton' and 'worth'.

A small number of major ports (Ipswich, London, Southampton and York) developed spectacularly in the 8th century and by the 10th century a more extensive urban network was in place. And at least two royal palaces were built in Britain around this time — at Yeavering in Northumberland and at Cheddar in Somerset (which was a rural palace for the kings of Wessex).

But what of religious beliefs during this period which came to be known as the Dark Ages? In 597 AD, a monk called Augustine, dispatched by Pope Gregory the Great, led a mission to Canterbury, the capital of Aethelbert's Kent. Augustine had some success at converting the people of the south-east to Christianity — but it was the church of Ireland that was the base for the conversion first of Scotland and then, via Northumbria, of most of England. There

was a pagan reaction in Northumbria in 632 AD but the Christian King Oswald won control there in 634 AD and, thanks to his influence, Cynegils of Wessex was baptised in 635 AD. Peada, heir to the vigorous pagan Penda of Mercia, followed in 653 AD, although paganism was difficult to eradicate. Signs of pagan burials throughout the Midlands, Essex, Kent and East Anglia have been useful historical indications of Saxon settlements.

There was also tension between the Northumbrian church and the authority of Rome. But, as a result of the support of King Oswy of Northumbria at the Synod of Whitby in 664 AD, Roman customs, such as the date of Easter, prevailed.

Christianity meant stronger links with the Continent. St. Wilfrid (634-709 AD), the Abbot of Ripon, studied in Rome, ministered in Lyon, and was consecrated bishop at Compiègne. Bishoprics were created and diocesan boundaries reorganised. A strong monastic tradition — as, for instance, at Jarrow, Monkwearmouth and Lindisfarne — influenced the nature of kingship, since many monasteries were founded by rulers and nobles of the period. From the late seventh century, monastic churches were constructed at important centres, though most local parish churches were not founded until the 10th and 11th centuries.

Christianity meant the beginnings of written law — not least to protect churchmen and their property — and the use of such documents to prove ownership of land. That is not to say that the pen was thought mightier than the sword; military and political strength still determined which kingdoms were to prevail. Skirmishes saw the rise of Offa of Mercia (757-796 AD), who boasted a disciplined society and impressive resources and who controlled such formerly independent kingdoms as Essex, Lindsey, East Anglia, Kent and Sussex. Offa is most often linked with the earth dyke named after him, built to prevent the Welsh from raiding his wealthy kingdom. The combined length of Offa's Dyke (stretches of which still survive today) and the related Wat's Dyke was 240km (149 miles) — longer than the Antonine and Hadrian's walls — and the building of it must have entailed considerable organisation. It was a testimony to the administrative strength of Mercian England.

Mercia was weakened in the early 9th century AD by the effort involved in the occupation of North Wales and by dynastic feuds. Meanwhile further south in 825 AD, after defeating the Mercians at Wroughton, Egbert of Wessex conquered Kent, Essex, Surrey and Sussex. Mercia eventually fell to Egbert in 829 AD and Cornwall in 838 AD. In 829 AD, Northumbria also acknowledged his overlordship. This acceptance did not last for long however, and Mercia was soon independent again.

Thus, feuds within and between royal families and between tribes ensured that society of Anglo-Saxon England remained violent and unpredictable. As proclaimed in the epic poem *Beowulf*, it was believed glory could only be achieved through warfare.

Much had occurred in England in the early days of the second millennium. In 1066 King Harold resoundingly crushed a renewed Viking offensive in north-eastern England, then marched his exhausted troops south to the Sussex coast where yet another invasion force was challenging his supremacy. The resultant Battle of

Left: *A cross to the memory of St. Augustine, a religious philosopher and a major influence on England's first 'national' king, Alfred.*

Hastings — between King Harold's Anglo-Saxons and the northern French invaders of King William of Normandy — was the single most important turning point in the 'recent' history of the British Isles. For when, after a closely fought conflict, Harold was carried dead from the field of battle, the spoils of war fell to a French-speaking hierarchy who changed the old British lifestyle, language and culture for ever.

A chain of vast fortifications was thrown up across the land to maintain the Norman overlords' stranglehold on the recalcitrant islanders. It took many decades before the Normans could finally claim to have subdued their newly conquered lands.

When the Normans ventured to the north of the British Isles, they found a people who were, for the first time in its history, coming together almost as one nation. It was under the rule of Duncan, King of Strathclyde (1034-40), that we can first speak of the kingdom of Scotland. Indeed, it had virtually the same borders as it does today. Duncan was killed by Macbeth, who successfully ruled Scotland for 17 prosperous years, to be succeeded in 1057 by one of Scotland's most significant early monarchs, Malcolm III.

There was some uneasy unity when Malcolm took the throne. Most commonly known as Canmore, a Gaelic name literally translated as 'big-head', Malcolm married Margaret of the royal house of Wessex, giving him some interest in the English throne. But when William the Conqueror finally invaded Scotland in 1071, he forced Malcolm to pay homage to him at Abernethy. In the intervals between the fighting, amicable relations were maintained between England and Scotland, for Malcolm remained a popular figure at the English court. But his death in 1093, while raiding Alnwick, in Northumberland, plummeted Scotland into 30 years of turmoil, ruled over by a succession of weak, insecure kings.

The first of these was Malcolm's 60-year old brother Donald Ban. Donald clashed with William Rufus, the new king on the English throne, who made several attempts to usurp him. Donald's half-brother Edgar became king in 1097, followed by his brother Alexander in 1107. Alexander married King Henry I's daughter and his sister Maud became the wife of the king himself. Ties with England grew closer and the Norman influence even greater.

When Alexander died in 1124, he was succeeded by his brother David, the ninth son of Malcolm and already the ruler of most of southern Scotland. He was to reign for 30 years. Like his brothers, David had been brought up in England where he had had a Norman education and made many Norman friends. In addition to being King of Scotland, he was also Prince of Cumbria. Further, by his marriage to a rich Norman heiress, he held the title Earl of Northampton and Huntington. Because of this he was one of the most powerful barons in England as well as being the English king's brother-in-law. He was also to prove one of the most innovative of Scotland's early kings.

On returning to Scotland, David began distributing large estates amongst his Anglo-Norman friends and associates who then became landowners on both sides of the border. At the same time, David introduced something akin to a feudal system of ownership to the Lowlands of Scotland. In the Highlands, however, the king's ideals counted for little while the Northern and Western Islands and some coastal regions gave a loose allegiance to Norway.

David did his best to establish a national system of justice and administration with a specially selected governing body to advise him. He appointed sheriffs to administer justice. He also encouraged trade with foreign countries and established two royal mints and a standard system of weights and measures. David granted the status of burgh to a number of towns, together with a freedom from tolls and the right to hold markets and fairs. He was a devout man and established more parishes, built more churches and endowed monasteries. He died in 1153, ending a rule which had brought with it dramatic change.

The focus of this short narrative of Scotland's ancient history now turns to its central heartlands — to Stirling, the 'crossroads' of the nation. Set at the highest navigable point of the Forth, and on the line of the main pass through the northern hills, Stirling guarded both the principal north-south and east-west routes across Scotland. The coincidence of strategic significance and a naturally strong site meant that the great rock upon which old Stirling stands was a prehistoric fortress and the likely site of the city of Iudeu, which figures in accounts of British kings in the 7th century.

However, Stirling Castle does not begin to appear in recorded history until the early 12th century, by which time it is already a residence of Malcolm's Canmore dynasty. Alexander I had founded a chapel here, and probably died within the walls of the castle in 1124. The castle next comes on record exactly 50 years later, when it was handed over to Henry II of England, along with five other castles, to pay for Scottish King William the Lion's release after his capture at the battle of Alnwick. Scottish control of Stirling was regained in 1189, and 25 years later King William died within it.

In all this time, we have no idea of Stirling Castle's physical appearance, although most of the buildings would have been of timber. The castle probably began to assume more permanent masonry from the late 13th century — something the turmoil of the succeeding century was to obliterate.

Edward I of England was the scourge of the Scots. Nicknamed 'Longshanks', he had long coveted the Scottish kingdom. As one of the most important castles in the kingdom, Stirling naturally played a major part in the Scottish struggle for independence of English overlordship. In 1291 Edward I took custody of all Scottish royal castles while he adjudicated on who was the rightful king of Scotland, and the castle's history over the next 50 years is mainly that of a struggle for its occupation by the forces fighting on behalf of the rival claimants. During the course of this struggle, Stirling was the scene of several of the finest triumphs of the Scottish patriots — although the benefits derived from these triumphs were short-lived.

In 1297 an army led by that great Scottish hero William Wallace overthrew the English in a famous victory at Stirling Bridge, and thus secured the castle for a time. Wallace was forced to defend his victor's crown the following year at Falkirk, and this time Edward I wrought his revenge. The English and Welsh archers shot down the Scottish foot and so enabled a charge by Edward's heavy cavalry to prove decisive.

By 1304 Stirling was the only castle left to the patriots. In that year Edward I instigated a successful siege, using fire-throwing equipment and a siege machine known ominously as the 'War Wolf'. The castle was again in English hands. The country seemed to lie at his mercy. And when the Scots' champion Wallace was captured and put to death at the king's orders in London in 1305, hope ran out and final surrender seemed inevitable.

Scotland was occupied from end to end and a foreign garrison lay in every town from Annan to Dingwall. Yet some did not

Above: *An impression of the Sutton Hoo ship burial by artist Peter Dunn.*

despair and, in 1306, Robert the Bruce was crowned King of Scots at Scone, with a mission to recover his kingdom and regain freedom for his subjects. For the victories won by the first Edward were not followed up by his son. In the years which followed the tide slowly turned, almost imperceptibly at first and then with gathering impetus, to the chagrin of Longshanks's successor, Edward II. One by one the towns and fortresses were retaken until by the spring of 1314, of only three castles which were still in English hands, Stirling remained the most important.

In that year, Stirling Castle was under siege by a Scottish force commanded by King Robert's brother, Sir Edward Bruce. Extraordinarily, under the laws of chivalry of the day, an agreement had been made between Edward Bruce and the English governor of Stirling castle, Sir Philip Moubray, whereby it was to be surrendered if not relieved before Midsummer Day (24 June 1314).

Edward II of England, realising the blow that failure would mean to his prestige, determined to relieve the castle in time. In doing so, he believed that he could draw the main Scots army out to oppose him, rather than allow them to conduct the campaign by their previous, highly successful guerrilla tactics. With one mighty stroke, Edward felt that he could recover all the ground lost since his father's death. Robert the Bruce was made aware of the English king's intentions by March 1314 — and determined to accept the challenge.

8 The Viking Scourge

Meanwhile, the Vikings had arrived — and for the Saxons who farmed Britain it was the dawn of a terrifying new age. The year was 793 AD and their prosperous world was about to be turned on its head. Few, if any, had even considered that their wealth would be a target for plunderers from across the sea. Certainly none could have imagined the ruthless, bloodthirsty warriors who would soon be pouring onto their shores.

As for the tall, fair-haired invaders from the Scandinavia, they must have been astounded at the lack of resistance they met. Very often their sleek longboats would come racing towards a beach to be confronted by locals standing around gaping in disbelief. It was never much of a fight. The well-armed, powerful Vikings would slaughter all who crossed their path before stripping nearby villages of valuables or livestock and putting back to sea. Even if the Saxons had a mind to organise defences, it would have been an impossible task; there was no telling when or where the enemy would strike next and the remote coastal settlements of northern and eastern England had no hope of summoning reinforcements in time. It meant rich easy pickings for the raiders, and a typical ship carrying 30 or so men was usually more than sufficient to see off the native opposition.

Above: *An example of a stone grave marker, in Viking style, dating from the late 9th century AD. The figures represent an attack on either a Scottish or Scandinavian settlement.*

Right: *The Brough of Birsay from where Viking lords ruled a substantial empire and set out for the rich pickings of coastal England.*

So who were the Vikings — or Northmen as they were first called — and what drove them to make war? The Vikings originated from the lands that are now Norway, Sweden and Denmark.

The Norwegian people tended to build their settlements around fjords, sheer-sided sunken valleys, penetrating far inland and well-protected from the worst of the weather. Some historians believe the name Viking may actually stem from the old Icelandic word '*vic*' which describes an sea inlet or cove. The Norwegians were excellent seamen but their agricultural land was limited by the country's topography.

Sweden was easier to cultivate because the land was generally lower and flatter but the winters were much colder and longer than those in Norway. The farmers had only a short growing season and the frozen rivers made travel and trade difficult.

Denmark's problem was the quality of crops. Although the country was low and flat and the climate reasonably mild, much of the land was covered by thin, unproductive soil. Denmark had to rely on its position at the centre of trading routes across the Baltic Sea and the Atlantic for its prosperity.

Shortage of good farmland was certainly one reason why young Vikings took to their ships in search of a better life. Any rise in the Scandinavian population quickly led to a food crisis. This didn't matter much to the wealthier chieftains or 'jarls' who owned most of the land, but it badly affected the middle classes, known as 'karls', who tended to be farmers, tradesmen or sailors. Lowest of the low were the 'thralls', or slaves, they had the worst-paid and dirtiest jobs and were happy to take on a hazardous sea adventure if it meant even the slightest chance of improving their lot.

To make matters worse the size of farms tended to grow smaller. A farmer would divide his land among his sons when he grew too old or sick to continue himself, and these smaller farms were less efficient. No surprise that a majority even of the landed classes decided it was easier to take than to grow...

The limited amount of land available for cultivation in Scandinavia and the vulnerability of nearby prosperous and fertile lands overseas led to an explosion of activity from the late 8th to the late 11th centuries. The most dramatic results were the establishment of Swedish power in Russia and Norwegian settlements in Iceland, Greenland and possibly Newfoundland (Vinland). In western Europe, the Danes campaigned extensively in northern France, establishing themselves in Normandy. The British Isles, close to Scandinavia and with a long coastline prone to marine raids and invasion, were extensively attacked. The Norwegians overran the Orkney and Shetland islands, the far north of Scotland and much of its west coast, as well as coastal regions of Ireland.

The Viking raiders inspired such terror that for more than 300 years all of Europe lived in fear of their coming. The appearance of these warriors must have been awesome: their main weapons of attack were the two-edged iron sword, heavy battleaxe, a hefty 'stabbing' spear and a lighter 'throwing' spear. They would also

use bows and arrows. In defence, a warrior relied upon his large, round shield, a helmet and a mail shirt. One Arab traveller, who had seen them fight at close quarters, wrote:

'The Vikings are a mighty nation, with huge bodies and great courage. They do not know the meaning of the word defeat — they never turn their backs on their enemies but slay or are slain. It is customary for each warrior to carry with him some craftsmen's tools, such as axe, saw, hammer and so on, while he is wearing his armour. He fights on foot with spear and shield. He wears a sword and dagger and has a throwing spear slung across his back'.

The Vikings were not very well disciplined fighters — war for them was very much a 'death or glory' affair. They had little time for tactics if it meant a delay in engaging the enemy, whom they preferred to catch unawares with a ferocious wave of warriors. They even had 'shock troops', the so called 'Beserkers', who according to the *Ynglinga Saga* 'were frenzied like mad dogs and wolves, biting their shields in their fury. They were as strong as bears or wild boars and struck men down right and left. Neither fire nor steel could stop them.'

England had been free from continental invasion for two centuries but in 789 AD the Danish ships were first recorded, and in 793-794 AD the pagan Danes brutally sacked the great Northumbrian monasteries of Lindisfarne and Jarrow. Viking pressure increased in the 830s and 840s AD, with frequent attacks on southern England. The kings of Wessex played a major role in resisting these attacks. Egbert defeated a joint Viking-Cornish army at Hingston Down in 838 AD, and his son Aethelwulf defeated a Danish force at Aclea in 851 AD. The latter's son Alfred was later to save Wessex by his efforts.

So, as we can see, the first incursions of the Scandinavians did not amount to invasion. From the early nuisance raids on northern England and Ireland in the eighth century, it was to be more than seventy years before the first full-scale Viking armies arrived. From the mid-ninth century the Vikings came not to plunder but to conquer and stay. Danish invaders took up winter quarters in Thanet in 850 AD and Sheppey in 854 AD. The Danish 'great army' abandoned operations in northern France and overran East Anglia in 865 AD and Northumbria in 866-867 AD.

In 865 AD a force of about 500 to 1,000 men landed in north-east England under the leadership of Ivar the Boneless, Ubbi and Halfden. These three men were sons of the unlikely-named Ragnar Hairy-Breeches, and were apparently seeking revenge for his death. Ragnar was reputed to have come to England with two ships some years earlier only to be roundly defeated by King Ella of Northumbria. Ella had Ragnar killed by throwing him into a pit of snakes. But before he died the Viking warned the Englishman that his sons would avenge him. He was right. In 867 AD the Danes defeated Ella at York and killed him. Gradually they overcame the little resistance that they encountered in central and southern England. But the kingdom of Wessex was a different enemy altogether.

Wessex, which was attacked in 871 AD, owed its survival in part to the skill of its young King Alfred, although the struggle was a desperate one and Wessex came very close to total defeat in 871 AD when the Danes won four of six major battles. Brief periods of peace came at a price: Alfred's dealings with the Danes involved both the paying of tribute and the exchange of hostages. Wessex's resistance encouraged the Danes to turn to the conquest of Mercia. King Burgred fled to Rome in 874 AD, and his successor Ceolwulf paid tribute to the Danes. In 877 AD Mercia east and north of Watling Street became Danish.

Throughout these dramatic years, however, Alfred fought on. The young king incurred the wrath of the Vikings when, extraordinarily, he beat them in a naval battle in 875 AD, capturing one longship off the south coast and putting seven others to flight. It was the first time the invaders had found their sea power challenged and they determined to seek revenge. Hearing of Alfred's success, the Viking king Guthrum marched south with a large force and began the occupation of Wessex.

Most of the locals gave up their struggle against him but Alfred fought on as a resistance leader from a secret hideout in marshes at Athelney in the West Country. According to the *Chronicle of the Kings of England*, by William of Malmesbury:

'Alfred wished to find out the plans of the Viking army, so he disguised himself to look like a wandering minstrel and went boldly into their camp. He was able to get right into the innermost place where the Viking leaders were holding a council of war. There, playing his harp in a dark corner, he listened and looked as hard as he could and found out all their secret plans. He stayed in the camp several days until he was satisfied that he knew everything. Then he stole back to Athelney, gathered together all his leaders and explained to them how easily they could beat the Vikings'.

The *Anglo-Saxon Chronicle* tells us that Alfred then:

'... rode to Egbert's Stone, east of Selwood, where he met all the people of Somerset, Wiltshire and Hampshire and they rejoiced to see him. And after one night he went to Iley and after another night to Edington and there fought against the whole Viking army and put it to flight.'

The Vikings were pursued to the Bristol Channel, where a peace treaty was drawn up at Edington, Wiltshire. Guthrum swore to leave the kingdom of Wessex in peace and even agreed to be baptised, with Alfred as his sponsor. Edington was a great victory for the English king and until his death in 899 AD he kept the invaders at bay throughout his lands (conquering London in 886 AD). Alfred's successful opposition to these further sporadic Danish attacks enabled him to accumulate wealth and begin minting 'good pennies'— to historians, always a clear sign of a well-ordered kingdom!

Above Right: *A modern sculpture of St. Aidan, founder of the great monastery at Lindisfarne; he set up his outpost of Christianity on this remote stretch of the Northumberland coast in 635 AD, following an invitation from King Oswald.*

Far Right: *A stained glass image of St. Hilda, founder of Whitby Abbey, as she appears in the north-west window of Oxford Cathedral's Latin Chapel.*

LINDISFARNE PRIORY

The monks of Lindisfarne were so successful at finding converts to Christianity in the North that they became rich and famous — too much so for their own good for they suffered a series of attacks over the centuries by those jealous of their success and wealth.

The Vikings were the first to attack in 793 AD. Despite the isolated position of the place they called Holy Island, linked to the mainland by nothing more than a causeway, the monks were unable to repel them. They fled with their most precious possession, the one which attracted pilgrims from all parts: the body of St. Cuthbert, at whose shrine miracles were performed.

Following the Viking destruction, it was 400 years before Lindisfarne was re-established, and it is the ruins of a mediaeval Benedictine priory that is seen today. The dramatic 'rainbow arch' over the nave of the priory church still stands. Nothing remains of the original monastery, which was founded in the 7th century by St. Aidan, who became the first bishop of Lindisfarne in 635 AD. Under him, Holy Island became known internationally as a centre of learning and culture. The Lindisfarne Gospels, now in the British Library, were copied and illuminated here in around 698 AD. They are one of the finest examples of the skill and artistry of the early English monks.

A view of the decorated pillars which adorn the nave at Lindisfarne Priory church.

9 The Danelaw: A Country Divided

Despite King Alfred's success in keeping the Vikings out of his own kingdom of Wessex, a vast slice of the British Isles was now under their occupation. The Treaty of Edington, reported in the previous chapter, left the Danes with what became known as the Danelaw — that is, England east and north of a line from Chester to London.

Extensive Danish settlement is indicated by the large number of Scandinavian place-names ending in 'by' and 'throb' and, in the north-east today, by the many Scandinavian surnames ending in 'son'. The centre of Danelaw was Northumbria, while the Norwegians established a base at Dublin in 841 AD and in the first two decades of the 10th century colonised the coastline of north-west England, invading the Wirral from Dublin in 902 AD. Scandinavian place-names are extensive in Cumbria and coastal Lancashire.

Meanwhile, a separate lifestyle continued in those parts of Britain not controlled by Danelaw. Freed from Viking insurgences, Alfred had turned to strengthening Wessex, building a fleet, creating a more effective system of military recruitment, and constructing a system of fortified towns. Existing towns had their walls restored or new ones constructed, while new burghs were established. It was a process that was continued by Alfred's successor Edward and by his daughter Aethelfled, who ruled English Mercia, the area south and west of Watling Street not settled by the Danes.

Defence under Alfred was followed by conquest under his heirs. Edward the Elder (899-924 AD), Athelstan (924-939 AD) and Edmund (939-946 AD) conquered East Anglia, eastern Mercia and Yorkshire; the kings of Wessex brought modern England under their authority. Edward overran the Danish bases in eastern Mercia and built forts in the north-west Midlands, including Manchester (919 AD) and Rhuddlan (921 AD), to limit the danger of attack from the Norwegian kingdom of Dublin. The defeated Danes were allowed to keep their lands and the Danelaw retained distinctive features, including its own legal system.

English Mercia was absorbed by Wessex after the death of Aethelfled (918 AD). In 923 AD the rulers of Scotland, Northumbria, Strathclyde and the Welsh kingdoms accepted Edward's lordship, giving the idea of a 'kingdom of Britain' some substance at last.

In 927 AD Athelstan captured York, in 934 AD he invaded Scotland, and in 937 AD he defeated a united army of Scots, Strathclyde Britons and Norsemen (Norwegians) from Ireland at Brunanburh. He formed alliances with leading continental rulers, fixed the Wye as the boundary with South Wales and restricted Cornish power to west of the Tamar. Despite formidable resistance from the Yorkshire Danes, they were finally reduced — Eric Bloodaxe, their last king, being killed in an ambush in 954 AD.

The areas reconquered from the Danes were quick to abandon their old gods and to adopt Christianity. Ultimately it was their conversion to Christianity which ended the Vikings' warlike habits and turned them into more peaceable farmers and sea traders.

Their conquering reign had lasted little more than 300 years but in that time they bequeathed much more to Western Europe than savagery and brutality. Their burning desire to explore the world made them truly the lords of the sea — an inheritance which, by their knowledge of shipbuilding and navigation, they bequeathed to Britain, thus shaping that emerging nation's great naval tradition.

England was now making remarkably swift progress in political and social terms. Royal authority had been re-established under an expanding state ruled by the house of Wessex. A county or shire system extended into areas reconquered from the Danes. The shires were in turn divided into hundreds and, in Scandinavian areas, wapen-takes, responsible for maintaining law and order. Their public courts were a link between rulers and the fairly numerous free groups in society. The coinage was improved, with seventy mints set up around the country, with a flexible rate of exchange boosting foreign trade. There was also a system of assessment for taxation and military service based on hides, the hide being the amount of land deemed necessary to support a peasant family.

The church made sure that it was closely linked with royalty, and an ecclesiastical revival took place that was largely monastic in inspiration. Following the decay of monastic life in the ninth century, Edmund's son Edgar (959-975 AD) reformed the monasteries, and Canterbury, Sherborne, Winchester and Worcester all became monastic cathedrals.

The church was well endowed (the total income of monasteries and nunneries by the early 11th century was far greater than that of the king). The Anglo-Saxon church had long provided missionaries, such as Boniface and Willibrord, to help convert Germany and the Low Countries to Christianity, a sign of the vitality of English Christianity. It sent others to Scandinavia in the late 10th and early 11th centuries. This religious revival provided a literary and cultural activity which revealed itself in brilliant manuscript illumination, stone carving and embroidery.

The kingdom of Wessex had by now become what was later termed the 'Old English Monarchy'. This state was still very much centred on Wessex, Athelstan alone among the 10th century rulers spending much time in Mercia. Wessex was administered from its four heartland shires of Hampshire, Wiltshire, Dorset and Somerset the regions where the kings spent most of their time. However, the precariousness of nationhood was indicated in 957 AD when the

Opposite: *The ruins of St Augustine's Abbey, Canterbury, founded in 598AD as a shrine for burying the kings and archbishops of Kent. There was further large-scale building on the site for the next four centuries, although much was demolished in 1070 to make way for Abbot Scotland's great Norman Abbey.*

Mercians and Northumbrians renounced allegiance to Eadwig in favour of his brother Edgar. The schism was healed, although Edgar also became King of Wessex on Eadwig's death in 959 AD. The allegiance of Northumbria to whomever ruled at Winchester remained uncertain until well into the 11th century.

The country prospered, however. As a result of agricultural advances and the production of wool and cloth, England became wealthy by the standards of contemporary northern Europe, and a tempting prize to foreign rulers. The power of the old English monarchy was displayed in 973 AD when other British rulers made a formal submission to King Edgar at Chester. The Winchester monk and chronicler Aelfric wrote:

'... *King Edgar*
furthered Christianity, and built many monasteries,
and his kingdom still continued in peace,
so that no fleet was heard of,
save that of the people themselves who held this land;
and all the kings of the Cymry and the Scots
that were in this island, came to Edgar
once upon a day, being eight kings,
and they all bowed themselves to Edgar's rule.'

The peace and unity of England was not to survive Edgar's death in 975 AD. Both his sons were young. The elder, Edward, succeeded but was unpopular and was murdered in 978 AD by supporters of the younger son, Aethelred 'the Unready' (978-1016). Aethelred has been the subject of scorn throughout history, not least because of the hostile tone of the *Anglo Saxon Chronicle*. In fact Aethelred made major efforts to improve the state's defences but he lacked the presence and natural authority to command or elicit trust. This limited his ability to deal with the next crisis to hit the British Isles — the return of the Vikings.

England under the recent kings of Wessex, Scotland under its outstanding ninth century ruler Kenneth MacAlpin and much of Wales under the rulers of Gwynedd, had all experienced a welcome measure of statehood. But so too had the Viking lands — enabling them again to organise themselves into larger armies.

Soon after Aethelred's accession, the Danes started mounting major attacks, in one of which they defeated the Essex militia under ealdorman Brihtnoth at Maldon (991 AD). Aethelred used a mixture of bribes (Danegeld) and violence, such as a pitiless massacre of English-resident Danes in 1002 to maintain his power. The Danes retaliated with fearsome vengeance over a decade and in 1013 resistance collapsed. The following year Aethelred was briefly driven into exile in Normandy by King Sweyn of Denmark, who was recognised but never crowned as king of England.

Aethelred returned on Sweyn's death. But the struggle was continued by Sweyn's son, Cnut, while resistance was hampered by divisions among the English, especially that between Aethelred and his eldest son, the energetic Edmund Ironside. After Aethelred's death, England was divided between Cnut and Edmund in 1016 by the Peace of Alney, Cnut receiving Mercia and Northumbria. Edmund, however, died and Cnut became King of all England from 1016-35.

England was now, almost by default, part of a greater Scandinavian empire. Cnut, following the death of his older brother Harold, had also become king of Denmark and thereby the newly conquered Norway. The Vikings now largely ruled the western seaboard of Europe including, significantly, Normandy which still bears their name as 'home of the northmen'.

Cnut chose to rule these dominions from England, where he largely followed the peaceable practices of the local kings of Wessex, although he introduced a number of Danes into the aristocracy and divided the kingdom into a small number of earldoms. The earldom of Wessex was given to Godwin, an English protégé of Cnut, who married a Danish princess and gave Danish names to four of his six sons, including Harold. An Anglo-Viking aristocracy was being created, as England looked increasingly overseas to the lands of her Scandinavian conquerors.

But for the most extraordinary catalogue of events that were to follow, the British Isles might have developed as the centre of a Viking empire.

Above and Right: *Two views of Whitby Abbey in North Yorkshire. The original structure was founded by St. Hilda in 657 AD but its proximity to the north-east coast made it an easy target for the Vikings, who destroyed it in 867 AD. It was rebuilt as a Benedictine house in 1078 although today's ruins are the remnants of a later 13th and 14th century design.*

10 The Norman Conquest

Above: *A reconstruction of the most famous battle ever fought on English soil — the Battle of Hastings. The engagement was dominated by the Normans' skilful use of archery, supported by cavalry charge, which effectively broke up King Harold II's massed infantry. Both sides suffered heavy losses but Harold's death, allowed William, Duke of Normandy to claim the English throne.*

Right: *The Great Gatehouse at Battle Abbey, near Hastings. The Benedictine Abbey was founded by William in 1067 to celebrate his victory and offer prayers for the souls of the fallen. He ordered that the high altar be placed on the precise spot where King Harold fell.*

Edward 'the Confessor' had spent 25 years in exile as a refugee from the Vikings in Normandy before his popularly acclaimed return to England in 1042. Following the reigns of Cnut's sons, Harold and Harthacnut, the ancient house of Wessex was now restored. Edward's reign, although brief, was prosperous for Britain — but it was overshadowed by the problem of the succession.

When Edward died childless on 5 January 1066 the Witan, the great council of the realm, elected as their king Harold Godwinson, Earl of Wessex, who claimed that Edward had made him a deathbed promise of the throne. The largest landowner in the country, Harold had acquired considerable prestige from successful campaigns against Gruffydd ap Llywelyn, King of Gwynedd, who had conquered all of Wales and sacked Hereford in 1055. At Rhuddlan in 1063 Harold defeated Gruffydd, who was soon after murdered by his followers, his head being sent to Harold. The next threat to the peace of England was to come from Scandinavia, where the Vikings were again casting greedy eyes upon the British Isles. In these dangerous times, Harold, the popular war hero, was seen as the one man whose prowess in battle could maintain the unity of England.

Having vanquished the Welsh, and fearing invasion by Vikings from the north, King Harold came to the throne facing yet another threat from a third quarter. Duke William of Normandy, the head of a warlike people descended from Viking settlers, laid claim to the English succession — on the faint grounds that he was the late King Edward the Confessor's illegitimate second cousin once removed. However, he alleged that, when visiting Edward in 1051, the old king had solemnly promised the throne to him. And, with a strong army assembled on the Norman side of the English Channel, he was out to get it. That he managed to do so was only down to a series of extraordinarily unlucky breaks for King Harold…

To thwart any invasion by William, Harold initially concentrated his forces along the south coast. When bad weather prevented William from sailing in September 1066, Harold disbanded his forces and left for London. There he heard that the Norwegians under Harold Hardrada, King of Norway, had landed in Yorkshire. They defeated the local earls at Gate Fulford on 20 September and seized York, winning a measure of local support. King Harold and his men were now called upon to perform an unparalleled feat in military history.

• On 18 September he learned of the Yorkshire landings.
• Harold marched his army north at miraculous speed.
• On 25 September he decimated the Norwegians at Stamford Bridge. Hardrada was slain and his defeated army needed only twenty ships of the invasion force of 300 to ferry the survivors home.
• Then to his horror, Harold heard that the Normans had landed at Pevensey, Sussex, on 28 September.
• He force-marched his men back to London, recruited fresh soldiers and arrived in the deep Weald of Sussex on the night of 13 October — an astonishing 400km (250 miles) in all.
• At nine o'clock the following morning, the Normans, after two weeks' preparation, joined them in battle.

What really happened on 14 October 1066, the most celebrated date in English history? Myth and legend have clouded the dramatic reality of the conflict. But the truth, as we now know it, is more amazing than any fiction.

At nine o'clock that Saturday morning, two armies were drawn up in the Sussex countryside. That led by Harold Godwinson was utterly exhausted — 5,000 men weakened by battle and fatigue after their victory in the north and their astonishing march south. William's Norman army of 7,000 men were fresh from an easy Channel crossing. Apart from the difference in preparedness, there was one other crucial difference between the two armies. Norman cavalry fought on horseback, wielding swords and thrusting lances. Those of the English who rode to battle dismounted and fought on foot.

The English line, a dozen close-packed ranks of infantry and archers, were drawn up on Senlac Hill, just oustide of the town of Battle which subsequently grew on the site. In the centre stood

Harold, surrounded by his 'housecarls', an elite bodyguard of crack troops, the best in Europe and wielding the dreaded two-handed battleaxe.

William attacked first. His infantry, many of them mercenaries, made little impact against the brave and unbudging English. They retreated in disarray, passing the word that the day was lost and that William himself had been killed. The English soldiers were jubilant. With equal vigour, they beat off an awesome Norman cavalry charge which followed.

Then came the error that changed the course of the battle and English history.

Repulsed, the Norman knights turned back to regroup — a manoeuvre that appeared to the English to be a disorderly retreat. The front lines of the Saxon army broke ranks and charged down Senlac Hill in pursuit of the horsemen. William saw his chance and staged a further series of feigned flights, successfully enticing his enemy to break ranks. Depleted, King Harold's army reformed — 'withstanding as though rooted to the soil', according to one chronicler. But there were now too few of them. Harold had foolishly arrived in Sussex ahead of the reserves (the fyrd, a sort of Territorial Army) whom he had recruited in London.

The final push came as dusk fell. The professional Norman archers, using short or 'Danish' bows, advanced to within 100 yards of the English, as they had done throughout the day. Attacking uphill, they fired their showers of arrows high into the air. It was this hellish hail of death that brought the collapse of the English army.

King Harold was struck in or near the eye — wounding though not killing him — as so graphically depicted in the Bayeux Tapestry. As he desperately tried to pull the arrow out of his head, a few rampaging Norman knights came upon him and cut him down with their swords. The disintegrating English fled, with William himself in pursuit on his fourth horse of the day, the previous three having been killed beneath him. The fyrds arrived six hours later — far too late to turn the tide of war.

As penance for the dreadful slaughter of that day, the newly-proclaimed William I of England built an abbey on the site of the battle. He placed the high altar on the very spot where his noble adversary Harold had fallen.

In a way, the unification of England under the house of Wessex ensured that it fell rapidly to William the Conqueror — unlike the more lengthy processes by which the Iron Age and Romano-British kingdoms had fallen to Rome and the Anglo-Saxons. Following his victory at the Battle of Hastings, the victorious William crossed the Thames to the west of London and, as he approached the city, morale among the defendants crumbled. At Berkhampstead they submitted to William. And on Christmas day he was acclaimed king in Westminster Abbey.

At last, some stability was coming to England. The Normans recognised that although the country they had conquered was wealthy, a proper administrative system had to be established to ensure future prosperity.

Indeed, it became a time of great power building by a people who were basically warriors. Castles were built to emphasise the Norman presence and authority. These were initially earth and timber constructions which could be quickly erected in areas where defence was considered of immediate importance. These later gave way to mightier and more permanent stone castles such as the White Tower in London and Windsor Castle. Stone cathedrals soon dotted the landscape too, and again, those such as Durham cathedral are testimony to Norman architectural skills. All such buildings were evidence of the conquerors' control, providing centres for both political and religious rule.

Now, too, came the beginnings of a defined social structure, with Norman lords the masters and lower orders very much their servants. Creating what was to become known historically as the feudal system, the lords pledged support and protection of their people and provided them with land in return for service — principally military service. For the understanding was that this 'military tenancy' meant Norman lords were obligated to provide a number of knights for service roughly proportionate to the size of their estate.

At this time in English history, the island's boundaries were becoming more defined, with an area to the east and south and the highland ranges of Wales and Scotland being drawn up to come under written administration. Despite the teething problems of feudalism, newly introduced laws, higher taxes and different tongues, the nation slowly became unified.

But while the common people adapted to their servitude, the Norman hierarchy fought amongst themselves. Nobles and monarchs wanted more power and land. Inheritance was almost always disputed, leading to the establishing of a rule under which the eldest male child automatically enjoyed a rightful claim. Even this

Left: *The large Norman motte and bailey of Berkhamsted Castle in Hertfordshire. The earliest work was begun by William the Conqueror's half-brother, Robert of Mortain.*

Above Right: *Stonework at Dover Castle, one of England's largest and best-preserved fortresses.*

Below Right: *The Tower of London by floodlight. In its time it became the most feared — and the most famous — prison in England. The central White Tower was built by William the Conqueror around 1080.*

was not without its problems. William I (1066-1087) died after being thrown from his horse in the French town of Mantes which he had burnt as a result of a border conflict. William left Normandy to his eldest son Robert and England to his second son William II, believing that he was the right man to rule an often troublesome country. Robert, however, wanted to be lord of both nations. He and William, known as Rufus (1087-1100) because of his red hair, became bitter foes. Eventually Robert resigned Normandy to William in 1096 in order to raise funds to embark on the First Crusade.

William had an impressive military record. In 1092 he took an army to Cumbria which, although in the hands of an English family, had Malcolm III of Scotland as its recognised overlord. William created a town and built a castle at Carlisle, established a Norman ally at Kendal and made the Solway and the Liddel the northern border of his kingdom. He was also successful against Norman rebels and the French. But William earned a reputation not only as a fine soldier but the patron of fine buildings too. His greatest achievement was Westminster Hall, whose vast interior is still used on state occasion.

William died in 1100, in what some say was a suspicious hunting accident in the New Forest, while out with his brother Henry.

Henry I moved quickly to secure power and eventually defeated older brother Robert at Tinchebrai (Normandy) in 1106. Robert was imprisoned in Cardiff where he died in 1134.

Henry was not a man with whom to come into conflict. Those who crossed him were subjected to appalling torture. Anyone, for instance, considered responsible for irregularities in minting money was blinded and castrated. It was his tight administration of the currency that laid the groundwork for today's exchequer (named after the chequer or chess board).

The wars Henry was forced to wage in Normandy were a considerable drain on his resources — he was significantly poorer than Rufus had been — but this was compensated for by his efficient management. Henry was also respected more by the church than his brother — despite talk of siring more than 20 children, only two of whom were legitimate. His only legitimate son, William, died at sea in 1119.

But the Norman kings, like their Anglo-Saxon predecessors, worked closely with the church and the fervently supported the reforming Popes of the late 11th century. New religious orders were introduced to England, previously home only to Benedictine houses, the sole monastic order in Saxon England. First came the Cluniac order from Burgundy, then the Augustinian priories, with groups of canons (priests who lived together under a common rule). These orders were later joined by the solitary Cistercians, who founded the famous abbey at Tintern.

Henry I married Matilda, daughter of Malcolm III of Scotland, in 1100. By 1107, his throne was finally secure. With his brother incarcerated at Devizes and a victory over the church to appoint his own bishops, the king felt a confident ruler. He had also sealed a treaty with Archbishop Anselm of Canterbury under which bishops must pay homage to Henry for the estates that accompanied their office. The deal ended the feuding which began under William and gained Henry the support of the Pope.

Henry I died in France in 1135 from food poisoning, after gorging on lamprey fish. Only one child, his illegitimate son Robert, Earl of Gloucester, was at his deathbed. Because his only legitimate son was dead, Henry left behind him a disputed inheritance. His daughter Matilda had married Geoffrey Plantagenet, Count of Anjou, in 1128. Her father's death made Matilda and her husband rightful rulers of England. But Geoffrey, at war with Normandy, was never to set foot in England.

So, far from uniting the kingdoms of England and Anjou, Henry's death led to twenty years of destructive civil war. Matilda, despite her husband's detachment, was determined to take the throne — and one man was equally determined she should not. As soon as he heard of Henry's death, his nephew Stephen of Blois, son of William the I's daughter Adela, sailed from Boulogne to seize power and was crowned by a reluctant Archbishop of Canterbury. Ironically, the woman Stephen chose as his queen was also called Matilda.

The period of his reign is known as 'the anarchy' when 'Christ and his angels slept'. And not without good reason. Stephen was

Above: *The distinctive outline of Carisbrooke Castle, on the Isle of Wight. The fortress is of mostly 13th century construction, although considerable improvements to the defences were made by Elizabeth I to ward off invasion. Charles I had the dubious pleasure of being imprisoned here in 1647-48.*

Right: *Only the great square keep survives intact at Rochester Castle, Kent. The castle was once the largest and most luxurious in Britain, containing a magnificent great hall within its merged second and third storeys.*

recrowned king in 1141 after an astonishing year which had seen him defeated, captured, deposed and finally victorious.

In February that year, while he was besieging the rebellious Earl 'Moustaches' Ranulf of Chester in Lincoln Castle, he was overwhelmed by the superior forces of Matilda, led by her half-brother Robert of Gloucester. Refusing to flee, Stephen fought until he was captured. He was held in Robert of Gloucester's castle while Matilda made her way to London to seek the succession. But the citizens of London, already wary of her, became hostile when she demanded large sums of money from them. While preparing for her coronation, the Londoners rose and drove her out. Stephen's supporters, led by his wife, defeated her army outside Winchester and captured Robert of Gloucester. He was exchanged for Stephen who once again sat on the throne. In 1148, Matilda left England and returned to her husband in Normandy, dropping her claim to the throne.

King Stephen died in 1154, two years after his beloved wife. The question of succession had been resolved only a year earlier, when Stephen had dramatically disinherited his son, Eustace, in favour of Henry Plantagenet — son of his old adversary and thwarted claimant to the throne, Matilda. A new royal house now had the task of trying to end England's anarchy.

Above: *The massive keep of Castle Rising, in Norfolk, was built in 1138 by William de Albini, Earl of Lincoln in the same year that he married Henry I's widow Queen Alice. The castle's Norman earthwork defences are unusually well preserved.*

Right: *A splendid aerial view of Dover Castle – the 'Gateway to England'. Dover Castle is possibily the most important fortress in England. The Romans knew its strategic value and so did the Conqueror who, on defeating Harold at Hastings, made straight for Dover. He built a motte-and-bailey castle in, it is said, only eight days. Only when his crossing point with France was secure did he continue his march into the heartland of England.*

BUS STOP

11 The Plantagenets

The crowning of King Henry II in 1154 healed the rift between England's royal rivals, Stephen and Matilda. Henry was the son of Matilda. The death of Eustace, son and heir to Stephen, paved the way for a compromise deal in which Henry took the throne. Stephen's second son William was paid off handsomely with large tracts of land. Henry's father was Geoffrey Plantagenet, Count of Anjou, and the dynasty became known as the Plantagenets.

Although king of England, Henry was much concerned with matters in France. After all, he was born in Le Mans, did not visit England until he was nine yèars old and was to eventually die in France, in Chinon. His queen was Eleanor of Aquitaine, a union which brought vast new lands to the south of this dual nation. Henry certainly had his work cut out. There were troublesome Scots to contend with as well as brooding Celts and greedy and unpredictable barons from the Scottish borders to the Pyrenees. Energetically, he tackled the challenges that dogged his reign.

Yet his 'new broom sweeps clean' approach, which undoubtedly helped restore some semblance of order to England, is largely forgotten by history. Henry is remembered as the king responsible for the death of St Thomas à Becket.

Becket was the son of a London merchant, who rose to become Chancellor to the king and later Archbishop of Canterbury. Henry was convinced he had a tame churchman in the form of Becket, who was a personal friend. On that count, the appointment suited Henry well as he was aiming to reduce the power of the church. He wanted an end to the system in which the church punished its own, often more leniently than would a civil court. Likewise, appeals to Rome, Henry felt, flew in the face of his own authority and should be scrapped.

Henry's spearhead into the church was known as the Constitutions of Clarendon of 1164 and contained fifteen points. There Becket and his bishops fought the proposals for two days before caving in. Almost immediately Becket regretted his decision and stood once again for the interests of the church, in opposition to the king. Henry had Becket arrested and in 1165 the country's most eminent churchman fled into exile. It was five years before he returned to England to resume his battle of wills with Henry.

In a fit of outrage at his court in Normandy, Henry burst out: 'Will no one rid me of this turbulent priest?' In response, four knights made their way to England, found Becket in Canterbury Cathedral and on 29 December 1170 slayed him with their swords.

Henry was grief-stricken when he heard about the killing. He donned sackcloth and ashes and loud lamentations were heard from behind the door of his chamber, where he imprisoned himself for three days. Three years after his death, Becket was canonised. A year after that Henry had monks flog him in the street as a mark of his repentance, although he always maintained that he had never ordered the killing.

If Henry believed his worst enemies were abroad, he was sadly mistaken. In the last years of his life, his wife and three of his four sons plotted against him. Eleanor slaughtered the king's mistress, 'Fair' Rosamund Clifford, and was so disagreeable that she was eventually imprisoned.

When his eldest son, also called Henry, was crowned successor in 1169, his second son Richard was incensed. By a coincidental quirk both later joined forces with Philip II of France and waged war on their father. John, Henry's favourite son, joined them. By now both Henry the Younger and Geoffrey, Henry's other son, were dead. The aggressors compelled a heartbroken King Henry to accept a shamefully humiliating peace. A month later he died.

Richard was crowned king of England on 3 September 1189 in Westminster. It was one of the few occasions he visited the country during his reign. It is calculated that during a decade of rule he spent less than a year with his feet on English soil.

Nor was it the happy occasion he might have wished. By his own decree, Jews were banned from the coronation. When some turned up they were attacked by Richard's courtiers. Many were killed and those released were badly injured. The incident sparked a pogrom in London and Jews were rooted out and slaughtered by the score.

Richard, despite his foreign travels, was a popular king. His upbringing at the court in Poitiers, France, with its emphasis on chivalry and knightly courage, served him well. He won the name 'Lionheart' — although whether his personal integrity matched up to his bravery is open to question.

It was the lure of the Third Crusade that took Richard overseas. Jerusalem, the centre of Christianity, was once again under control of Muslims led by the charismatic Saladin. Prompted by attacks on pilgrims, the Pope sanctioned another Crusade.

Richard stayed in England long enough to raise taxes to pay for the expedition. He jokingly said that he would have sold London if only he could have found a buyer. In 1190 he set off for the Holy Land with his old ally, Philip II of France. Their relationship was soured, however, when Richard failed to marry Philip's sister Alice as promised. Instead Richard wed Berengaria of Navarre, the choice of his mother Eleanor.

Deserted by Philip, Richard fought on and delivered a brutally decisive blow to the Saracens at Acre. Now he fell out with Duke Leopold of Austria over the spoils of victory and the Duke withdrew from the Crusade. Wisely, Richard negotiated with Saladin when he arrived at Jerusalem. The two men got along famously and agreed that pilgrims had a right of entry to the Holy City while the Muslims remained in charge.

Returning from Palestine, Richard was captured by the irate Duke Leopold and held to ransom for more than a year. At home his ambitious brother John was in league with the disgruntled Philip. Both undoubtedly contemplated abandoning Richard to Duke Leopold but decided the repercussions would be too great.

Right: *A fine 14th century oriel, or windowed recess, is the splendour of Prudhoe Castle in Northumberland, which also has its gatehouse, curtain wall and keep.*

Above: *Henry II is believed to have added the dominating great keep to the existing structure of Richmond Castle which lies above the River Swale in North Yorkshire. Although the castle fell to ruin after the 16th century the keep with its magnificent archway remains almost intact.*

Right: *The remains of Clun Castle on the Welsh borders are dominated by a ruined keep and a pair of 13th century towers.*

As a result of the collusion between Philip and John, further English territory was lost. Richard went to war in Europe to try to redress the losses. But in 1199, in a siege of the castle of Chalus, near Limousin — so minor an engagement that he did not even bother to don his armour — Richard was hit in the shoulder by a crossbow bolt. The wound festered and he died.

Richard's younger brother John succeeded him to the throne. King John has long been cast as the arch villain of English monarchs. Under scrutiny, there seems little to recommend the man who connived against his father, King Henry, even though he was the favourite son, tried to usurp his brother, Richard, and according to rumour did away with his nephew, Prince Arthur, who had a legitimate claim on the throne. Treacherous, impetuous, foolish and unwise, John found a capacity to alienate one and all. Before his succession in 1199, he had been sent to Ireland by his father to rule. He and his companion rudely laughed aloud at the beards worn by the Irish chieftains who came to pay homage to him.

His rule there was a disaster. John, like his brother before him, fell out with Philip of France and lost many further English possessions on the Continent in the ensuing conflict. In a bid to fund the war against Philip, John taxed his people mercilessly. Perhaps that is how the tale of folk hero Robin Hood sprang up. The legend of someone who stole from the rich to give to the poor — who were becoming still poorer thanks to the greedy king — was an irresistible one. Still, there is scant evidence to suggest that the legend of a virtuous Robin Hood is anything other than folklore.

Sensationally, John rowed with Pope Innocent III by refusing to sanction Rome's appointee to the archbishopric of Canterbury; instead John nominated his own candidate. In 1208 the Pope placed all of England under an interdict, cutting off the entire country from the church. The dead were buried in unconsecrated ground while Mass was banned. The following year the King himself was excommunicated. Only when Philip II of France was poised to invade did John make his peace with the Pope. He effectively bought his way back into favour.

John's row with the powerful English barons left the most enduring legacy. With barons in the north and east poised to revolt, John was pressured into signing the *Magna Carta*, or Great Charter. Much later the *Magna Carta* was hailed as a statement of civil rights. It was not. The campaigning barons cared as little for the plight of the common man as the king himself.

The *Magna Carta* defined the role of the barons in government, limited royal powers and set out the spheres of power of the English church. Prime among its purposes was to declare that no one — not even the monarch — was above the law.

Yet the 39th article of the charter is perhaps responsible for its progressive reputation. It reads: 'No free man shall be arrested or imprisoned or dispossessed or outlawed or harmed in any way save by the lawful judgment of his equals under the law of the land. Justice will not be sold to any man nor will it be refused or delayed'. And so the *Magna Carta*, signed at Runnymede, near Windsor, Berkshire, in 1215, became one of the cornerstones of British justice. It was restated several times in later years.

When John reneged on his Charter signature later that same year, he sparked the first Barons' War. Outraged barons offered the English Crown to the future King Louis VIII of France who attempted an invasion.

At the height of the conflict, John died in agony at Newark-on-Trent Castle, in Nottinghamshire. The theory that he was poisoned has been largely discredited. He died in grief, days after his baggage train was tragically lost in quicksand while crossing The Wash.

Above: *When Henry II built Orford Castle in Suffolk in 1165 it was a state-of-the-art design with no fewer than 18 sides to defend. The number of sides was crucial in defeating the commonly used enemy tactic of undermining the corner of a beseiged castle.*

Right: *Conisborough Castle in Yorkshire was built by Hamelin Plantagenet, half-brother to Henry II, and features one of the first round keeps ever built in Britain.*

Arundel Castle was originally built by the Normans in the early 11th century, Henry II built much of the stone castle in 1176 - 89. From the 13th century the castle has mainly been in the hands of the Earls of Arundel, and from 1580 the Dukes of Norfolk.

12 The Medieval Period

With the death of John in 1216, his son, the boy-king Henry III, came to the throne with a coronation held at what is now Gloucester Cathedral. Although only nine years of age, he was an acceptable royal figurehead. Accordingly, the warring barons rallied to drive the invading French King Louis from English shores.

Hubert de Burgh was among Henry's loyal regents (or 'Protectors') and it was he who secured a damning victory against the French at sea off the Kent coast at Sandwich — by bizarre means. Powdered lime was tossed into the eyes of the French sailors, blinding them at the height of the battle. Another victory on land at Lincoln dispatched the French and from 1217 there was peace between the two countries.

In effect, it wasn't until 1232 that Henry was able to assume full control of his country. One of his first acts was to rid himself of the loyal de Burgh by placing him under arrest. Hubert escaped from prison and sought sanctuary in the parish church at Devizes. It was customary to grant the right of asylum to those in the boundaries of a church. Hubert was nonetheless dragged from the church and returned to gaol. Furious, the Bishop of Salisbury intervened and insisted he was taken back to the sanctuary of the church. The king's men had the place surrounded until de Burgh's supporters stormed it to rescue him.

Henry's reign was long but not particularly distinguished. There was a series of disastrous wars in France as he set about trying to recoup territories lost by his father. At home there was some shameful anti-Semitism which would escalate until Jews were finally expelled from England in 1290 by Henry's son Edward I.

On a more positive note, there was the arrival of spectacles during the 12th century, a tremendous benefit to those elite men of letters. Universities were founded at Oxford and Cambridge and the studies of science and medicine began in earnest. Henry did much to refurbish Westminster Abbey, work which he carried out as a tribute to his personal hero, St. Edward the Confessor.

The ineptitude of Henry III and his corrupt advisors inspired the wrath of some barons. The king's own brother-in-law, Simon de Montfort, led a rebellion which began successfully enough. De Montfort's army, entirely English-based, routed the king's forces at Lewes in Sussex on 14 May 1264. Lining up for the royalists were a significant number of foreign mercenaries as well as Henry's brother Richard of Cornwall and his son Edward.

Edward, a commanding figure, displayed some of the military flair which would later earn him respect as a warrior king. He was 1.8m (6ft 2in tall) — which earned him the nick-name 'Longshanks' — and physically fit. Incensed by the rebels, he pursued them for miles. But in his absence, de Montfort captured Richard and ultimately Henry and Edward.

De Montfort had ideas ahead of his time about a Great Council or Parliament with members drawn from all over England. However, his choice of representative was irksome to the barons. The thuggish behaviour of some of his supporters worried them even more. Overseas, a Royalist rescue mission was being summoned. At this point, key figures in the civil war switched sides, leaving de Montfort with seriously depleted ranks.

Above: *The flip side of a penny from the reign of King Edward I, now housed in the Lindisfarne Priory Museum.*

Right: *Berkeley Castle, Gloucestershire. The original castle was built by William FitzOsbern shortly after the battle of Hastings. In the 12th century Robert Fitzharding received permission to build a castle of stone and the Berkeleys are his decendants. Edward II is said to have been murdered horribly here — by having a red hot poker inserted into his nether regions.*

Edward escaped from captivity after persuading his guards that he should race each of their horses in turn to see which was the fastest. After driving the animals hard Edward suddenly leapt on to a fresh steed and galloped away, leaving the frustrated guards with horses too weary to make chase.

A vengeful Edward confronted Simon de Montfort in battle at Evesham in August 1265 and secured the freedom of his father and a decisive victory. During the battle de Montfort was killed and his head severed, to be displayed on a pike by way of warning to other prospective insurgents. The battle also claimed the lives of 18 barons, 160 knights and 4,000 soldiers.

As peace returned to England, it was Edward who was king in all but name. When Henry died in 1272 Edward was fighting a Crusade. So confident was he about the security of his tenure on the throne that he did not return for two years for his coronation.

Although firm to the point of cruelty, Edward was a rational man with patience, foresight and fortitude. On a personal level he was a devout Christian and a devoted husband to his Queen,

Eleanor of Castile. Just a decade after de Montfort, he instituted the Great Council with two representatives drawn from each borough. Ironically, the chosen representatives were so reluctant to appear that they had to be threatened with fines in order to ensure their attendance.

Edward was determined to quell rebellion among the Welsh and the Scots. His main adversary in Wales was Llewelyn ap Griffith, who called himself the Prince of Wales, although his sphere of influence was in fact restricted to Caernarfon, Anglesey, Merioneth and part of Denbigh. After Llewelyn refused to pay homage to Edward following his coronation, Edward replied by seizing his bride-to-be, Eleanor, daughter of Simon de Montfort.

In 1276 Edward followed up with an invasion. Llewelyn was beaten back into the Snowdonia mountains and was starved into submission. A shaky peace came into force but within four years Llewelyn had been killed in a border skirmish. His duplicitous brother Dafydd, who at one time supported the English, was hanged by Edward as a traitor. From the Welsh wars came Caernarfon Castle, one of a string of fortresses built to subdue the Welsh. It was at this imposing castle that Edward's son and successor was born. The baby, also called Edward, was publicly declared Prince of Wales.

Edward fared less well on the northern borders, where the Scots refused to submit. When the Scottish throne fell vacant, Edward was asked to pick one of 12 claimants. John Balliol was chosen as the incumbent. Although Balliol began by paying homage to Edward, he was soon moved to rebellion — providing Edward with the excuse he'd been eagerly awaiting — to invade. In 1296 he won the victory he craved and contemptuously removed the Stone of Destiny, the Scottish coronation stone of Scone, to London.

An uprising two years later was suppressed with the same ruthless efficiency. But still the rumblings of rebellion swept through the glens. Edward had yet to face the most successful of his Scottish foes, Robert the Bruce.

A campaign against the English by Bruce got off to a faltering start. He blundered badly by stabbing an eminent rival in a church at Dumfries. After the Red Comyn died at Bruce's hand, Edward and the Pope were united in anger at such a violation of the church's sanctity. Still, Bruce was crowned by the bishop of St Andrews.

A first conflict with the English and the furious Comyn clan left Bruce reeling. However, as he pondered his plight in hiding, he watched a spider try, try and try again to build a web. According to fable, this humble sight inspired him to renew his efforts. In 1307 he prepared for battle. Edward, now 68 and close to death, travelled to meet him. The English king failed to make the battlefield, dying in Burgh by Sands, Cumbria.

Edward wanted his bones carried before his army until Scotland was won. This was impractical. Instead his body was taken to Waltham Abbey and finally to Westminster Abbey where he was laid close to St. Edward the Confessor. His tomb was inscribed, according to his instructions, with the words '*Scottorum malleus*' ('hammer of the Scots'). It was a defiant but not entirely accurate tribute.

It was Edward's deathbed wish to have his 23-year old son continue the fight. Yet he must have known in his heart of heart's that this would not and could not happen. Edward II was a pleasure-loving homosexual, as feeble as his father was bold. His father was a hard act to follow, and perhaps Edward II's downfall was that he inherited none of the soldierly bearing that was a prerequisite of kingship in those days.

The new king was less concerned with Scotland than he was with the fate of his favourite companion, Piers Gaveston. Edward I had insisted the snide Gaveston was banished. Now Gaveston could be reinstated, much to the fury of the barons. They loathed him and were deeply suspicious of the amateur theatre which delighted both Gaveston and Edward II. In 1312 Edward's close companion was seized by some of England's most notable earls, sentenced to death by a kangaroo court and hanged at Blacklow Hill in Warwickshire.

Matters went from bad to worse for Edward. It was 1314 before he found the enthusiasm to march on Scotland. He went north with a large army but found himself outmanoeuvred at every turn. The Scottish victory at Bannockburn ensured independence from England, and a fiery new nation with Robert the Bruce (Robert I) at its helm.

Despite his sexual preferences, Edward had married a French noblewoman, Isabella, and sired four children. She grew to hate him, however, and fled to France where she plotted with her lover, the rebel baron Roger Mortimer, to oust Edward.

After they landed in Suffolk in 1327 they gathered popular support. From behind the walls of Kenilworth Castle, Edward was compelled to abdicate in favour of his fourteen year old son, another Edward. He was then taken to Berkeley Castle in Gloucestershire where he was treated with contempt. In the corner of his cell was a pit where the rotting carcasses of animals were thrown in the hope that he would be smothered by the terrible stench.

Still, he survived and his enemies decided to murder him. Armed with a red-hot poker his assassins entered the cell and impaled him from the rear. His piercing screams could be heard echoing outside the castle walls.

An era of chivalry again returned with King Edward III despite the opening episode of his 50-year reign when he tried and executed Roger Mortimer, the ambitious nobleman who had deposed Edward II on his behalf. At the same time he banished Mortimer's mistress — his own mother — to an isolated castle.

Robert the Bruce was now dead and, as the claimants to the Scottish throne squabbled, Edward saw his opportunity to invade. In 1333 Edward won a great victory against the Scots at Halidon Hill. In his armoury was a brand new weapon — the cannon. Thereafter the town of Berwick became English although the county of Berwickshire remained Scottish.

Activities north of the border drew Scotland's ally France into the conflict. When Philip VI opened up a southern front by ousting Edward from Gascony in 1337 it signalled the start of the Hundred Years War. There was little genuine purpose to the war, which amounted to a series of skirmishes, except to confirm the reputation of the English bowman as the best in the world.

Right: *Construction first begun in 1083, however it took 168 years to build Ely Cathedral as the rampaging Black Death decimated its workforce. Due to the shortfall in labour the nave and transepts were roofed in wood instead of stone.*

Edward, still harbouring a claim to the French throne through his mother, nevertheless mistrusted French ambition. By now the wool trade was a vital one to England and so was trade with Flanders, where the craft of weaving flourished.

With a victory at sea against the French fleet already behind him, Edward invaded France. Using gunpowder and canon-fire to great effect, he secured a victory at Crecy, near Calais in 1346. One observer revealed that the English archers 'shot their arrows with such force and quickness that it seemed as if it snowed.'

There followed a siege at Calais. The waiting game was eventually won by Edward who demanded six burgers bring him the keys of the town with nooses already around their necks, ready to be hanged. Only when his Queen, Philippa of Hainault, went on bended knee on their behalf did he show mercy.

A peace treaty in 1360 halted the hostilities only temporarily and, bizarrely, the Hundred Years War lasted for a total of 116 years.

Such was King Edward's respect for the legend of King Arthur that he had his own round table constructed during the first years of his reign. He created the Order of the Garter, the highest honour intended for the bravest of his knights. The Order won its name and motto when his cousin Joan dropped her garter at a ball in 1348. Edward picked it up and fastened it to his own leg. To counter the sniggers, he boldly declared: '*Honi soit qui mal y pense*' ('Let he be ashamed who sees evil in it'). Incidentally, Joan — who was wooed but not won by the king — was in love with the steward of the Earl of Salisbury. To be closer to her lover she wed the earl. But when both died she became the bride of the Black Prince.

Also in the time of King Edward III came the creation of the Courts of Quarter Sessions. These were new courts established in 1363 to deal with low grade offences under the stewardship of justices of the peace. These courts remained in existence until 1971.

Edward died from a stroke in 1377. The crown went to Richard — son of the Black Prince and grandson of Edward III — who was just ten years old.

BLACK DEATH

At home Edward III's subjects faced the ravages of the Black Death. This was the name given to the bubonic plague, a dreadful disease carried by the fleas of rats which stowed away on ships travelling from the east. Its symptoms were hard black spots and tumours under the arms. The breath of one victim was sufficient to infect the next. Once infected, the victim could expect to survive no longer than a few days.

When it struck in 1348 doctors had nothing with which to combat the menace. The population of Bristol was all but wiped out. Thomas of Bradwardine died two days after arriving in London having been consecrated by the pope as Archbishop of Canterbury.

As the epidemic ran its course, it claimed between one fifth and one third of the English population. In Europe it is estimate the disease killed a quarter of the population, some 25 million people. Sporadic outbreaks continued for two centuries, wreaking havoc in the rural economy by slashing the number of available labourers.

At the time, diarist Henry Knighton wrote: 'Everything was low in price because of the fear of death, for very few people took any care of riches or property of any kind. A man could have a horse that had been worth 40 shillings for half a mark (6s 8d — or 33 pence). Sheep and cattle ran at large through the fields and among the crops and there was none to drive them off or herd them; for lack of care they perished in ditches and hedges in incalculable numbers throughout all districts and none knew what to do.

'Believing that the wrath of God had befallen the English, (the Scots) assembled in Selkirk forest with the intention of invading the kingdom, when the fierce mortality overtook them, and in a short time about 5,000 died.'

Above: *Photograph of a deserted medieval village at Gainsthorpe in Lincolnshire.*

Right: *Aydon Castle in Northumberland is a fine example of a medieval fortified manor house. Virtually unchanged it survived thanks to its conversion to a farmhouse in the 17th century.*

BLACK PRINCE

At the battle of Crecy, the king's son, also called Edward, distinguished himself. A well-meaning knight summoned the king to help the young Edward, who was clad in black armour, only to be told 'Let the boy win his spurs, for I am determined, if it please God, that all the glory of this day shall be given to him and to those into whose care I have entrusted him.'

The Black Prince, as he became known, fought so valiantly that he was knighted on the battlefield. It was there that he picked up three feathers and the motto '*Ich dien*' (I serve) from the fallen Prince John, the blind king of Bohemia. Both have remained emblems of the title to this day.

At the end of the encounter, the bodies of 11 princes, 1,200 knights and about 30,000 soldiers lay dead on the ground.

Throughout his part in the Hundred Years War the Black Prince fought with valour and astonishing bravery all over France. Sadly, the Black Prince died the year before his father. From the little we know of him, we can assume he would have instituted a just rule.

Left: *A 15th century fireplace in the upper chamber of the castle at Ashby de la Zouch.*

Below Left: *Ashby de la Zouch Castle was first established in the 12th century but was reconstructed in the 14th century and most of today's remains date from then.*

Right: *Durham's Barnard Castle on the River Tees was built by Bernard de Balliol whose grandson John founded Balliol College at Oxford. His great-grandson was chosen by Edward III to be king of Scotland.*

Below: *Clifford's Tower, York*

Bottom: *At Baconsthorpe Castle in Norfolk there remain the grand gate-houses of a large 15th century fortified manor house.*

Top Left: *Although it existed from Saxon times Bamburgh Castle owes much to Henry III who made many additions, including the impressive, double-towered east gate.*

Far Left: *Dating back to the middle ages, Berry Pomeroy Castle in Devonshire illustrates a typical medieval construction centring on a rectangular courtyard.*

Left: *Medieval fortifications at Berwick Castle proved useless against the fearsome artillery fire of the 16th century. The strategic site received a major overhaul in Elizabethan times but it was mostly destroyed when the railway station was built.*

Right: *Belsay Hall in Northumberland.*

Above: *Fortified in 1385 to repel a threatened French invasion, the efforts made at Bodiam Castle in Sussex were somewhat wasted as England quickly gained control of the Channel.*

Overleaf: *Beeston Castle, perched on the Cheshire plain, was built in the 1220s by Ranulf de Blundeville but soon became crown property and was further fortified by Edward I.*

Above: *Hever Castle, Kent. Begun in the 1270s Hever Castle was refortified by Sir John de Cobham in the 1380s and was purchased in 1462 by the father of former Lord Mayor of London, Sir Geoffrey Boleyn whose daughter Anne became Henry VIII's second wife. She was Queen Elizabeth I's mother and was beheaded on 19 May 1536. On Henry VIII's death the castle was given to his widow, Anne of Cleves.*

Left: *John of Gaunt, a son of Edward III, takes credit for the grandeur of Kenilworth Castle. He redesigned the existing castle in the 1370s, transforming it into a magnificent palace.*

Right: *Dunstanburgh Castle was another castle which bears the hallmark of John of Gaunt. So successful were the fortifications added by him in the 1390s that the castle withstood years of Scottish attacks.*

Overleaf: *An aerial view of Kenilworth Castle reveals the scale of improvements embarked upon by John of Gaunt.*

Above: *Leeds Castle, Kent originated in Norman times and was rebuilt by Edward I. However much of what can be seen today is 19th century reconstruction.*

Left: *Old Scotney Castle, Kent. Fears of French attack led wealthy landowners to fortify manors or build castles. So around 1378 the manor house at Scotney was fortified by its owner. Today Old Scotney comprises a 17th century house and some of the original castle.*

Right: *Another frontline castle in the clashes with the Scots — the shell of Pickering Castle in North Yorkshire indicates its glory days.*

Overleaf: *Stokesay Castle, Shropshire, is in fact a fortified manor house, a priceless relic from the medieval era. Its appearance is due mainly to Lawrence de Ludlow who bought it in 1281 and built the hall and top storey of the north tower.*

Above: *When King John stayed at Warkworth Castle in Northumberland in 1216 it was already a strategic stronghold. It remained a royal castle until 1332 when Edward III sold the property to Henry, 2nd Lord Percy of Alnwick.*

Right: *Warwick Castle is another that started life in Norman times — William I built a castle there in 1068, then in the 14th century the Earls of Warwick built the structure we see today.*

Left: *After it was stormed by Prince Louis of France during the reign of King John, Dover Castle — a key English defence — was rebuilt. Henry III invested in new fortifications, including 'Constable's gate' built in 1227.*

Far Left: *The undercroft of Whitfield Manor. Once fortified, Wingfield Manor in Suffolk boasted a drawbridge, portcullis and gate after being modified by King Richard II's Lord Chancellor, Michael de la Pole, in 1384. Yet its earliest use was as a college.*

Bottom Left: *The isolation of Dunstanburgh Castle was intended to protect its owner Thomas, Earl of Lancaster who was in conflict with Edward II. Alas for Thomas he was captured in Yorkshire where he was executed.*

Below: *Much of what remains of Wingfield Manor was put in place in Tudor times. However, the older outer walls and towers are still evident.*

13 Rebellion and Civil War

The rule of King Richard was put to the test when he still only a teenager. As the Black Death had cut the labour supply so drastically the peasant classes felt for the first time a sense of power. When continued high taxes threatened their very existence they put this power to the test.

Wat Tyler led the Peasant's Revolt of 1381 with assistance from a radical priest called John Ball. In his sermons, Ball preached emotively about the woeful inequality of the baronial system. 'My good friends, matters cannot go on well in England until all things shall be in common; when there shall be neither vassals nor lords; when the lords shall be no more masters than ourselves. How ill they behave to us! For what reason do they thus hold us in bondage? Are we not all descended from the same parents, Adam and Eve?'

Peasants known as villeins — those with only limited rights — marched from Kent to London, gathering all the time in numbers. In the capital they burned down John of Gaunt's palace of the Savoy and broke into the Tower of London where they killed several dignitaries, including the Lord Chancellor and the Archbishop of Canterbury. Another victim in London was the wealthy Richard Lyon. He had once been Tyler's master and had beaten him badly. Now Tyler and his followers wrecked a terrible revenge.

It seemed the fourteen year old king was showing similar steel to his father when he rode out to Mile End to meet the peasants. When he asked them what they wanted they replied: 'We wish you to make us free for ever. We wish to be no longer called slaves, nor held in bondage'. Instantly, Richard offered to meet all their demands and granted a pardon to all those who dispersed.

However the leaders of the revolt and some 30,000 followers were not appeased. At a second meeting held at Smithfield, the horse market, on 15 June, Wat Tyler spoke impudently to the King while fingering a sword. He was stabbed by William Walworth, the Lord Mayor of London, who feared the king would die at the hands of the rebel. As Tyler lay dying his followers rose in uproar. The King rode among them shouting 'I will be your leader; follow me'. And they did, until the king's guard broke up the demonstration. A bloody rebellion was undoubtedly averted by his presence of mind. Yet Richard was callously duplicitous. He instantly went back on his word, undid all the fine promises he made to the crowds and saw the remaining leaders hanged.

This shed a more accurate light on Richard — who was so effeminate and fastidious that he introduced the handkerchief to England! His chief pleasures came from gold and jewels. He became deeply unpopular with his nobles with his choice of ministers, particularly when he made merchant's son Michael de la Pole his Lord Chancellor. A rebellion by leading nobles known as the Appellants in 1388 had the majority of Richard's favourites executed.

Richard sought revenge and contrived to have two of the rebels, Thomas Mowbray, Duke of Norfolk and Richard's uncle, and his cousin Henry Bolingbroke, Earl of Derby and son of John of

Above: *The battlefield at Tewkesbury in Gloucestershire was christened 'Bloody Meadow' after the Prince of Wales was killed there on 4 May 1471 and King Henry VI captured and imprisoned.*

Right: *For centuries churches remained the central focus of village life.*

Gaunt, banished. While he was abroad, Bolingbroke's father died. The exile meant he lost his inheritance to the greedy King.

Bolingbroke was furious. To his advantage, he accurately forecast the mood of the country and, while Richard was conquering Ireland, mounted an invasion at Ravenspur in Yorkshire — an area which has since been swallowed up by the sea. Bolingbroke won the majority of the nobles around to his cause and when Richard returned he was imprisoned at Flint castle on the Dee estuary. He was forced back to London to abdicate in favour of Bolingbroke in 1399 and was then held prisoner at Pontefract Castle in West Yorkshire. Richard died there in 1400, either of starvation or violence. It was a brutal end to the Plantagenet line.

The fresh complexion on the monarchy in the shape of the Lancastrian Bolingbroke after he was crowned Henry IV did little to bring peace to England. To the west there was an uprising engineered by Owain Glyndwr and discord in Ireland, while to the south the French continued to chisel away at English-held provinces, most notably Aquitaine.

Even within his own borders Henry had insurgents with which to contend. The Percy family had once lined up with him. Now they were dissatisfied with his rule and plotted his overthrow. Leading light of the rebel family, which now allied itself with Glyndwr, was Henry Percy — known as Hotspur. On 21 July 1403 Hotspur was killed in the Battle of Shrewsbury by Henry IV and his son Prince Hal, the future Henry V.

Within two years the rebels regrouped. Now the ranks alongside the Earl of Northumberland — father of Hotspur — and Glyndwr were Archbishop Scrope of York and Edmund Mortimer, Earl of March, who had a legitimate claim on the throne as a descendant of Edward III. Henry moved quickly and Scrope was executed, Northumberland killed in the Battle of Bramham Moor in 1408 and the Welsh were slowly but surely subdued.

Like many in the Middle Ages, Henry IV was bewitched by mysticism. When it was foretold that he would die in Jerusalem he prepared to meet his fate by making a pilgrimage to the Holy Land. It was a journey he never found the time to make.

He collapsed in 1413 praying at the tomb of St Edward the Confessor in Westminster Abbey. His dying body was carried into a nearby ante-room decorated with tapestries depicting the story of Jerusalem. It was the Jerusalem chamber, known simply as Jerusalem.

His son, Henry V, who had been at his side in the thick of numerous battles, came to the throne. The truth about this warrior king is much blurred by the Shakespearean legend. Some historians have put a question mark over his reputed wisdom and grace, highlighting his brutality. He thought nothing of putting to death prisoners of war or those who had surrendered on the battle field.

As Prince of Wales he attended the burning of John Badby, a Protestant in the rebel Lollard movement who was convicted of heresy in 1410. After the execution was underway Henry ordered that the flames be doused. In agony Badby was hauled before the Prince and told to recant his beliefs. When he would not the execution continued until Badby's death. Henry would doubtless have justified his cruelty by declaring that it was carried out for the most noble and religiously devout reasons.

It was in pursuit of a claim to the French throne that Henry V arrived on the northern coast of France on 14 August 1415. Having taken Harfleur his forces were severely depleted by an outbreak of dysentery. Accordingly, Henry marched on Calais in order to meet a convoy of ships and return home. The French seized their opportunity to attack. Despite overwhelming odds, Henry and his army won a tremendous victory at Agincourt on 25 October, thanks for the most part to the longbow men of the ranks. Nearly 7,000 French fighters were killed compared to no fewer than 1,000 English fatalities. Battle observer Jehan de Wavrin, on the French side, wrote afterwards:

'When the battalions of the French were formed, it was grand to see them; and as far as one could judge by the eye, they were in number fully six times as many as the English. And when this was

Right: *Richard II, the crouch-back king, was defeated and killed at the Battle of Bosworth Field in Leicestershire in 1485.*

Overleaf: *The octagonal Dunster Yarn Market is a tribute to the medieval influence in the Somerset town which is overshadowed by a romantic castle.*

THE DEER LEAP HOTEL
THE
DEER LEAP
HOTEL

FORTE
Heritage

done the French sat down by companies around their banner, waiting the approach of the English and making their peace with one another; and then were laid aside many old aversions conceived long ago; some kissed and embraced each other which it was affecting to witness; so that all quarrels and discords which they had had in time past were changed to great and perfect love . . .

'The said French were so loaded with armour that they could not support themselves or move forward. In the first place they were armed with long coats of steel, reaching to the knees or lower, and very heavy, over the leg harness, and besides plate armour also most of them had hooded helmets; wherefore this weight of armour, with the softness of the wet ground...kept them as if immovable so that they could raise their clubs only with great difficulty, and with all these mischiefs there was this, that most of them were troubled with hunger and want of sleep.

'Then the English archers . . . began to send their arrows on the French with great vigour. The said archers were for the most part in their doublets, without armour, their stockings rolled up to their knees, and having hatchets and battle-axes or great swords hanging at their girdles; some were bare-footed and bare-headed, others had caps of boiled leather, and others of osier, covered with harpoy or leather'.

After the battle, fearing a further attack, Henry ordered all prisoners to be killed, wiping out great numbers of French noblemen at a stroke. At home, the triumph did much to distract from domestic tensions. In 1417 Henry returned to France to conquer much of Normandy. By an alliance with the Duke of Burgundy and his betrothal and marriage to Catherine of Valois, daughter of the French King Charles VI, Henry V was declared regent and heir to the throne of France.

This was his aim. Henry felt it his bounden duty to unite England and France. Impressed by his strength and discipline and appalled at the insanity evident in their own shambling monarch, many French people concurred.

The face of Europe might have been much changed had the bold Henry taken this second crown. In fact he died of dysentery while on a soldiering campaign in France. Two months later the French king was himself dead.

Henry's only son was just nine months old when he was proclaimed King of England and, soon afterwards, King of France. The English forces under the leadership of the king's uncle, John, Duke of Bedford, at first maintained a strong foothold in France. However the reversal of fortunes inevitably occurred, in a most romantically sensational way thanks to Joan of Arc.

Henry VI was but a child when the gains his father made in France were lost. He was crowned in Paris in 1430 aged 10 but never returned and would not countenance leading an army there. Few French people took the coronation of the foreign king seriously. Even had he been fully grown, the outcome would probably have remained much the same, for Henry lacked the passion for war that his father and grandfather both had had and he abhorred violence and bloodshed. It was his peaceable nature that earned him the affection of his people and the contempt of his wife Margaret and the warrior nobles.

His interests lay in academia and it was he who founded both Eton College, the exclusive private school near Windsor in Berkshire, in 1440, and King's College, Cambridge, a year later.

Although there were some military successes for the English, France consolidated its strength. The tide turned against the English and by 1453 their cause was utterly lost. It was the same year that Henry VI was struck down by the same madness that blighted his maternal grandfather. Calais was held until 1558 although it was a full 200 years after that before the claim on the French throne by the English monarchy was dropped once and for all.

The loss of possessions in France was a serious blow to English prestige. The murmurings of discontent were finally translated into a fully fledged rebellion by Richard, Duke of York, in 1455. He was descended from the third son of Edward III while Henry VI's claim to the throne was through the fourth son, John of Gaunt, Duke of Lancaster.

The dispute between the two sides was to last thirty long years, and was known as the War of the Roses because of the antagonists' emblems — a red rose for the Lancastrians, a white rose for the Yorkists. The impact of the civil war on ordinary folk was not great, although there were battles in eight counties, with campaigns which in total accounted for about fifteen months out of three decades. Worst affected were the noblemen, as it became customary to execute aristocratic prisoners of war in the aftermath of every battle.

Richard, Duke of York, scored an immediate success by forcing the king to accept him as regent. Then a son was born to the ambitious Queen Margaret, nicknamed 'the She-wolf of France'. Now there was an heir to the throne, an unwelcome complication as far as the Yorkists were concerned but a rallying point for the Lancastrians.

When Richard was killed at the Battle of Wakefield, his son Edward assumed leadership of the Yorkist cause. His forces defeated the Lancastrians in a battle fought in blizzard conditions at Towton, in Yorkshire, on 29 March 1461. Henry and his queen escaped to Scotland and plotted a counter-revolt. When the bid to overturn Edward failed in Northumberland, Margaret and the Prince of Wales only narrowly escaped capture. It is said that a vicious robber who then seized them took pity on the queen and her young son, and spared them, not wishing to have royal blood on his hands.

In 1474 the Lancastrians repeated the bid, only to be defeated at Hexham. Margaret and her son fled to France while Henry disguised himself as a beggar and contentedly wandered the hills and dales of Yorkshire until he was recognised and taken to the Tower of London. By then Edward was on the throne.

A switch in allegiance by the powerful Richard Neville, Earl of Warwick, helped to oust Edward in 1470. The earl, whose perpetual power-plays earned him the title 'king-maker', was perturbed by Edward's choice of bride. The handsome king had fallen in love with Elizabeth Woodville, a low-born widow of a Lancastrian stalwart. When Edward began to favour her family above the earl's, Richard Neville changed sides, received aid from King Louis XI of France and placed Henry once more on the throne.

Right: *An artist's impression of strip farming which predominated in the Middle Ages.*

Left: *The exterior of a typical medieval merchant's house during the age when England began its tradition as 'a nation of shopkeepers'.*

Right: *At Ospringe in Kent, Maison Dieu, an ancestor of today's hospitals, looks much the same as it would have done when it was built in the 16th century.*

Below Right: *The 14th century tithe barn in Bradford-on-Avon, Wiltshire, is among the best preserved in the country.*

It did not take the exiled Edward long to summon assistance from Charles the Bold, Duke of Burgundy and long-time adversary of Louis XI, and return from Holland with an army which took London in 1471. On a foggy Easter Day, Edward fought a decisive battle at Barnet, in Hertfordshire, in which the Earl of Warwick was slain.

On 4 May the same year, a battle was fought at Tewkesbury in Gloucestershire, at a site which was afterwards christened 'Bloody Meadow'. The Prince of Wales was killed and Henry VI was captured and committed once again to the Tower of London. Within three weeks he was dead. Although the cause of death was officially given as 'pure displeasure and melancholy' he was undoubtedly murdered, probably by Edward's brother Richard, as he prayed in a small chapel in the Tower. Every year, on 21 May, the authorities of Eton school mark the anniversary by placing a wreath of lilies and roses at the spot where he died.

The tussle between the Yorkists and Lancastrians was not over yet, however. Edward IV died prematurely in 1483, his reign perhaps best marked by the construction of St George's Chapel, a fine building at Windsor which he had built to outshine Henry VI's chapel at Eton.

Next in line was his son Edward V, who was just 12 years old. He was king for 77 days before his uncle, Richard, Duke of Gloucester, took the crown. The facts of the *coup d'etat* are murky. Richard cloaked it as concern for the boy king, however Richard was popular and there was little dissent. It was allegedly with the safety of the young Edward and his 10-year old brother Richard, Duke of York, in mind that the pair were dispatched to the Tower of London. They were never seen alive again.

It is believed the boys were killed in the Tower of London at a place known ever since as the Bloody Tower. Bones of two children were discovered in the vicinity in 1674 and they were removed and buried in Westminster Abbey. In 1933 examinations of those bones revealed that they belonged to two brothers, aged 12 and 10 and at least one had been suffocated. Later findings had those same bones belonging to younger children who were perhaps girls. In short, nobody knows for sure the fate that befell the little princes.

Theories about the perpetrator and means of their murder are legion. Most popularly accepted is that Richard killed them or had them killed. Having declared himself king, he would have been unwilling to hand over the trappings of rule to his nephew. He never denied being responsible for the murders, even when he was openly accused of them by the French. The princes vanished at a time when Richard carried out a spate of executions to secure his position. Romantics have Sir James Tyrell, a supporter of Richard's, as the murderer. He was apparently a descendant of Walter Tirel, the man thought to have fired the arrow which killed William Rufus back in 1100.

Could the future Henry VII have been responsible for the killing of the little princes? He already had designs on the throne and would, like Richard, have had to make way for the young Edward when he came of age. Supporters of Richard claim the Tudors blackened his name to disguise Henry's complicity in the killings.

Richard was mildly deformed from birth, which earned him the nickname 'Crouchback'. To call him hunchback would have been too strong a term. He was a disciplined ruler, faced as he was with widespread corruption and intrigue among the noblemen. He was a forceful leader at a time when forceful leadership was needed. But the string of executions he ordered diminished his popularity. The Duke of Buckingham, once a close aide, opened covert negotiations with Henry Tudor, Earl of Richmond, whose claim to the throne was that he was grandson of Queen Catherine, widow of Henry V and her lover Owen Tudor, and descendant of John of Gaunt.

The traitorous Buckingham was caught and killed but Henry continued his plans to overthrow Richard. In August 1485 he landed at Milford Haven in Wales with an army of mercenaries recruited in Brittany. At Bosworth in Leicestershire the armies clashed. A secret deal struck by Henry with the nobles deprived the king of crucial forces on which he was reliant — Richard was killed and there was victory and a the throne of England for Henry Tudor.

STOP
Maison Dieu

Above: *A rainbow illuminates the dreamy spires of Oxford.*

Left: *Leigh Court Barn is a magnificent 14th century wood-framed barn — the largest of its kind in England — originally intended for the accommodation of monks.*

Right: *Age-old traditions are still observed at Balliol College, Oxford, the home of English academia.*

SCHOLA METAPHYSICAE

14 The Tudor Age

Henry VII was determined to bring peace to his kingdom. He united the Lancastrians and Yorkists by marrying Edward IV's daughter Elizabeth. Diplomatically, he adopted as his emblem a double rose — the famous Tudor rose — blended with white and red, the two colours of the warring houses. There were uprisings to quell, of course, as usurping had become something of a habit in England in previous years.

A usurper who was posing as a nephew of Edward IV and Richard III caused a stir by getting himself crowned Edward VI in Ireland — however he was actually a carpenter's son by the name of Lambert Simnel. In 1487 he attempted an invasion of England. Alas for him, the real nephew was being held in the Tower of London and was duly paraded to prove that Simnel was a hoaxer. Henry must have been amused about the impostor; instead of executing him the king set Simnel to work in the royal kitchens.

Perkin Warbeck was not so fortunate after asserting that he was the younger of the princes in the Tower. With the support of French and Scottish kings, he made several bids to destabilise Henry until he was captured and hanged at Tyburn in 1499.

By his careful management, Henry brought about new prosperity, not least to his own purse. Mindful of waste, he insisted upon checking and initialling every receipt issued by the Treasury. He fostered trade with foreign countries while protecting the domestic market. When he died in 1509 he was a millionaire.

One outstanding problem remained — the succession: his eldest son and heir had already died. Arthur, Prince of Wales, was an important instrument of new European union. He had been betrothed to and subsequently married Catherine of Aragon, the daughter of Ferdinand and Isabella of Spain. On 1 November 1499 when he was 13 years old Arthur wrote her a love letter which began: 'Most illustrious and excellent lady, our dearest betrothed . . .'

Within five months of the marriage he was dead. Now the sole surviving son would be king. But first there was a dilemma to resolve. Henry VII had been delighted at the political match made by his elder son and decided it was too good an opportunity to waste, not least because of her wealth. It was his intention that the widow should wed again, this time to Henry, the brother of her dead husband. That way the politically valuable union with Spain was maintained and Henry got to keep the huge dowry that Catherine had brought with her.

The problem lay with the church, which opposed a man marrying his dead brother's wife, however, Pope Julius II was persuaded to grant dispensation for the marriage which finally went ahead. Henry succeeded to the throne and married in 1509.

At first he seemed like a breath of fresh air in England which had been yoked by the sobriety of his penny-pinching father. Henry VIII cut a dashing figure when he attended tournaments and banquets adorned in fine clothes. An attempt at invasion by the Scots under James IV was spiked, thanks mostly to the efforts of Queen Catherine who dispatched an army headed by the Earl of Surrey to thrash the intruders at Flodden Field in Northumberland. A short, sharp burst of aggression against France gave way to peace. Enmity between England and France was laid to rest after a meeting near Ardres, northern France. The site was tagged the Field of the Cloth of Gold because of the breath-taking the spectacle of royal regalia.

Henry found plenty of opportunity to pursue his pleasures, including lute-playing, eating and bedding pretty women. On New Year's Day in 1511, to Henry's immense delight, Catherine gave birth to a son. Within seven weeks he died. Four more babies died before one, Princess Mary, survived infancy. Then the affliction of infant mortality returned to haunt Catherine. It was a source of irritation and then anger for the king, who had meanwhile noticed and become besotted with Anne Boleyn, a former lady-in-waiting to his sister Mary.

Troubled by the absence of a male heir, Henry began to convince himself that his marriage to Catherine was wrong in the eyes of God. He sought to disentangle himself, seeking an annulment from Rome. At this stage, Henry was anti-Protestant and happily ensured that so-called heretics were burned in accordance with the

Above Right: *It took 14 years to build Dartmouth Castle which was started in 1481. Outstanding not only for its thrilling profile but also because it was the first English castle built specifically to use artillery.*

Below: *On 9 September 1513 the English forces led by Thomas Howard, Earl of Surrey, defeated the Scots at Flodden Field.*

teachings of Rome. A well-worded broadside against the Lutherans who were gathering momentum in Germany had already earned Henry the title of 'Defender of the Faith' from Pope Leo X.

Using his considerable expertise in theology — Henry was trained in the subject having been earmarked as a boy for the post of Archbishop of Canterbury — he aimed to bring the Pope round to his way of thinking. Yet Pope Clement VII was unwilling to help Henry, primarily because the armies of Catherine's nephew Emperor Charles V were on his doorstep.

For five years there was a stand-off between Henry and the Pope. In that time Henry summoned a parliament, the House of Lords, which acted to change the face of the English church. Henry was still reluctant to break off all links with Rome, not through any loyalty to Catherine, his wife of twenty-three years, but because of an innate mistrust of Protestantism.

His patience ran out in January 1533 when he discovered that Anne Boleyn was pregnant. Optimistic that the unborn child was a boy, Henry employed a tame Archbishop of Canterbury, Thomas Cranmer, to invalidate his marriage. Within days Henry was married to his beloved black-haired Anne, scarcely bothered by the fact that he had once taken her sister as a mistress or that she had a deformed hand with a sixth finger.

To his crushing disappointment, the child was a girl, Elizabeth. It was probably due to this that the relationship between Henry and Anne rapidly cooled. Henry also found his bride to be something of a shrew. Some historians claim Henry was already impotent, although Anne is said to have found her husband in bed with Jane Seymour at Hampton Court Palace.

Duly Anne herself was accused of adultery and sentenced to be burnt alive or beheaded. It was only 'out of kindness' that Henry agreed the sentence could be carried out by sword to spare her the prolonged agony of the stake.

On 19 May 1536 Anne was paraded through the crowds from her prison in the Tower of London to a prominent scaffold constructed on Tower Green. Her dark hair was hidden beneath a close fitting cap. White ermine fur lined the grey cape that she wore and a crucifix dangled from the belt of a crimson skirt. She carried a handkerchief and a small, gold-bound prayer book. She prayed and spoke aloud of her innocence and loyalty to the king before she was blindfolded. Now the French swordsman, brought over especially from Calais at Anne's request, pulled his weighty blade from beneath the straw on the platform. While Anne was distracted by his assistant, he struck a single blow. Afterwards, the eyes and mouth of the queen were seen to flutter for some seconds.

The executioner was paid 100 crowns, a considerable amount. As for Henry, he was engaged to Jane Seymour the day after the execution and married her a week later.

Jane Seymour was the woman of Henry's dreams, not least because she provided for him a son and heir. Edward was born in 1537, although the royal joy was muted after complications set in and killed the mother within two weeks. Although it was undoubtedly Jane Seymour who won his heart — it was next to her that he chose to be buried — the grief of his bereavement did not stop him seeking more wives.

With Henry and England now deeply immersed in Protestantism, a match with Germany's Anne of Cleves was made in 1540. When they met, Henry was filled with dread at her plain face, describing her as 'this Flanders mare'. The marriage remained unconsummated and was annulled amicably in the same year.

Within months, Henry had got the matrimonial habit once more, this time choosing the eminently unsuitable Catherine Howard as a wife. Like her cousin Anne Boleyn, Catherine was bored by Henry, mocked his sexual shortcomings and had affairs elsewhere. And like her cousin, she was also convicted of adultery and beheaded. Henry's treatment of his wives revealed a cruel disregard which was evident elsewhere in his reign. Here was the king who introduced the horrible penalty of boiling alive for poisoners.

His sixth and final wife was the amiable Catherine Parr who married Henry in 1543, four years before he died. Upon his deathbed, Henry's swollen belly measured some 137cm (4ft 6in). There has been speculation that some thyroid problem was to blame for his immense girth, yet his gluttony was legendary and was most likely the cause of his incredible bulk.

During the reign of King Henry VIII, the church had changed beyond recognition in England. Henry had the utmost respect for the legislature but had a habit of making laws which suited his own ends. Accordingly, an Act of Parliament was passed which made it treasonable to deny the king's titles. The key title was Supreme Head of the Church of England. Of course, all good Catholics believed the Pope was the indisputable head of the church. A further act required an oath to be sworn throughout the kingdom. Accompanied as it was by vast amounts of pro-Henry propaganda, many people took the oath with varying degrees of enthusiasm.

Those who refused, most notably his Chancellor, Sir Thomas More, and John Fisher, Bishop of Rochester, paid with their lives. The abbot and monks of the Charterhouse in London refused to take the oath and were hanged, drawn and quartered. Henry's first wife Catherine and their staunchly Catholic daughter Mary were placed under house arrest when they would not take the oath. Catherine died in 1536 and Mary, against her better judgement, relented and voiced the necessary vow.

Until this time, monasteries and abbeys had flourished in England. Many of the fundamental monastic virtues like poverty and chastity had long since disappeared, and many monks and priests had been amassing sizeable fortunes for years while they indulged in sexual pleasures. Yet these were generalisations. At the same time there were plenty of monasteries providing a haven to the poor, and also food and education to the needy. They were a place of safety from which no one was turned away.

Henry wanted the church to fall into rank behind him, having broken all relationships with Rome. He sent out inspectors to scrutinise the religious institutions. The inspectors did not have to look too far to find misuse and abuse of monasteries and they furnished Henry with the evidence he was seeking. They reported: 'Manifest sin, vicious carnal and abominable living is daily used and committed amongst the little and small abbeys'. Another report described the Abbot of Langdon as: 'The drunkenest knave living. All his canons be even as he is, not one spark of virtue amongst them; arrant bawdy knaves every man.'

In response to reports like these came The Suppression Act of 1536 which effectively dissolved much of the old-style church to make way for the new Church of England. Property and treasures were swallowed up by the state, although the ousted abbots and abbesses were allocated a pension. Monks and nuns were compelled to join the few remaining large houses. Many of the grand Catholic buildings fell empty and crumbled into disrepair. Curiously, ardent Protestants were still being burned in the midst of this anti-Catholic fervour. It is a measure of Henry's tyranny that objections to this wholesale religious change in the church were both small-scale and piecemeal.

Right: *When the combined powers of France and the Holy Roman Empire threatened invasion in 1539, the English replied by building Deal Castle on the exposed Kent coast.*

There were other positive aspects to his 38-year reign, the improvements of the palace at Hampton Court and most notably the overhaul of the navy which left it with more and faster ships and better trained crews than ever before.

In 1535 it had been said that God's judgement would fall on Henry after his split with Rome and 'that the dogs would like his blood as they had done Ahab's'. And en route to St George's Chapel, Windsor, as his body lay at Syon Abbey — later to become Syon House — the coffin mysteriously fell open and the next day dogs were found mauling his remains.

His only legitimate son, Edward VI, was just nine years old, a sickly child and as likely to listen to his nurse Sibel Penn, known as Mother Jack, as he was to the Lord Protector, the Duke of Somerset. This duke was Edward Seymour, nominated by Henry because he was brother to the dead queen Jane. Somerset and his colleague Thomas Cranmer, Archbishop of Canterbury, continued the religious reform. Together they produced the Book of Common Prayer, significantly entirely in English instead of Latin. Somerset was duly ousted by the ambitious John Dudley, Earl of Warwick and later the Duke of Northumberland, who implemented the more radical Second Book of Common Prayer. This was the era of the Protestant nobles and the purists were appalled to see them behaving much as the Catholics had in terms of greed and exploitation.

Edward was every bit as zealous about Protestantism as his noblemen, although his beliefs were more pure and less borne of self-interest. He had to be a key figure if England was to continue down the road to Protestantism. To the alarm of the nobles, the frail Edward contracted consumption and died before his 16th birthday.

Next in line to the throne was Mary, Henry's first daughter and a dogmatic Catholic. Greatly perturbed, Dudley had plotted for a usurper to take the throne. He alighted on Lady Jane Grey, the daughter of the Protestant Duke of Suffolk, who had recently married his son Dudley. The plan even won the support of the king as he lay dying. Jane was a great-niece to Henry VIII but her claim to the throne was further removed than both Mary's and his other daughter Elizabeth. Jane was unwilling to embark upon state treachery but was shamefully manipulated by her ambitious father-in-law.

None had bargained for the national uproar. Mary — for perhaps the only time in her life — was the focus of popular support. Jane, crowned at Syon House, ruled for just nine days before the leading players in the coup were compelled to admit defeat. Mary was proclaimed queen of England by the Lord Mayor of London on 19 July 1553.

At first Jane and her husband, along with Archbishop Cranmer, were spared by Mary who avenged herself with a modest three deaths after coming to power. However, following a Protestant revolt in 1554, Mary decided Jane had to die.

The death of the beautiful, learned 17-year old Jane, who was beheaded on Tower Green, sparked off a chain of anti-Protestant repression. The Archbishop of Canterbury, Thomas Cranmer was burnt at the stake as a heretic. In prison he recanted against Protestantism no less than eight times but went to his death affirming his beliefs, claiming he had denied his true faith 'for fear of death, and to save my life'. At the stake he thrust forward the hand which had offended by writing such untruths so it would be the first part of his body to be punished.

Above: *Hurst Castle was also built in response to a threat of French invasion as part of a chain of forts along the Solent.*

Above Right: *The brick-built Kirby Muxloe Castle in Leicestershire was never completed. Its owner Lord Hastings, a Yorkist, was executed by Richard III for treason.*

Far Right: *Pendennis Castle in Falmouth, with its tall circular tower and 16-sided walls, was one of many defensive forts built by Henry VIII.*

Below Right: *Portland Castle in Dorset and its pair Sandsfoot, which stands opposite, were fortifications ordered by Henry VIII, convinced that war with the French was imminent.*

Mary sought to strengthen the newly returned grip of Catholicism on the country and secure the Catholic succession by marrying Philip, Prince of Spain, a devout guardian of the faith. When the marriage took place in Winchester Cathedral on 25 July 1554 Philip became King of England, although he was rarely on the shores of his adopted land.

The burning of heretics was unremitting and earned the queen the title of 'Bloody Mary'. English people, who so disliked foreigners, saw their kinsmen being slaughtered at the stake on behalf of the Pope in Rome and a Spanish king.

Meanwhile, war was provoked with France, where its ruler King Henri II was fearful over the unification of his two time-hon-

oured enemies, England and Spain. England was defeated and thrown out of its last remaining French possession, Calais.

This was a humiliating body-blow to Mary who was already grieving at the prolonged absences of her husband on affairs of state. (In truth Philip had quickly wearied of the dour, devout Mary and willingly stayed away.) A few days before her death she told her ladies-in-waiting: 'When I am dead and opened you will find Calais lying in my heart.'

Above: *Walmer Castle is another fortification inspired by Henry VIII out of fear of the French. It was built along a stretch of coast in Kent along with Deal and Sandown Castles. Its main purpose was to aim artillery seaward at an approaching enemy.*

Right: *Buildwas Abbey in Shropshire was founded in 1135. It was run by an order of Cistercian monks from 1147 until its dissolution by King Henry VIII.*

Above Left: *Among the religious houses dissolved during the reign of Henry VIII was the Benedictine priory at Binham in Norfolk.*

Left: *Founded in the 12th century Denny Abbey in Cambridgeshire was in 1342 taken over by Mary de St. Pol, Countess of Pembroke and the founder of Pembroke College, Cambridge. The Franciscan nunnery she established existed until the Dissolution.*

Above: *Easby Abbey survived the centuries because, following its dissolution, it was used as a granary.*

Top Right: *Egglestone Abbey at sunset — the splendour of the Abbey, which stands on the River Tees, before it fell to ruin is apparent.*

Right: *Transepts, the chancel and the east side of the cloisters at Furness Abbey in Cumbria are remarkably well preserved.*

Far Left: *The west tower of Furness Abbey, which was begun in 1500, was never completed. By 1537 the Abbey had been dissolved.*

Above Left: *Although the church at Haughmond Abbey in Shropshire was pulled down, the abbot's chamber and hall is remarkably well preserved. After Dissolution the site became a squire's home.*

Left: *During the Dissolution the abbot and one monk at Jervaulx Abbey in Leyburn, North Yorkshire, were executed and the church was blown up. Its stonework was carried away for use elsewhere.*

Above: *The secluded limestone valley which is home to Roche Abbey in Yorkshire was landscaped by Capability Brown in the late 18th century.*

Right: *Kirkham Priory, founded in 1110, was once prosperous thanks to the patronage of local nobility. Now only fragments of the Yorkshire priory remain.*

Left: *From the Chapter House at Westminster Abbey a mural telling the story of St John.*

Below: *A reconstruction of St Augustine's Abbey shows how grand religious houses had become in early Tudor times.*

Right: *The tiled floor of the Chapter House at Westminster Abbey is rich in detail.*

15 Good Queen Bess

At the death of Mary, beacons of celebration were lit around the countryside and there was joy at the succession of the Protestant Elizabeth. The optimism of the people of England was well-placed.

Elizabeth, who was born at Greenwich in 1533 but grew up at Hatfield House, Hertfordshire, had witnessed the country swing from zealous Protestantism to rabid Catholicism but had declined to become involved in intrigue. Instead she spent her time in study, distinguishing herself as a musician. She spoke French, Spanish and Italian and had a good grasp of the classics. Thanks to her taste for poetry, an era of fine verse was ushered in.

Elizabeth rode to London at her half-sister Mary's side when the rebellion with Lady Jane Grey as its figurehead collapsed. While Elizabeth shared the religious beliefs of the usurpers she had youthfully strong principles regarding the sanctity of the royals and 'Sacred Majesty'.

She got a taste of what plotting might bring when she was imprisoned in the Tower of London because of an alleged involvement with a rebellion again Mary. Outraged, she refused to enter the palatial prison by Traitor's Gate. Instead, she sat herself on a rock protruding from the Thames riverbed and declared: 'Better sit here than in a worse place.' One of the ramparts at the Tower where the future queen was fond of exercising is still called Elizabeth's Walk.

She was sitting under an oak tree in the grounds of Hatfield House when she first learned that she had succeeded to the throne. She held her first council in the Great Hall there, now the only remaining part of the house which Elizabeth knew so well. The rest was rebuilt in a subsequent century.

Her position was, on the face of it, a tricky one. Here was the product of the liaison between Henry and Anne Boleyn — which had caused the fissure of the national faith in the first place — taking the throne. Catholics at home and abroad believed her illegitimate. And she was ruling a country that had been brow-beaten by the intense religious persecution inspired by Mary.

With the counsel of her most trusted advisor, the able William Cecil (later Lord Burghley), Elizabeth chose a wise path. She set about national meet-the-people tours which evoked a fresh unity of purpose. Instead of seeking retribution for the Protestants martyred by Mary, she accepted that judges and the like had been merely following orders. If they once again followed orders and accepted the ethics of Protestantism, none would be harmed. The Bishop of London, 'Bloody' Bonner, and Nicholas Harpsfield, the archdeacon of Canterbury, refused to accept the edict and were thrown into jail. As they were deeply implicated in the burning of Protestants, the move delighted many people. The celebration of Mass was banned; yet those who pursued the Catholic religion behind closed doors were for the most part left alone.

In 1563 a book compiled by the Protestant scholar John Foxe helped to establish Protestantism more firmly in England than anything that had gone before. In an astonishing four million words, the *Book of Martyrs* related the suffering of Protestants both at home and abroad, swaying the sympathies of many who were hitherto unconvinced about the new faith. The book, reproduced in 1570, was as widely read as the Bible. Not only did it bring waverers into the Protestant fold but it also engendered a deep hatred and mistrust of Catholicism and the papists.

Elizabeth was determined to preserve a moderate Protestant England. Even though she embraced the new faith, she disliked its more radical aspects, like the abolition of bishops, which was being called for by the Calvinists of Geneva.

Walking this fine line, she politely declined numerous marital matches with foreign crowned heads, Catholic and Protestant alike. Her true love appears to have been Robert Dudley, Earl of Leicester, who wooed her for nineteen romantic days in Kenilworth Castle in July 1575. Even now her sense of duty prevailed. The courtship was never formalised. With his wife dying in suspicious circumstances shortly before the affair got underway, a scandal would have ensued and would have dented the prestige of the flame-haired royal.

The most pressing problem thrown up by the religious divide was that of Mary, Queen of Scots. Mary was the Catholic daughter of James V of Scotland and the French noblewoman Mary of Guise. She was also a great niece of Henry VIII which gave her a claim on the English throne. Elizabeth may have been uncomfortable in this knowledge but she was not half as concerned as her

SHAKESPEARE

Few Englishmen have made as much impact on the world as playwright William Shakespeare. The giant of English literature, he was born in the opening years of Elizabeth's reign and produced his first plays before her death. He was the son of a merchant who became the mayor, and went to grammar school in his home town of Stratford-Upon-Avon where he married Anne Hathaway. In his 20s the lure of the stage drew Shakespeare to London. He became an actor with the Lord Chamberlain's Company of players, later to become the King's Company. After he graduated to writing plays, his first works, produced after 1589, were *Henry VI*, *Richard III* and *The Comedy of Errors*. Although he bought New Place, a large house in Stratford, he stayed mostly in London, absorbed as he was with productions at the Globe Theatre in Southwark which he partly owned. His last play *The Tempest* was penned in 1611 before he retired to Stratford. He died in 1616, leaving an indelible mark on not only English but world theatre.

Above: *Hampton Court was a favourite residence of Henry VIII who jealously purloined the palace from Cardinal Wolsey in 1528. His daughters — Queen Mary and Queen Elizabeth — both used Hampton Court extensively: it was there that Mary waited in vain for Philip of Spain's child. Elizabeth was kept captive here for much of Mary's reign but must have liked the place for she continued to spend Christmas there each year.*

closest advisors. For if Elizabeth died, the crown would go to Mary. And while Mary lived, there was every chance of a Catholic assassination attempt on Elizabeth so that England would be restored to popery.

After growing up in France, Mary married the heir to the French throne, Francis. Following his death in 1561, she returned to Scotland and, at the age of twenty-two, wed her cousin, the nineteen year old Lord Darnley. Six years later he was murdered and she married for the third time. This time her groom was the Earl of Bothwell, the man thought to be Darnley's killer.

Scotland was divided in its support between Mary and her son, James (who later became James I, the first Stuart king of England). There was keen suspicion that she was involved in the killing of Darnley. Many of the nobles were now Protestant. It was the Protestants who eventually imprisoned Mary on an island in Loch Leven in Scotland where she was forced to abdicate in favour of James.

Mary was ultimately exiled from Scotland and fled to England. She expected asylum from Queen Elizabeth who was undoubtedly sympathetic to her plight. However, her very existence posed a threat to the English queen. Even if Mary herself did not propose to harm her, she became the focus of plots against the monarch. Elizabeth at first used Mary to control the Catholics of Scotland. She could not find the enthusiasm to have her killed; if nothing else, the authority of the crown would be severely weakened by such a regicide. Only when dubious evidence was produced by spies of the duplicitous Sir Francis Walsingham that Mary had twice plotted against the queen, did a treason trial take place.

Mary was convicted some nineteen years after arriving in England and, albeit reluctantly, Elizabeth signed the execution warrant. Afterwards the English queen claimed she did not send off the vital document but that an under-secretary of state had dispatched it without telling her. The official was jailed for two years.

The execution took place indoors on 15 February 1586 in the Great Hall of Fotheringhay Castle, near Peterborough. When the executioners asked for forgiveness, Mary told them: 'I forgive you with all my heart, for now, I hope, you shall make an end of all my troubles'. With a serene smile, she prepared herself for death. Her ladies-in-waiting removed religious jewellery from her neck and her top clothes until she was stripped to a fulsome petticoat. Her loyal attendants could not bear the torment and broke down into tears. Mary soothed them with words spoken in French, embracing each one in turn. Before they withdrew, one pinned a cloth across her face.

There were no signs of fear as the Scottish queen knelt on a cushion and quoted a psalm in Latin before laying her head on the block. The executioner must have been overcome with awe for the first blow of the axe only succeeded in knocking her senseless and it took three swings to completely sever her head. Afterwards he held up the head and cried: 'God save the Queen'. Observers saw her lips move for some 15 minutes after the impact of the axe.

Only after the deed had been carried out did the executioner find her small, faithful dog hiding in her petticoats. The hound's hairy coat turned red with blood as it sat between his mistress's head and shoulders, snapping at those trying to retrieve him.

Mary's death outraged the rest of Europe. Elizabeth had long benefited from the politics of hate which existed between France and Spain. Neither acted against England because each was too concerned with the activities of the other.

Elizabeth and her navy had been aggravating the Spanish with attacks on the motherland and the colonies. Now Philip of Spain decided to move against England. He gathered a mighty Armada with the aim of obliterating the English navy and then invading. An early blow to his plan came when Sir Francis Drake sailed into Cadiz harbour in 1587 and let rip into the flotilla of galleons, causing massive damage.

Not until the 15 July 1588 did the Armada, with its 8,000 sailors and 18,000 soldiers, reach the English Channel heading for Calais. As legend has it, Drake was playing bowls on Plymouth Hoe when the Spanish ships were sighted and he insisted on completing the game before setting sail. Small English ships, stealthy and swift, harried the Armada in the Channel. Then Drake once again inflicted serious damage by sending fire-ships into Calais harbour.

The invasion plans were shelved but further tragedy was to come for the Spanish. As they headed back out to sea, gales devastated the remainder of the fleet. Only a few escaped by sailing around the top of Scotland and returning to Spain via Ireland.

It was to her troops at Tilbury on 8 August that Elizabeth famously said: 'I have the body of a weak and feeble woman but I have the heart and the stomach of a king, and of a king of England too'. Even as she spoke, the menace of the Armada had been destroyed. Afterwards she had a medal struck inscribed with the words '*Deus flavit, et dissipati sunt*', meaning 'God blew, and they were scattered'.

Elizabeth died on a bed of cushions at Richmond Palace in Surrey in her 70th year. The body of Good Queen Bess lies in the same tomb as her sister Mary in Westminster Abbey.

Above: *At Tilbury Fort Elizabeth I assured her troops: 'I have the body of a weak and feeble woman but I have the heart and the stomach of a king, and a king of England, too.'*

Below: *Queen Elizabeth's Pocket Pistol at Dover Castle, the fort which was a vital Channel defence.*

Above Right: *Although it has been abandoned since the beginning of the 19th century, the local limestone of Kirby Hall in Northamptonshire has weathered the years well and still evokes a picture of Elizabethan grandeur.*

Right: *Sir Thomas Pomeroy was lord of Berry Pomeroy Castle until 1549 when he refused to give up Catholicism. As he fell from grace his lands were snapped up by Edward Seymour, Duke of Somerset, a leading proponent of the new faith under the Protestant King Edward VI.*

16 Regicide and Restoration

At the death of Elizabeth, a horseman galloped from London to Edinburgh in 60 hours to inform the heir to the throne, James VI of Scotland, that his hour had come. When he made the journey south to London, James marvelled at the wealth of his new kingdom, so apparent in the homes and castles of his noblemen. In Scotland life was much more dour. With his coronation in 1603, he became James I of England, the first of the Stuarts. He returned but once to his native Scotland.

The king declared, like the succession of monarchs who had gone before him, that he was the divinely chosen head of the Church of England. As the son of Mary, Queen of Scots and the murdered Lord Darnley, he was religiously suspect in the eyes of the Protestants. Yet neither was he accepted by the Catholics.

In 1605 a determined group of Catholics led by Robert Catesby and Thomas Percy plotted to blow up the king and members of the House of Lords during the opening of Parliament on 5 November. In the cellars beforehand, a veteran of the Spanish army, Guido Fawkes, was supervising the use of the explosives. He was seized after one of the plotters wrote a letter to a friend warning him not to attend the formalities. The letter was handed straight to the authorities.

Although the use of torture was illegal under England's justice system, Fawkes endured appalling suffering until he named his co-conspirators. They were hanged, drawn and quartered on 31 January 1606. Their activities are still marked annually in England with Fireworks Night on 5 November.

The question mark over state religion continued. Puritans, plain-living Protestants who worked as lawyers, sought to colonise the New World. Catholics took refuge in Spain and France where their religion was strictly observed.

There were other ways in which James lost favour with his people. He was a homosexual who showered rewards on his lover George Villiers, finally elevating him to Duke of Buckingham. Ultimately, Buckingham was killed on 23 August 1620 by an ex-army lieutenant, John Felton, who claimed he was both owed money and bypassed for promotion. Felton fought his way to the duke through a collection of army personnel to lunge a dagger into him. His victim turned around, uttered the word 'villain' before collapsing. Reflecting the unpopularity of Buckingham in the country, Felton wrote: 'He is unworthy of the name of a Gentleman or Soldier, in my opinion, that is afraid to sacrifice his life for the honour of God, his King and Country'. He was hanged on 27 November 1620.

James inspired a panic about witchcraft which led to mass persecution. He was convinced in the power of the occult, firmly believing that a storm which lashed the ship bringing himself and his fifteen year old bride Queen Anne from Denmark was witches' work. Two women were burned at the stake — one while still alive — after admitting as much. In 1597 he had written *Daemonologie*, all about witches, to counter Reginald Scot's sceptical book *Discoverie of Witchcraft* which appeared in 1583. The superstitious king went on to introduce harsh new laws against witches. Yet he was enough of a scholar to study the legal cases brought against witches and grew to realise that many trials were unsound.

Above: *This painting from the studio of Sir Anthony Van Dyck, 'The three eldest children of Charles I' hangs in the Ranger's House.*

Right: *Charles I after Cornelius Johnson; this too hangs in the Ranger's House.*

He ended one of the most dubious forms of condemnation, that of denunciation by children, at a time when the courts were prepared to accept any flight of fancy by youngsters as evidence. John Smith of Leicester feigned fits and the vomiting of pins to frame old women for casting spells on him. Nine had already been hanged on his evidence before James I intervened. At the king's behest, the boy was dispatched to the care of the Archbishop of Canterbury. Within weeks he broke down, confessing his tale had been fabricated. No more would the words of children wield so much deadly power.

This act went virtually unnoticed. Alas, the same could not be said for the execution of Sir Walter Raleigh. As a court favourite in the Elizabethan Age, Raleigh had enjoyed royal patronage. But he was suspected of plotting against James who also loathed smoking, the habit introduced by Raleigh to English society after one of his forays to the New World. The king described smoking as: 'Loathsome to the eye, hateful to the nose, harmful to the brain, dangerous to the lungs and in the black stinking fume thereof, nearest resembling the horrible Stygian smoke of the pit that is bottomless'.

Generally well-placed the sentiments may have been, but Raleigh nevertheless did not deserve to die for importing the weed. Raleigh had been condemned to death for treachery in 1603 but lived for 13 peaceful years in the Tower of London from where he wrote his *History of the World*. Perhaps yearning once again for a life of adventure, Raleigh convinced the king he could find gold in Guiana. When he returned empty-handed, having stirred up trouble

by attacking a Spanish settlement, Raleigh was executed in Old Palace Yard, Westminster, on 29 October 1618.

James's obsession with a union between England and Spain also severely dented his popularity. Spain was a long-time enemy yet he was determined his son Charles would marry the Infanta, the Spanish princess. To secure the agreement, James was even prepared to pave the way for a return to Catholicism. Parliament was outraged. His dream fell apart when Charles, accompanied by the Duke of Buckingham, visited Spain and behaved rudely towards his hosts.

James, a man whose hands were constantly black because he refused to wash them, was once branded by France's Henry IV as 'the wisest fool in Christendom'. By the time of his death in 1625 he had foolishly sacrificed much of the goodwill won for the crown by Elizabeth.

As the king's eldest son Henry died of typhoid in 1612, it was his second son, Charles, who took the crown. Charles was an art lover who was patron to van Dyck and Rubens. He had built for his wife, Henrietta Maria of France, the fabulous Palladian Queen's House at Greenwich. But his artistic bent was lost on politicians who grew to loathe him.

It was rampant taxation that caused the greatest rub. In 1628 the House of Commons presented Charles with a Petition of Right, aimed at protecting people from royal taxes which did not meet with the approval of Parliament. It also banned martial law and declared that no one could be arrested by the king's order without a named charge. Furious at the challenge to his authority, Charles dissolved Parliament in 1629 and ruled without it for eleven years. During this time, he continued to raise money from taxes which was now, thanks to the Petition of Right, illegal.

Charles was trounced in a war with Scotland in 1639. The following year he was compelled to recall Parliament to secure more funds. The Long Parliament, as it was called because it lasted 20 years, released Charles's enemies and imprisoned his advisors, Sir Thomas Wentworth, Earl of Stafford, and the zealous Archbishop William Laud. Charles was forced to sign the assent needed to execute Stafford, who died at Tower Hill on 12 May 1641. When he tried to avenge the death, Charles met open antipathy in London. He left the capital for Oxford, effectively leaving the city to the Parliamentarians. Now King and Parliament were on a collision course. The result was Civil War.

In essence, the king's supporters were the majority of noblemen and the Catholics. Geographically, the heartland of the king's camp was in Wales, the south-west and the north. They were called Cavaliers, a name derived from the Spanish word '*caballeros*' used by their enemies to denote that they were papists.

Followers of Parliament were the crop-haired apprentices, the merchants and a few of the noblemen in the London, the south-east and East Anglia, where support for the anti-royalists was greatest. Crucially, the country's main ports were in the hands of Parliament.

The first clash was in Warwickshire at Edgehill on 23 October 1642. That battle was indecisive but the Cavaliers had the best of the fighting in that and the following year. In September 1643 the Roundheads attracted the vital support of the Scots. In return the Church of England was by law made Presbyterian.

Oliver Cromwell rose to prominence in the ranks of the Roundheads. A member of the Long Parliament, he achieved brilliance as a military tactician and propagandist. He despaired of the rambling strands of the Parliamentarians and moulded the highly organised New Model Army, which by his order was composed of clean-living Puritans.

When the king's forces were eventually defeated at Naseby, in Northamptonshire, on 14 June 1645, the eventual outcome of the Civil War was certain. Yet still the fighting continued with Charles witnessing for himself a further rout at Rowton Heath, Chester. He finally surrendered himself to the Scottish Army at Newark, Nottinghamshire. For a fat ransom, he was handed over to the Parliamentarians.

There was discord among the Protestant victors, centring on the degree to which the faith should now be followed. Charles made capital out of the grievances, carrying out secret negotiations and hoping to win back the throne. For a while he was imprisoned on the Isle of Wight, in Carisbrooke Castle, to remove him from intrigue. When fresh fighting erupted in May 1648 Charles was roundly blamed and was put on trial for his life. The charge against him was that he was a 'tyrant, traitor, murderer and public enemy of the Commonwealth'.

Charles refused to plead, signifying that he did not recognise the court. There were 78 commissioners at the hearing held in Westminster Hall, many of them unwilling to find against the king. It was thanks to enthusiastic efforts by Cromwell that they were persuaded to return a guilty verdict. Charles lived long enough to see the 'Rump' of the Long Parliament, as it was known, declare itself a republic at the start on 1649.

On 30 January 1649 Charles marched from St James's Palace to the sombre sound of beating drums, steadying himself on a gold cane. The scaffold on the balcony of his palace at Whitehall featured an especially low block, a calculated insult to his dignity. Two executioners were present, both heavily disguised for fear of revenge attacks by Royalists. Dressed in black, they wore masks, false beards and heavy coats to alter their shape. One of them was Richard Brandon, nicknamed 'Young Gregory', and it was he who wielded the axe against King Charles. His assistant was William Lowen.

The king asked the executioners not to swing the axe until he gave a sign. The signal was to be the stretching of his arms. With the aid of the executioner and an attendant bishop, he tucked his long hair beneath a white satin cap and stretched himself on the floor of the scaffold with his neck on the block. A devout man, he began to say prayers. A movement by the executioner momentarily panicked the king. 'Wait for the sign, wait for the sign!' he called urgently. Moments later he spread his arms. The axe fell and Britain was without a monarch.

It is said Brandon was reluctant to take the life of a king and had to be escorted to the scaffold by armed guards. As payment, he was given £30 in half crowns, an orange spiked with cloves and the king's handkerchief. Not long afterwards he fell ill and died. Many believed 'he died of remorse at killing a king'.

Above Right: *On 14 June 1645 the fate of Charles I was sealed when his troops were routed by the New Model Army under Fairfax and Cromwell at Naseby, Northamptonshire.*

Right: *Boscobell House, dating from the 16th century, sheltered the future King Charles II after the Battle of Worcester. Charles hid in an oak tree while two Parliamentarian soldiers loitered below.*

Although hundreds attended the execution, the atmosphere was muted. Most felt the forebodings of a national disaster. One bystander was seventeen year old Philip Henry, who wrote: 'The blow I saw given and can truly say with a sad heart at the instant whereof, I remember well, there was such a groan by the thousands then present as I never heard before and desire I may never hear again'.

In 1813 the coffin of Charles I was exhumed from a vault at St George's Chapel, Windsor. Observer Sir Henry Halford cut off a lock of the dead king's hair and removed a vertebra, which he used as a salt cellar on his dinner table. Only when a furious Queen Victoria heard of it some 30 years later was the section of backbone reunited with the body.

The king's execution diminished support for Cromwell, whose so-called 'Commonwealth' further became unpopular through a Puritanical ban on theatre and May fairs. His insistence on religious toleration for Protestant sects infuriated the Presbyterians who considered themselves to have the only acceptable faith. Consequently, the Scots backed the Prince of Wales, who was in exile in Holland, and on 1 January 1651 had him crowned Charles II. However, a bid to install Charles on the English throne was smashed when Cromwell fought the Scots and remaining Cavaliers at Worcester on 3 September 1651.

The adventures of Charles II thereafter became legendary. He is said to have hidden in a oak tree in the grounds of Boscobel House, in Shropshire, while Commonwealth soldiers gossiped below. Dressed as a woman, he finally arrived at Shoreham in Sussex, and set sail for France in a coal brig by the name of *Surprise*.

History puts Cromwell in a bad light given his vicious repression of the Catholics in Ireland and the dreary existence he inflicted on the English. While he was undoubtedly flawed by his bigotry against Catholics, he was in fact highly-principled and strongly motivated. Until his death on 3 September 1658, Cromwell continued to wrestle with the dilemmas thrown up by bickering colleagues. He became so frustrated with the fellows of his party that he dissolved Parliament and made himself Lord Protector. His son Richard briefly held the title until he was overthrown by army generals in April 1659. Disputes continued until Parliament voted to restore Charles II to power.

When Charles entered London on 29 May 1660, the streets were lined with cheering supporters. Charles was a handsome, intelligent *bon viveur* who loved theatre, horse racing and women. Among his mistresses was Nell Gwyn, an orange seller turned actress, who caught the roving eye of the king. Honest and true, Nell became a folk heroine. When her carriage was mistaken for one carrying another of the king's Catholic lovers and stoned by a mob, she popped her head out of the window and bellowed: 'Don't hurt me, good people! I'm the Protestant whore'. The dying words of Charles to his brother James were reputedly: 'Let not poor Nelly starve'.

The atmosphere of paranoia between the two main religions during Charles's reign culminated in the 'Popish Plot'. Protestant Titus Oates spread a scurrilous rumour that Catholics were planning to assassinate King Charles. Several Catholics were executed on his word while a wave of anti-Catholicism swept the country.

In Parliament the Whigs — a Protestant political group — pressed for an Exclusion Bill which would bar James, the Catholic brother of the king, from taking the throne. Charles refused it and dissolved Parliament, furnished by cash as he was by the King Louis XIV of France. Until he died in 1685 he ruled as a dictator.

Above: *On top of a rocky outcrop in the Isles of Scilly, Cromwell ordered the construction of a defensive castle.*

Right: *Portrait of Oliver Cromwell, Lord Protector and signatory to the death warrant of King Charles I.*

Far Right: *Built by persecuted Catholic Sir Thomas Tresham in 1593 the Rushton Triangular Lodge symbolises the triple aspects of the Holy Trinity.*

Below Right: *Lulworth Castle was built as an ostentatious hunting lodge by Thomas Howard in 1607. Badly damaged during the Civil War it was revitalised by rich Londoner Humphrey Weld who bought it in 1643.*

The reign of James II opened in 1685 with an invasion by the Duke of Monmouth, the illegitimate son of Charles II and a popular Protestant. Monmouth's inferior forces were crushed by the army at Sedgemoor, Somerset. It was the last battle to take place on English soil.

Afterwards James pursued his Catholic interests vigorously and elevated fellow believers to the highest ranks of government. The outlook got even bleaker for Protestants when his second wife, Mary of Modena, gave birth to a son who would be raised a Catholic and would one day inherit the throne. James' enemies were convinced the child was an impostor who had been smuggled in to the palace in a bed-pan to ensure a Catholic succession.

It was the last straw. A committee of seven eminent Protestants pleaded with William of Orange, the Dutch ruler, to intervene. William was married to Mary, James II's daughter by Anne Hyde, and was himself grandson of Charles I. A north wind brought William and his forces from Holland to Brixham in Devon on 5 November 1688. James soon realised his cause was hopeless and fled to France, hot on the heels of his wife and son.

There was no armed resistance to William and Mary so the 'Glorious Revolution', as it was known, was gratifyingly bloodless. However, an attempt by James and his supporters, the Jacobites, to win back the English crown was fought out on Irish soil and was decided in William's favour at the Battle of the Boyne on 1 July 1690. The harsh penalties imposed subsequently on the

Irish Catholics who fought for James have scarred Ireland to this very day.

Asthmatic William escaped the city smog by having Kensington Palace built for him by Sir Christopher Wren, the architect who designed London's St Paul's Cathedral. Wren also redesigned much of Hampton Court for William and Mary. William outlived his wife but died in 1702 after a riding accident in the grounds of Hampton Court when his horse stumbled in a molehill and threw him.

Queen Anne, Mary's sister, was his successor. Parliament passed the Act of Settlement in 1701 to ensure a Protestant would always take the throne. For her survival, Queen Anne had to thank the soldierly skills of the Duke of Marlborough. His prowess in the field ensured a clutch of victories against the French King Louis XIV, who was backing James Stuart, the 'Old Pretender', for the English throne. Only after the Treaty of Utrecht in 1713 did Louis XIV withdraw his support for James and recognise Queen Anne as rightful ruler of England.

Queen Anne suffered ten miscarriages. Unable to provide a successor, the crown would go to Germany, to the Hanoverian offspring of a granddaughter of James I. The colourless Queen Anne died in 1714, bringing to a close one of the most vivid eras of English history.

However, the foundations had been laid for a new age — the future 'glory years' of industrial might and empire. England's ancient history was at an end. Her centuries of prosperous nationhood and world power were dawning. The fledgling born out of the migrant waves of prehistory was about to spread her wings . . .

17 The Georgian Period

Historically the Georgian period began when George I, elector of Hanover, succeeded to the British throne on the death of Queen Anne in 1714. The term Georgian however, which was used to describe the elegant style of architecture and decoration strongly influenced by the buildings of the ancient Greeks and Romans, was not used in this sense until the beginning of the next century. The succession of George I was determined by the Act of Settlement of 1701, which passed over the legitimate but Roman Catholic representatives of the Stuart line in favour of the Protestant house of Hanover, descended from the daughter of James I. After succeeding to the British throne, he remained staunchly German in his attachments and objectives and caused much controversy by his uncompromising support for the Whig party against the Tories and by his tendency to take advice on matters of state from his Hanoverian counsellors. The Whig oligarchy, though purely selfish in its aims, brought peace, toleration and prosperity to the land so there was little English support for the half-hearted Jacobite uprising of 1715 on behalf of James II's son, the 'Old Pretender'. The new interest in gambling with speculative trade in the tropics culminated in the spectacular and ruinous crash of the South Sea Company and the burst of this bubble brought Sir Robert Walpole into power in 1721 with a mandate to clear up the economic mess. For 21 years he ran the Whig machine and by developing the Cabinet system was really the first British Prime Minister.

George II succeeded to the British throne on the death of his father, George I, in 1727 and although he remained largely Hanoverian in his interests he learned fluent English, unlike his father. George II has been represented as a king manipulated by his own ministers — notably Sir Robert Walpole and the Duke of Newcastle — and by his highly intelligent wife, Queen Caroline but he was by no means a weak monarch. He played a larger part in the direction of foreign and military policy than most contemporaries suspected, and at Dettingen (1743), in the War of the Austrian Succession, was the last British monarch to appear in person on the battlefield. His reign witnessed the final collapse of the Jacobites after their uprising of 1745 when King James II's grandson, the 'Young Pretender', 'Bonnie Prince Charlie', sailed from France to the west coast of Scotland, assembled an army and marched down into England as far as Derby. Because of lack of

Right: *The Georgian period saw the growth and, ultimately, the independence of the British colonies that would become the United States. This is a map of Boston showing the harbour where the famous 'Tea Party' took place in 1773.*

Below: *The great houses of the 18th century sat in a landscape that, while man-made, was softer and more rural than the formal gardens of before. Chatsworth's were designed by Capability Brown who produced the beautiful parkland we see today.*

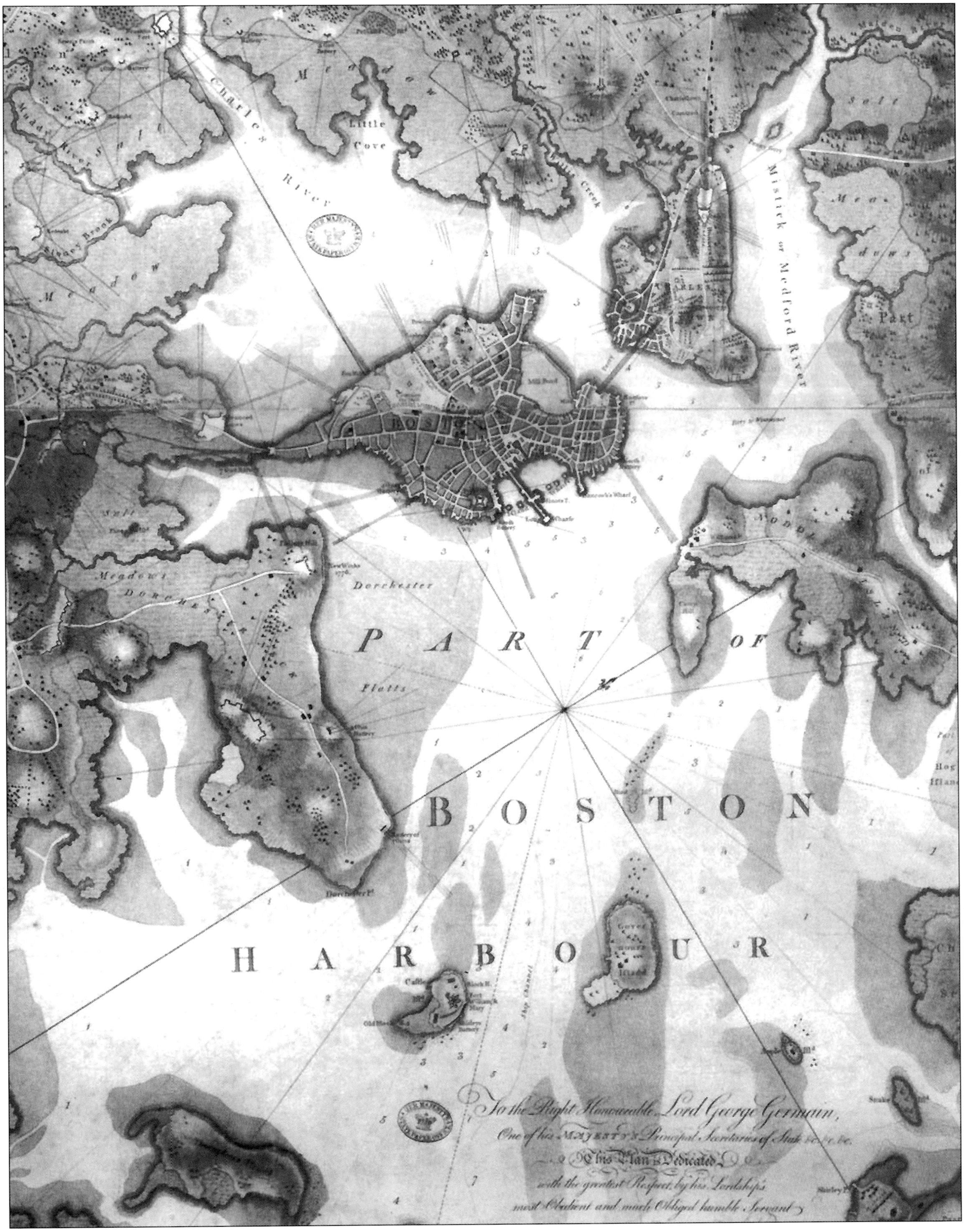

Charles River
Little Cove
Mistick or Medford River
Muddy River
Meadow
Dorchester
Meadows
Platts
PART OF
BOSTON
HARBOUR
Ship Channel
To the Right Honourable Lord George Germain,
One of his Majesty's Principal Secretaries of State &c. &c. &c.
This Plan is Dedicated
with the greatest Respect, by his Lordship's
most Obedient and much Obliged humble Servant

support the rebels soon lost heart and retreated back to Scotland where in a battle at Culloden, near Inverness — the last land battle to be fought on British soil — they were slaughtered by the King's son, the Duke of Cumberland.

George's son, Frederick, predeceased him, so when George II died on Oct. 25, 1760, he was succeeded by Frederick's son, George III, who was to become the longest reigning of male British monarchs. George had high but impractical ideas of kingship. On his accession he sought to rule without regard to party, to banish corruption from political practice, and to abandon the Hanoverian preoccupations of his predecessors. He resumed the royal patronage and, with the suspension of Cabinet government, England endured ten years of disastrous rule by the King and the 'King's Friends' which ended only in 1770 with the appointment of Frederick, Lord North, an able and congenial minister. Although never an autocratic monarch in the sense that his opponents contended, George III was always a powerful force in politics. He was a strong supporter of the war against America, and he viewed the concession of independence in 1783 with such detestation that he considered abdicating his throne.

After 1801 George was increasingly incapacitated by an illness, sometimes identified as porphyria, that caused blindness and senility. His recurring bouts of insanity became a political problem and ultimately compelled him to submit to the establishment of a formal Regency in 1811, the regent being his oldest son, the future George IV.

This period of British history (1811-1820) is known as the Regency and is associated with what is generally regarded as Georgian England. The period gave its name to a style of architecture and furniture design incorporating neo-classical styles based on the ancient Greeks rather than Romans and on Egyptian ideals, inspired to a certain degree by the contemporary French Directoire and Empire styles. In this era of considerable social and moral permissiveness, literary and artistic romanticism reached its climax.

Although George III was bitterly criticised by Whig historians of his own and later days he is now seen as a strong-minded but public-spirited monarch and was the best loved of the Hanoverian rulers. He enjoyed a personal reputation that stood his house in good stead during the disastrous reign of his son George IV who succeeded to the throne on his death in 1820. George IV brought the standing of the British monarchy to its lowest point than at any other time in its modern history. Although long an ally of the Whigs, he declined to bring them into power when he became Regent, and he was thereafter associated with deeply conservative causes, especially the maintenance of official discrimination against Roman Catholics and Protestant dissenters. His personal profligacy and his treatment of Queen Caroline brought him great unpopularity during his reign and he died on June 26, 1830, to be succeeded by his brother, William IV.

Left: *King George IV was the eldest son of 'mad' King George III and regent in his place from 1810. He acceded to the throne in 1820 and is best remembered for his debts, reckless extravagance, extreme unpopularity, and dissipation.*

Overleaf: *The splendid grand conservatory at Syon House which has been home to the Dukes of Northumberland for more than 200 years.*

Above: *The first building on the site of Syon House was a nunnery founded by Henry V. It owes its interiors today to Robert Adam, the famous designer commissioned by the Duke of Northumberland in 1769 to remodel his new home.*

Previous Page: *Ironmaster Thomas Foley bought the Jacobean mansion Witley Court near Worcester after the Civil War and added two towers. In 1735 the lavishly baroque parish church was added by another member of the dynasty, the 1st Lord Foley.*

Right: *Extensions were made to Ranger's House during subsequent centuries but it remains in essence a typically Stuart house, with its lofty ceilings and orange brickwork.*

18 Victoria

Victoria emerged from a lonely, secluded childhood to take the British throne in 1837 at the age of 18 years on the death of her uncle King William IV and was to become the longest-reigning monarch in English history. She was the only child of Edward, Duke of Kent and son of George III, and Princess Victoria, daughter of the Duke of Saxe-Coburg. Victoria displayed a personality marked by strong prejudices and a wilful stubbornness and embarked upon establishing the monarchy as a respected and popular institution while it was irrevocably losing its place as an integral part of the British governing system. Victoria and her court were greatly transformed by her marriage to her first cousin, Prince Albert of Saxe-Coburg, in 1840. The term Victorian, when designated to this age, has taken on certain prudish connotations but it was Albert who made a point of strait-laced behaviour, and it was he who introduced a strict decorum in court. He also gave a more conservative tinge to Victoria's politics, leading her to become close to Sir Robert Peel. Albert taught Victoria the need for hard work if she was to make her views felt in the cabinet, and during the prince's lifetime Victoria did indeed make her opinions known and by insistent interjection she forced her ministers to take them into account. Her political importance was based, however, upon the temporarily factionalised state of the Commons, between 1846 and 1868, when royal intervention was needed to help glue together majority coalitions.

Victoria's reign saw huge benefits from the Industrial Revolution culminating in the Great Exhibition of 1851 whose aim was to demonstrate to the world the industrial supremacy and prosperity of Britain. The exhibition was housed in the Crystal Palace, a vast iron and glass structure with more than 300,000 panes of glass, designed by Joseph Paxton. This period of Victoria's rule saw Britain embroiled in the Crimean War of 1853-56. It was one of the long series of Russo-Turkish Wars, but it differed from the others as a result of British and French involvement. Tsarist Russia continued to seek expansion of influence in the Balkans at the expense of the Ottoman Empire but Britain deemed the preservation of the Ottoman Empire vital for her own imperial interests in the eastern Mediterranean and Asia. In military terms, the war was a blundering, needlessly costly affair. The commanders on both sides proved remarkably inept, squandering lives in senseless engagements. Supply services for both armies were hampered by inefficiency and corruption, and medical services were appalling. The Crimean War also introduced women in the important role of army nurses under the effective direction of Florence Nightingale who won fame by her efforts to improve the care of the sick and wounded. With the newly developed telegraph system it was the first major conflict to have almost up to the day press coverage allowing the populace to exert an influence on government decisions.

By the 1870s, like aristocratic Whiggism, the strait-laced Prince Albert was dead and his Ruskinian Gothic memorial in Kensington Gardens was also a memorial to an age that had ended. When her beloved Albert died in 1861 Victoria, always prone to

Left: *The Industrial Revolution would change the face of Britain during Victoria's reign. In particular, the 'Railway Mania' would lead to the construction of extraordinary track mileages and the locomotives to run on them. Engine works grew up around the country, such as this one at the major rail centre of Crewe.*

Right: *Queen Victoria lived from 1819 to 1901, acceding to the throne in 1837. She married Albert of Saxe-Coburg in 1840 and with him discovered the joys of Scotland. She continued to travel to Balmoral after Albert's death in 1861, although some say that this was more because of her affection for John Brown than her love of the place.*

self-pity, fully indulged her grief. She thereafter dressed in black and remained in mourning until her own death, making few public appearances and spending most of each year on the Isle of Wight and in her beloved Scottish Highlands with her closest companion, the dour Scottish servant, John Brown. As a result of this her popularity declined and a strong republican sentiment appeared during the late 1860s. Her attempts to influence government decisions ceased to carry significant weight as the doubling of the electorate, by the Reform Act of 1867, strengthened party organisation against dissenting factions in the Commons and eliminated the need for a mediator, namely the monarch.

With her characteristic stubbornness Victoria made a concerted effort to win back the affection of her people by her determined efforts to steer public affairs. She won particular esteem for defending the popular imperialist policies of the Conservative ministries of Benjamin Disraeli, who flattered her relentlessly and made her Empress of India in 1876. At the same time she made the life of William E. Gladstone, the Liberal Prime Minister, a misery; she intensely disliked him for pursuing policies which she thought weakened the empire. The great celebrations of her Golden and Diamond jubilees in 1887 and 1897 demonstrated her renewed popularity and the affection she held in the hearts of her British subjects. The Diamond Jubilee, in particular, glorified empire as a source of British greatness and provoked jingoistic assertions of nationalism in the face of threats to British supremacy.

Throughout the reign of Queen Victoria the British Empire grew without much competition from other European powers. British armies conquered Indian states and brought the whole subcontinent under British domination and by 1871 the British Indian Empire included over 250 million people. The whole of Australia was claimed by Britain, New Zealand was annexed in 1840 and British Canada was extended westwards to the Pacific. The sun never set on this empire and the large number of British emigrants who overlooked the these territories, and who were increasingly allowed to run their own affairs, were largely protected by the then rulers of the oceans, the powerful Royal Navy. British world supremacy was challenged towards the end of Victoria's reign at the close of the 19th century. France, Germany and Russia developed interests beyond Europe, the USA and Japan were emerging as world powers and within the Empire itself their were nationalistic stirrings of people beginning to demand the right to self-rule. Britain responded by occupying more territory, specifically in tropical Africa which had until then not been considered valuable. Great swathes of land were annexed by such freelance adventurers as Cecil Rhodes who, in the 1890s, built up a vast British domain in central Africa extending over what is now Zimbabwe, Zambia and Malawi. The challenge of the Afrikaner Boers in South Africa represented the most overt nationalistic movement against the British Empire at this time and it was only repressed by the costly and often brutal Boer Wars (1899 and 1902) at the end of Victoria's and beginning of Edward VII's reigns. On Victoria's death on January 22, 1901 the descendants of her and Albert's nine children occupied most of the thrones of Europe.

Below: *Queen Victoria distributing the Victoria Cross in Hyde Park, London in 1857. This bronze medal for conspicuous bravery in wartime was first instituted the year before. The medals were struck from metal of canons captured from the Russians at the Battle of Sevastapol (1855) until supplies ran out in 1942.*

Above left: *David Livingstone (1813-73), the famous Victorian explorer was an ordained missonary as well as a medical man. His extraordinary expeditions into central Africa revealed the Victoria Falls and the course of the Zambezi River amongst many other discoveries. He eventually died in Old Chitambo (now in Zambia), where his body was embalmed then sent back to England to be buried in Westminster Abbey.*

Above: *Sir Marc Isambard Brunel (1769-1849) fled from his native France to America during the French Revolution where he became an architect in New York and eventually the city's chief engineer. After moving to England he constructed public works at Chatham Dockyard and Woolwich Arsenal. His most notable achievement was the Thames Tunnel (1825-43) which runs from Rotherhide to Wapping.*

Left: *Florence Nightingale — the Lady of the Lamp — took 38 nurses to Scutari in 1854 to nurse wounded casualties of the Crimean War. Horrified at the insanitary conditions, where more soldiers died of disease than of their wounds, she imposed strict sanitation rules which reduced the hospital mortality rate. In later life she became deeply involved in improving nursing conditions and training, as well as public health in India.*

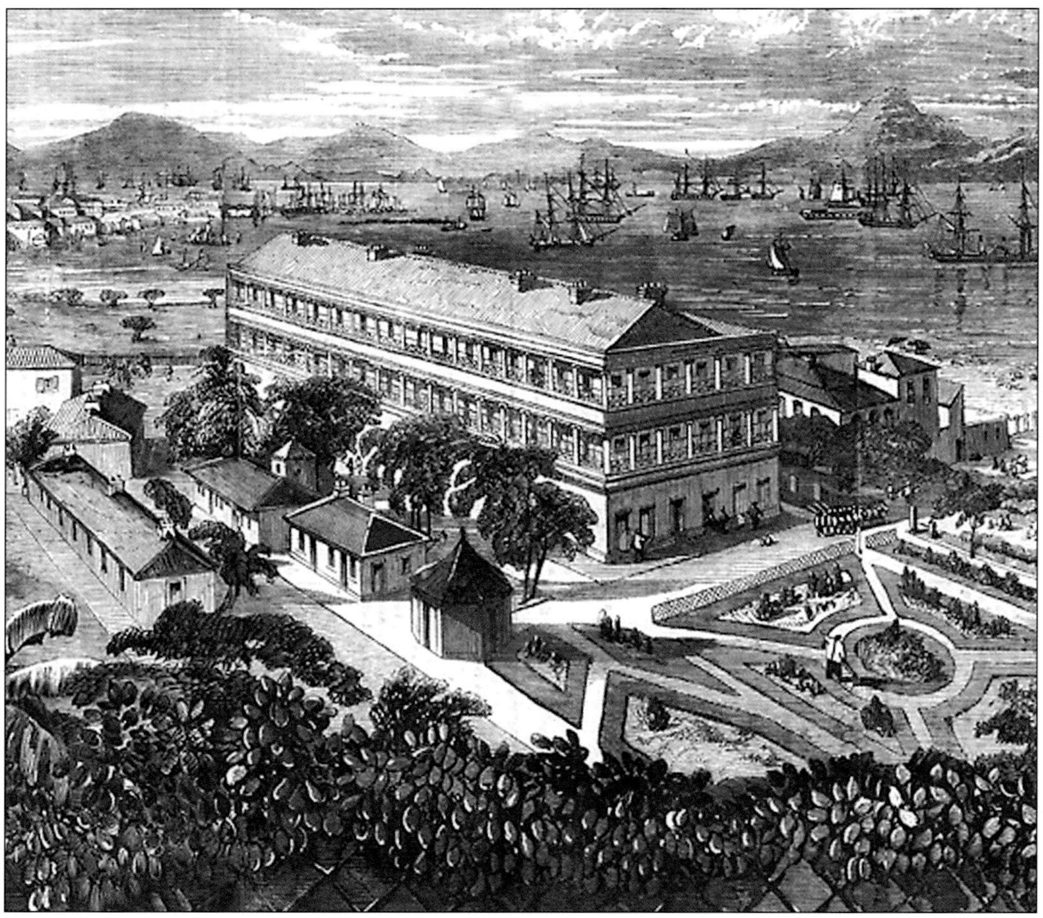

Above: *Fashions of the 1850s.*

Left: *Outpost of Empire — Victora Harbour, Hong Kong in 1856. This site was chosen for its natural, deep, sheltered harbour. A haven for colonialists, traders and rogues, the British Empire used Hong Kong as a major port and centre for trade of all kinds to all points of the compass. However, it was only leased from the Chinese and would be handed back in 1997.*

Above Right: *Marriage of first cousins Queen Victoria and Prince Albert at St James's Palace, 10 February 1840. Albert was not crowned king, but in 1857 he was given the title Prince Consort. He died in 1861, respected if not much loved by the public who considered him suspiciously German and feared his influence over the Queen who clearly adored him.*

Above: *George Stephenson (1781-1848). His invention of steam locomotion changed the face of Britian forever and brought railways, industrialisation and mechanisation to every town and city across the land.*

Left: *British soldiers at Isandhlwana during the Zulu War, May 1879. Five months earlier, on 22 January, British soldiers were massacred here by the Zulus — only 350 troops of the original contingent of 1,800 escaped. After reinforcements from Britain arrived, King Cetshwayo was defeated and captured in August. A peace treaty was signed on 1 September 1879, and Zululand would become a British Protectorate in 1887.*

19 The Twentieth Century

At the beginning of the new century Victoria was succeeded by her son, Edward VII. Edward was unarguably a Victorian by birth but was definitely not a Victorian by nature. The term Victorian was already in use in 1875 when Victoria had still over quarter a century to live and although it has been taken to imply a regard for hard work, thrift, strict morality and family virtues, it has also has a derogatory context meaning, according to one dictionary definition, 'exhibiting the characteristics popularly attributed to the Victorians, especially prudery, bigotry or hypocrisy'. The term Edwardian, as used to describe the period of Edward VII's rule, related mainly to the clothes of the era marked by the hourglass silhouette for women and long narrow fitted suits and high collars for men. Edward was nearly 60 years old when he succeeded his mother and as the Prince of Wales, he had acquired a reputation as a playboy and was heartily disapproved of by his mother. He was a noted sportsman, traveller, and patron of the arts and, with his wife Alexandra of Denmark, presided over an unconventional social set that included members of the upper middle classes as well as the aristocracy. When he succeeded to the throne he had little experience in government but was extremely popular during his short reign (1901-10) and because of his efforts to increase international amity the king became known as Edward the Peacemaker. Edward died at Buckingham Palace on 6 May 1910, having reigned for only nine years and was succeeded by his son George who became King George V.

As king the Sailor Prince, so-called because of his active career in the navy, won popular affection, despite his gruff personality, by his visits to the troops during World War I and later by his Christmas radio broadcasts. The outstanding event of the reign of George V was undoubtedly the First World War, 'the war to end all wars', during which the youth of the western world destroyed itself. Following England's declaration of war on Germany in August 1914 after the Kaiser's troops had invaded Belgium, the king renounced all the German titles belonging to him and his fam-

Below: *The sinking of the* Titanic. *Technology had boomed in the 19th century and when Harland & Wolff built the* Titanic, *people truly believed that the ship was unsinkable. How wrong they were!*

Right: *The opening of King Edward VIII's first parliament in 1901. Sitting beside him is Queen Alexandra. Parliament is always opened by the monarch in an elaborate ceremony of pagentry and privilege.*

Below right: *Charles Rolls in the racing car that beat the world record over one kilometre, recording 83mph in 1903.*

BUILDER &
VOTES

ily and changed the name of the royal house from the German Saxe-Coburg-Gotha to Windsor. At the height of the conflict Lloyd George replaced Asquith as Prime Minister and promised survivors of the war that he would undertake 'to make Britain a fit country for heroes'. For a time it appeared that this promise would be fulfilled but the post-war boom was over within two years and was followed in the 1920s by years of depression, strikes and hunger marches culminating in the General Strike of 1926. T. S. Eliot's writings of *The Waste Land* and *The Hollow Men* expressed the disillusion of the early 1920s. At the beginning of the 1930s, after the American economic slump, the country was once again faced with an economy close to collapse with over three million unemployed.

London and the south of England was largely immune to this new economic crisis and was only reminded of it by events such as the historic Jarrow March (1936), where shipyard workers walked down to London from Durham where two-thirds of the population were out of work. At this time London was a world of cocktails, night clubs and dancing; the world of Noel Coward, Somerset Maugham and W. H. Auden. This was also the age when the motor car came into its own and the expanding suburbs of London necessitated the metropolitan extensions of the underground railway system. The architecture of the new stations by Charles Holden on the Piccadilly Line out to Hounslow evoke a vivid image of those days in 1930s' London. To most of the pleasure-seekers of the 1930s the economic problems of the country seemed far away and they were oblivious to the storm clouds gathering over Europe with the threatening rise to power of Adolf Hitler and his Nazi Party in Germany. King George was not to witness his country's second world conflict, he died at Sandringham House, Norfolk, on January 20, 1936 and was succeeded by his oldest son Edward VIII.

Left: *Suffragettes fighting an election for the first time in 1910. Women had been fighting for the right to vote since before 1886 — the first attempt in Parliament. The campaign got seriously militant in 1906 when Emmeline Pankhurst and her daughters took the cause to the country. Their struggle continued until 1914 when they sidelined the issue for the duration of the First World War. By 1918 women's role had changed thanks to their war efforts and they were given limited franchise. By 1928 all women over the age of 21 were allowed to vote.*

Above: *A shell-filling factory at Chilwell. The First World War was a turning point for women's rights as the enormous loss of manpower forced society to accept women into professions that had been exclusively male. In Britain, the early months of the war saw a severe shortage of shells for the front culminating in the May 1915 'Shell Scandal', following reports in* The Times *that the initial failure of the Artois Offensive was caused by a shortage of ammunition. The crisis led to the fall of the Liberal government, which was replaced by a coalition at the end of May.*

Edward VIII became the only British monarch to abdicate voluntarily. Soon after becoming king he found himself at odds with the government of Stanley Baldwin over his determination to marry Wallis Warfield Simpson, an American divorcee, and it soon became clear that this marriage would not be accepted by either the political leaders or the public. In a moving radio address on December 11, 1936, Edward announced his abdication and was given the title of Duke of Windsor but because his wife was not

Above: *All sorts of methods of transport were used to get troops to the front during the Great War. Here double-deck buses have been impressed into service in Flanders during the May 1917 Battle of Arras.*

Right: *Imperial forces from Britain's huge empire fought valiantly during the war. The Indian Army contributed more than 1.3 million men, the bulk of their 72,000 casualties lost on the Western Front, where the Indian Corps of two divisions and a cavalry brigade served from September 1914 until it was withdrawn nearly a year later. This photograph shows the 129th Baluchis in October 1914.*

Above: *The British Front in Flanders, 1917.*

Above Right: *A wiring party of Guards crossing a captured canal in 1917.*

Right: *A month before the armistice that ended the war at the 11th minute of the 11th hour of 11 November 1918, Royal Tank Corps vehicles are seen in October at Bellicourt, during the Battle of the St Quentin Canal, the most important action in the battle for the Hindenburg Line.*

accorded the privileges of a royal duchess in England, they resided abroad. In 1937 he observed social and housing conditions in Germany and visited Adolf Hitler. During World War II he served as a major general in the British Expeditionary Force, and he was governor of the Bahama Islands from 1940 to 1945. After the war he lived as a private British citizen, chiefly in the US and France. At the funeral of his brother George VI in February 1952, he took part in a British royal ceremony for the first time since his abdication.

George VI succeeded to the British throne on the abdication of his brother Edward VIII in 1936. In 1923 he married Lady Elizabeth Bowes-Lyon, the present Queen Mother, who at the time of writing is still alive. George was ostensibly a shy man who had never been groomed for kingship and with his successful struggle to overcome a speech defect won wide respect for his dedication and courage. The first three years of his reign saw Neville Chamberlain become Prime Minister of Britain and Hitler grow from strength to strength in Germany. In England there were clashes between Communists and Oswald Mosley's Fascists, and the poets of the day, including Auden and Day Lewis, passionately protested against the drift to disaster. In 1938, German troops entered Austria then in 1939 Hitler seized Czechoslovakia, and when he turned upon Poland, Chamberlain, who had done all he could to avoid fighting by a policy of appeasement, was obliged to declare war on Germany. Chamberlain was not the man to lead his country in war and Winston Churchill took over as Prime Minister in which position he directed the fortunes of his country with erratic brilliance. During the war, to encourage morale, George VI risked his life visiting war zones and recently bombed cities and also created the George Cross for civilian gallantry, famously awarding it to the people of Malta for heroism under air attack.

In 1945, at the General Election which followed the cessation of hostilities, Churchill was heavily defeated in the polls, much of the voting being influenced by the 'khaki vote' as servicemen voted for the party that would demobilise and send them home. The Labour Party which came to power with an absolute majority for the first time energetically set about its task introducing a series of Bills which were to lay the foundations of the Welfare State. They also began to repair the havoc caused by air raids which had damaged or destroyed 3,500,000 houses in London alone as well as some of England's national treasures such as Coventry Cathedral.

Right: *The armistice that ended the Great War proved short-lived. Just over 20 years later the world found itself at war with Germany again. Here the leaders of the Axis powers — Mussolini (left) and Hitler — are seen with their coterie of henchmen, including Ciano (Italian Foreign Minister), Hess (behind and to the right of Hitler) and Himmler (behind and to the left of Hitler).*

Below: *Crowds celebrate Armistice Day outside Buckingham Palace while the British Royal Family watch from the balcony, 1918.*

Above: *Winston Churchill, seen in RAF uniform in 1948. He had been ousted from office in the general election of 1945 but returned to be Prime Minister in 1951 at the age of 77. He retired aged 81 after overseeing many of the bleakest years in British history both during and after the Second World War.*

Above Right: *A photograph of General Sir Bernard Montgomery taken in 1944. Previously commander of the victorious 8th Army in North Africa, in 1944 he was appointed Commander for the Ground Forces for the Normandy Invasion. He had a distinguished post-war career culminating in serving as deputy Supreme Commander of NATO forces from 1951 to 1958.*

Right: *Women workers producing Spitfire parts.*

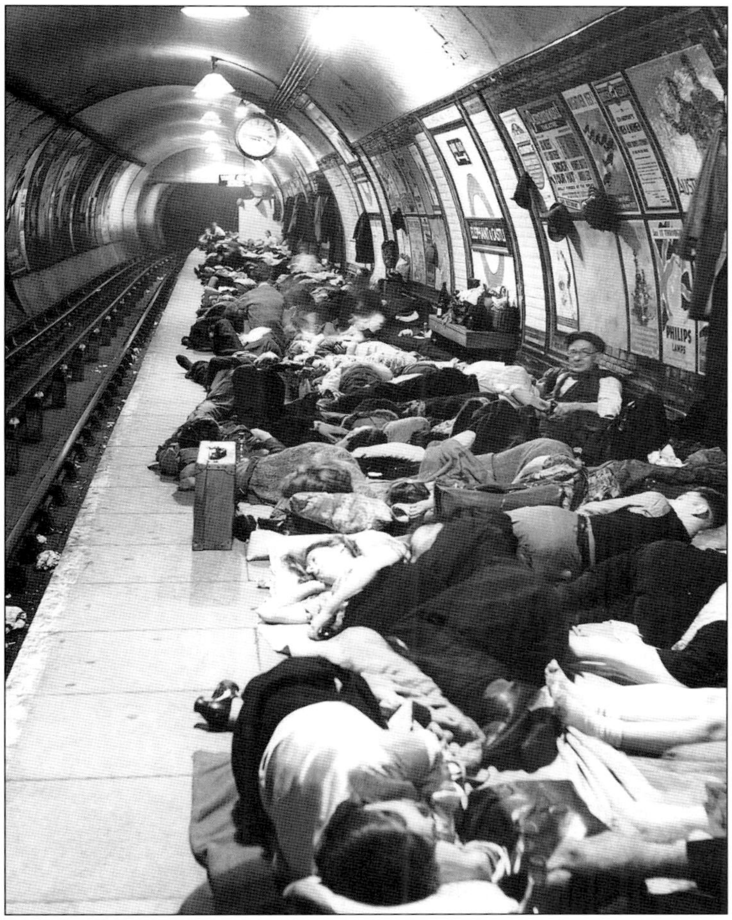

Above Left: *The Blitz — Luftwaffe attacks on British cities between September 1940 and May 1941 — and the 'Baby' Blitz, by V-weapons in 1944, placed civilians directly in the firing line. Over half of the 80,000 British civilian casualties of the war died as a result of the Blitz which destroyed two million homes (over 60 percent in London). Here the Elephant and Castle tube station is used as an air raid shelter.*

Above: *London's docks burn during the Blitz. The biggest port in England, it was a major target for the Luftwaffe on its nightly raids against London.*

Left: *The German V-1 and V-2s — the so-called vengeance weapons, designed to be reprisals for the bombing of Germany — were aimed at civilians mainly in London, Antwerp and Liège. This V-1 has been hit by anti-aircraft guns which (along with the guns of RAF fighters) accounted for over 7,000 of the 15,000 missiles fired at Antwerp and southern England.*

Above: *Buckingham Palace, the principal residence of the Queen, gets its name from the house built for John Sheffield, Duke of Buckingham, in 1702-05. The classical facade seen here was reconstructed in 1913 by Sir Aston Webb and overlooks a forecourt patrolled by the Guards' Division in full dress uniform. In front of the palace is the Queen Victoria Memorial.*

Right: *Selfridges, on Oxford Street, in the heart of London's West End, opened in March 1909 and benefited from the brief post war boom, becoming one of the biggest and most respected department stores in Britain. Since then, and despite a few recessions, London has become a paradise for shoppers.*

Above: *The King's Troop of the Royal Horse Artillery, equipped with guns from the Great War, is used for saluting and display purposes.*

The king and his queen consort resumed their royal visits abroad but George's frail health was weakened and his life probably shortened by his determination to carry on with his public duties despite serious illness. The latter part of the reign of George VI was marked by the relinquishment of the title of Emperor of India, following the partition of India in 1947 into Pakistan and India and the gaining of their independence. He died on 6 February 1952, and was succeeded by his elder daughter Elizabeth II who came to the throne at the age of 25.

By the time of the new Queen's ascension to the throne, the public duties of the British monarch were entirely ceremonial, but the Queen took her responsibilities seriously, inspecting state papers daily and consulting with Prime Ministers. She was educated in the role of constitutional monarch by her father and mother and by her grandmother Queen Mary, wife of George V. Harold Macmillan, Prime Minister from 1957 to 1963, wrote of her: 'She loves her duty, and means to be a Queen and not a puppet'. Elizabeth comes across as a colourless personality mainly because her constitutional role obliges her to keep opinions to herself but those who know her speak of her shrewdness and sense of humour. Queen Elizabeth is the wealthiest woman in Britain, having inherited the extensive royal family estates but, under pressure from public opinion, she volunteered in 1992 to become the first monarch to pay income tax.

The reign of Elizabeth II has seen the time when, according to Dean Acheson — an American Secretary of State — 'Britain had lost an Empire but not yet found a new role'. Few of Britain's old colonial possessions are left and most of these are being claimed by other countries: Gibraltar by the Spanish, Hong Kong has been returned to China and the Falkland Islands, a crown colony since 1892, by the Argentinians whose army launched an attack on them in 1982 — an attack which was vigorously repelled by a British task force sent to the South Atlantic. Britain's role in the modern world was also questioned by the French President, General de Gaulle, who believed that she was too closely involved with the United States to make a satisfactory member of the European Economic Community established by the Treaty of Rome in 1957. Twice de Gaulle vetoed Britain's application for membership and it was not until 1973 that she was at last admitted although even today the British people remain equivocal about the Community.

Britain today, in common with much of the Western world, suffers the afflictions of modern society with its economic problems as well as those posed by crime and violence, racial and class prejudice and decaying inner cities but the people are, as the poet Milton suggested over 300 years ago, 'not beneath the reach of any point that human capacity can soar to'. The story of England from Stonehenge to the Atomic Age is an indomitable narrative about the spirit of her people.

PART 3: THE ARTS

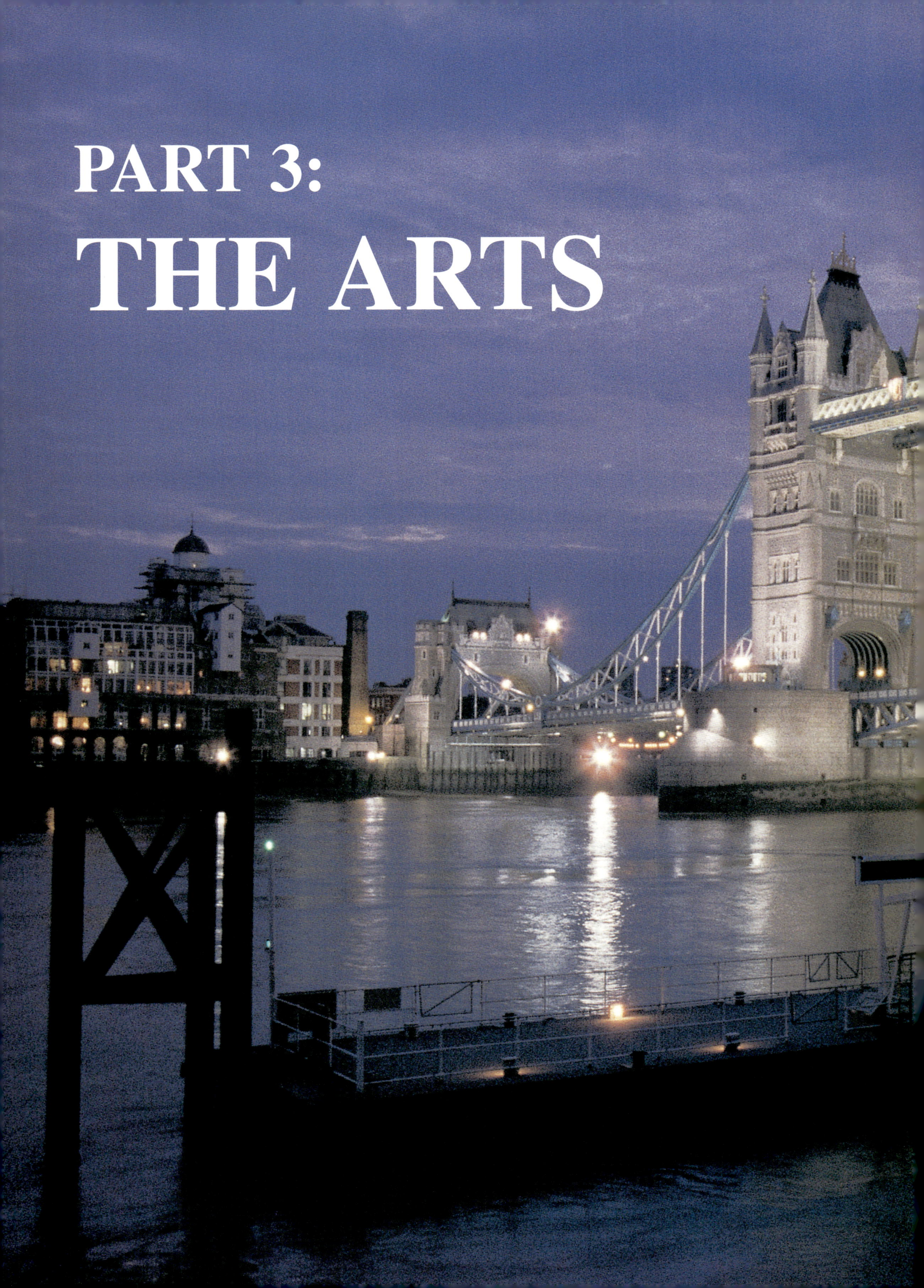

20 Architecture and Design

The architect Inigo Jones' patronage by Charles I allowed him to visit Italy (1613-1614) and he was the first Englishman to understand thoroughly the principles of Italian Renaissance architecture, which were exemplified for him in the work of Andrea Palladio. In the Banqueting House of Whitehall Palace Jones created the first building in central London to embody not only the classical orders correctly used, but also classical systems of proportion. Some of the private houses designed by Jones contained baroque features in their interior decoration, but it was not until the late 17th and early 18th centuries that the baroque style dominated English art and architecture. The leading architect of this phase was Sir Christopher Wren, whose masterpiece is Saint Paul's Cathedral (1675-1709) in London. With its great dome, solemn interior, and finely chiselled detail, Saint Paul's was a worthy centrepiece for the huge modern city that rose beside the Thames out of the ashes of the Great Fire of London (1666). Apart from the great cathedral, Wren and his assistant Nicholas Hawksmoor rebuilt nearly fifty City of London churches. Meanwhile, his pupils and younger contemporaries were designing enormous country houses, such as Chatsworth, Derbyshire (begun 1686), by William Talman and Blenheim Palace, Oxfordshire (1705-1724), by Sir John Vanbrugh.

Georgian is the term applied to the architectural and decorative art styles that flourished in England during the reigns of the first four Georges (1714-1830). The period began with the revived Palladianism of Richard Boyle and the baroque style of William Kent and by the middle of the century a rococo style was adopted for the interiors of some houses and a new informal type of garden design, the landscape or English garden, was invented by Lancelot 'Capability' Brown. Under the auspices of Richard (Beau) Nash, master of ceremonies at Bath, John Wood and his son were fashioning Bath into the most beautiful town in England with their great masterpieces of neoclassicism. The architects Robert Adam and Sir William Chamber were also contributors to this neo-classic movement with its elegant style and decoration strongly influenced by the buildings of the ancient Romans and Greeks. Neoclassicism found expression chiefly in architecture and perhaps the most important single example of the style was the Bank of England (1792-1823, rebuilt 1927) in London, by Sir John Soane.

Left: *St Paul's Cathedral.*

Above Right: *On the Thames between Richmond and Kingston is the 17th century Ham House, built as a modest manor house by Sir Thomas Vavasour but extended and redecorated after Charles II's restoration by the Duke of Lauderdale. The house contains a remarkable and rich interior decoration and furnishings that are well worth seeing.*

Right: *Salisbury Cathedral moved from the ancient Old Sarum to its current position in the 13th century. Building started in 1220 and finished over 100 years later. It is a perfect example of Early English Gothic style.*

Far right: *The remains of Old Gorhambury House, in Hertfordshire, illustrate the influence of the Renaissance in Elizabethan England.*

Previous Page: *Tower Bridge was built between 1886 and 1894 and cost £1.5 million. Between the towers (some 200ft apart) are walkways — open to the public — affording visitors wonderful views of the Thames. The central roadway lifts to allow large vessels through.*

The Prince Regent's (later George IV) favourite architect John Nash (1752-1835) was one of the leading British architects in the first three decades of the 19th century and is best known for his grandiose urban designs for London's West End. The king's patronage led to the commission for his greatest project, the design of Regent's Park and a processional way from the park to Buckingham Palace. Nash bordered the park with vast terraces and crescents of contiguous houses, incorporating them within gigantic, colonnaded palaces faced in white stucco. For the processional route Nash designed Park Crescent, Oxford Circus, Regent Street, Piccadilly Circus, Trafalgar Square, and the enlargement of Buckingham Palace as the route's terminus. Alongside the neoclassical art a revival of the Chinese taste was initiated by the Regent himself, who made extensive improvements to the Royal Pavilion at Brighton under the direction of John Nash with the interior decorated in the Chinese manner by Frederick Crace and Robert Jones. This Oriental pleasure palace, the Prince Regent's seaside retreat, remains as a monument to the extravagance of George IV and his cultural interests.

The Victorian age found its main architectural expression in the Gothic Revival seen in a renewal not only of church building and town halls but also in the Houses of Parliament by Sir Charles Barry, with assistance on the Gothic decoration by Augustus Pugin. Sir Charles Barry (1795-1860) was one of the leading architects in England in the second quarter of the 19th century and his design of Westminster Palace, the correct name for the building commonly called the Houses of Parliament, had an enormous impact on the Gothic Revival style of architecture in Great Britain and the United States during the 19th century. Apart from this famous work in London he designed many country houses, notably Cliveden in Buckinghamshire. In 1851 the English landscape gardener and architect, Sir Joseph Paxton (1803-1865), gained international renown for building the Crystal Palace which housed the Great Exhibition of the Works of Industry held in 1851 at Hyde Park in London. The vast, open architectural space that Paxton created was an entirely new concept and was an historically significant development inspired by work on a special conservatory that he designed for the Duke of Devonshire at Chatsworth. After the exhibition closed the framework of this immense enclosure of glass and iron was easily dismantled, and the whole palace was reassembled in Sydenham, a London suburb, where it remained in useful service until destroyed by fire in 1936. The Crystal Palace was the first work of distinctly modern architecture and it foreshadowed the curtain-walled buildings of the mid-20th century.

The Great Exhibition was a notable success and the profits realised paid for the transformation of a large part of Kensington where Exhibition Road, Queen's Gate and Cromwell Road — names all chosen by Prince Albert — were all built soon afterwards. Also built on land purchased in the 1850s was the Royal Albert Hall, the Victorian & Albert Museum, the Natural History Museum, the Science Museum and the Geological Museum. These great edifices of Gothic style, along with Barry's Westminster Palace and Sir George Gilbert Scott's Midland Hotel, Saint Pancras Station, changed a whole generation's attitude to architecture. The English writer and social reformer John Ruskin (1819-1900) passionately championed this Gothic style and he ultimately convinced most of his countrymen that it was far better suited than any other to reflect the glories of Britain's past. In an example outside of London the grandeur of the genre was exploited in the creation of Allerton Park, North Yorkshire.

The grandiose Victorian buildings create an image of London that is firmly etched in the minds of tourists and natives alike and it was not until the late 1920s/early 1930s that another architectural style was to pervade the country. Despite the economic hardships of the time the architecture reflected the mood of gaiety brought about by the pleasure seekers of London's high-society and the new age of the motor car. Scores of hotels were being built, including the Park Lane, the Mayfair, the Dorchester and the Strand and hundreds of cinemas from grand picture palaces in the capital to little cinemas in country towns sprung up. New theatres were constructed in London and the first great department stores were beginning to emerge on Oxford Street. The lines of London's underground railway system were constantly being extended and new stations,

Left: *A view of the northern edge of the Houses of Parliament from Westminster Bridge. The work of Pugin and Barry it exemplifies the late Gothic style of architecture so fashionable in Victorian England.*

Right: *Religious intolerance was one of the themes of English history during the years after the Reformation. Hatred for the papacy and Catholicism was followed by the bigotry of the rigid nonconformists. In the grounds of Lulworth Castle lies the first Catholic church built in England since the Reformation. Started in 1786, owner Thomas Weld was only allowed St Mary's if it didn't take on the appearance of a church.*

Left: *The Great Palm House at the Royal Botanic Gardens, Kew, London. Designed by Decimus Burton and erected in 1844-48, at 362ft long, 100ft wide and 66ft high, the Palm House was the biggest such structure in the world at that time. It is still impressive today, a wonderful example of Victorian technology and the burgeoning use of iron and glass as building materials.*

Above: *Hampton Court remained untouched from its completion by Cardinal Wolsey for more than 150 years until the reign of William and Mary. They asked Sir Christopher Wren to comprehensively redesign the palace. His initial plans were dropped as being too expensive but the frontage was changed and the gardens laid to a French style which has been recreated today.*

Left: *The Ranger's House is a brick villa built in the early 18th century by Admiral Francis Hosier between Greenwich and Blackheath in London.*

such as those by Charles Holden on the Piccadilly Line to Hounslow, were being built in a style which effected a change from the earlier, more decorative phase of Art Deco toward a simpler, bolder approach typical of the 1930s.

After the Second World War, thanks to the efforts of Hitler's Luftwaffe, there was much rebuilding to done in the country with no fewer than 3,500,000 houses damaged or destroyed in London alone. The influential British architect, Sir Basil Spence (1907-1978) won the architectural competition for a new cathedral at Coventry to replace the Cathedral Church of Saint Michael's, largely destroyed in an air raid and also directed the design of the Festival of Britain Exhibition (1951). The Royal Festival Hall, 'the first major public building in inner London designed in the contemporary style of architecture', remains a fitting memorial to the Festival enterprise although some of the subsequent buildings on the South Bank — notably the Hayward Gallery and the National Theatre — have not been so warmly received.

21 Literature

England's literary heritage is almost unrivalled in the Western world with names such as Chaucer, Milton, Wordsworth, Dickens, Eliot, Auden and of course the giant of them all, William Shakespeare. The great tradition of English literature really begins with Geoffrey Chaucer who is recognised as one of England's greatest poets.

Chaucer was born c.1340 and his masterpiece, *The Canterbury Tales*, was one of the most important influences on the development of English literature. In these tales the poet joins a band of pilgrims, a microcosm of 14th century English society ranging in status from a Knight to a humble Ploughman. The special genius of Chaucer's work lies in the dramatic interaction between their tales and the framing story. With this and his other works Chaucer greatly increased the prestige of English as a literary language and extended the range of its poetic vocabulary. Edmund Spenser paid tribute to him as his master and many of Shakespeare's plays show a thorough assimilation of Chaucer's comic spirit. Chaucer's reputation has been securely established as the English poet best loved after Shakespeare for his wisdom, humour, and humanity.

At the beginning of the Elizabethan age there was a spontaneous upsurge of the creative spirit when Philip Sidney was writing his *Arcadia* and Edmund Spenser published his *Shepherd's Calendar*. The fateful year of 1588, the year Drake defeated the Spanish Armada, was probably the year that Shakespeare arrived in London and saw Marlowe's first play *Tamburlaine* which voiced the heroic aspirations of the new men of the Renaissance:

'Nature that framed us of four elements,
Warring within our breasts for regiment,
Doth teach us all to have aspiring minds:
Our souls, whose faculties can comprehend
The wondrous architecture of the world.

And measure every wandering planet's course,
Still climbing after knowledge infinite,
And always moving as the restless sheres,
Will us to wear ourselves, and never rest
Until we reach the ripest fruit of all.'

This was the age of a great literary revolution when English drama was transformed into the greatest of all time. England had produced no major poet since Chaucer but was now enriched with such illuminaries as Spenser, Jonson and Donne. Marlowe had died in 1593 but Shakespeare had written some twenty plays, from *Henry VI* to *Hamlet* in the last decade of Elizabeth I's reign. It is no exaggeration to say that William Shakespeare (1564-1616) was the author of the most widely admired and influential body of literature by any individual in the history of Western civilisation. The richness of Shakespeare's imagination, and the subtlety with which he revealed the implications of thought and action, have made his plays endlessly amenable to reinterpretation by succeeding generations.

The Puritan Republic of Oliver Cromwell (1649-1660) was a barren interlude in English literature but the Restoration of the Stuarts, with Charles II, brought a restoration of joy with the new dramatists determined to enjoy themselves after a long spiritual exile. The first years of Charles's rule was a time when the Royalists were laughing at the ridicule poured on the Puritans by Samuel Butler in his satirical poem *Hudibras*, but they were also the years when Bunyan was conceiving *The Pilgrim's Progress* and Milton was writing *Paradise Lost*. This epic which attempts to 'justify the ways of God to men' is considered Milton's masterpiece and one of the greatest poems in world literature. He was arguably the greatest English poet to succeed Shakespeare and his sublime verse, devoted to the defence of civil and religious liberty, shaped the entire course of English poetry for three centuries. The London of this era was chronicled in the diary of Samuel Pepys of the Navy Office and amongst the momentous historical entries were reports of the Great Plague of 1665 and the Great Fire of 1666.

Soon after the death of Queen Anne the Hanoverians came to the throne and although there was discontent and poverty this early Georgian period was the age of Pope and Hogarth. This was also the age of the picaresque romances of Smollet and the novels of Fielding, the first real novels written in the English language, of the melancholy lines of Gray's *Elegy* and the more controversial scepticism of David Hume's *Philosophical Essays*.

The early period of George III's personal rule (1760-1820) saw the formation of the literary club whose members included Samuel Johnson, Sir Joshua Reynolds, Goldsmith, Garrick, Gibbon, Sheridan and Adam Smith. England was changing though and the Club reflected this with its membership increasingly admitting men of science as well as literary men. The Industrial Revolution was gathering momentum and within twenty years of Dr. Johnson's death William Blake was writing of the 'dark, satanic mills' whose high brick walls were the prisons of the poor. Later in his reign, the Twenty Years War with France inspired England's greatest poets of the day with the *Lyrical Ballads* of Wordsworth and Coleridge being arguably their best work. William Wordsworth was one of the earliest and perhaps the greatest of English romantic poets and did much to restore simple diction to English poetry and to establish romanticism as the era's dominant literary movement. His verse celebrates the moral influence exerted by nature on human thought and feeling. He set out to, 'choose incidents from common life and throw over them a certain colouring of the imagination, whereby ordinary things should be presented to the mind in an unusual aspect'.

Right: *Shakespeare's greatest creation? Hamlet, prince of Denmark.*

HAMLET.

OLIVER
CROMWELL
1599
1658

Although a prolific, long-lived poet, Wordsworth wrote most of his best verse during his so-called great decade of 1797-1807. The poet's major works are among the finest and most influential in the language and he was made Poet Laureate in 1843. Samuel Taylor Coleridge's contribution to the *Lyrical Ballads* was the *Rime of the Ancient Mariner*, which, together with his two other magical poems, *Christabel* and *Kubla Khan*, established his reputation as a poet and articulated the mysterious, demonic side of British romanticism. Coleridge became addicted to laudanum (opium dissolved in alcohol), a commonly prescribed drug, and, aware that his poetic talent was fading, he published *Dejection: An Ode* the last of his great poems.

The Regency period of English history (1811-1820) was the period of the great romantic poets Byron, Shelley and Keats.

Byron typified the romantic revolt and had a profound effect on the literature of Europe with his facetious and satirical poem *Don Juan* often considered his masterpiece. 'Mad, bad and dangerous to know' was how Lady Caroline Lamb described him and after many scandals, among the worst of which was his illicit passion for his half sister, Augusta Leigh, Byron left England. The poet's exile lasted until his death in 1824 when, after agreeing to go to the aid of the Greek patriots struggling against their Turkish masters, he landed at Missolonghi, where he died of a fever. Percy Bysshe Shelley stands with Coleridge, Wordsworth, Keats and Byron as one of the great English romantic poets demonstrating brilliant lyric power in such poems as *Ozymandias* and *Ode to the West Wind*. He drowned in 1822, not yet 30 years old, when his boat, the *Don Juan*, capsized on its way to San Terenso, his last Italian residence. The third of the second generation of British romantic poets was John Keats. His short poetic life is unprecedented in English literature; among the poems he wrote between the ages of eighteen and twenty-four are the six great Odes (including *Ode on a Grecian Urn* and *Ode to a Nightingale*) poems of such power that they rank with the greatest in the language. He died on February 23, 1821, in the house on the Spanish Steps that now forms a memorial to him and Shelley. The work of all three of the second generation of Romantics was concentrated within the seven years of Tory reaction after Waterloo, and by 1824 all of them had died tragically young.

In the Victorian age the great writers of the day were a deal less fanciful as illustrated by the compassionate realism of the works of George Eliot who in novels like *Middlemarch* described the slow dissolution of a rural community. The many powerful novels of Charles Dickens, even as early as *Oliver Twist*, show his deep concern about modern society and, as the first great urban novelist, he was a master storyteller whose works are laced with wit and social satire. Thackeray also considered the great social revolution of the Victorian age in his fiction.

'It was only yesterday but what a gulf between now and then. Then was the old world. Stage-coaches, more or less swift riding horses, packhorses, highwaymen . . .

Left: *This fine statue of Oliver Cromwell (1599-1658), Lord Protector 1653-58, is outside the Houses of Parliament. Interred inside Westminster Abbey on his death, at the Restoration his body was hung on the gallows at Tyburn and his head was set on a pole above Westminster Hall where it remained until 1684.*

Below: *Dove Cottage was where William Wordsworth lived from 1799 until he moved to Rydal in 1813. Open to the public, the cottage is on the shores of Grasmere. Wordsworth is buried in St. Oswald's churchyard in Grasmere and has a monument in 'Poets' Corner' in Westminster Abbey.*

Left: *Dame Agatha Christie (1891-1976) is justly famous for her detective novels and her unlikely sleuths, vain Belgian Hercule Poirot and elderly Miss Marple. Her play* The Mousetrap, *which appeared first in 1952, is still running in London. She is buried in St Mary's church, Cholsey, Berkshire.*

Right: *Thomas Hardy (1840-1928) was born at Upper Bockhampton near Dorchester. His ashes are in 'Poets' Corner' in Westminster Abbey, but his heart is in his beloved Wessex, in the churchyard of St Michael's, Stinsford.*

Far Right: *Charles Dickens (1812-70) was the son of a government clerk. He underwent great deprivation as a child and received little education — something that makes his vocabulary, writing style and characterisation even more remarkable. He is buried in 'Poets' Corner' in Westminster Abbey.*

Below Right: *Rudyard Kipling (1865-1936), best known for* The Jungle Book *and his poetry, was awarded a Nobel Prize for Literature in 1907. Born in Bombay, India, he too is buried in 'Poets' Corner' in Westminster Abbey.*

Below Far Right: *Herbert George Wells (1866-1946) was one of the great British writers, well regarded for both the vision of his imaginative work, such as* The Time Machine *and* The Invisible Man, *and the quality of his mainstream novels — such as* The History of Mr Polly.

But your railroad starts a new era . . . We who lived before railways and survive our ancient world, are like Father Noah and his family out of the Ark'.

Victorian contemporaries included the populist novel writer Anthony Trollope and the Bronte sisters with Charlotte's *Jane Eyre* and Emily's *Wuthering Heights* providing models for literature to come and both unique works of art in their own right.

Alfred, Lord Tennyson, was the pre-eminent English poet of his time establishing his eminence with *In Memoriam* which was largely responsible for him being named Poet Laureate in 1850. As laureate, Tennyson composed a number of poems on national occasions, notably *The Charge of the Light Brigade*. Robert Browning ranks with Tennyson as one of the greatest Victorian poets and his work *The Ring and the Book*, that finally established his reputation as a major poet, is considered by some modern critics to be the most important long poem in Victorian literature.

Thomas Hardy, one of the most widely read and respected English novelists, created an important artistic bridge between the 19th and 20th centuries. In Victorian England he had faced accusations of blasphemy as all his novels are pervaded by a belief in a universe dominated by the determinism of the biology of Charles Darwin and the physics of the 17th century philosopher and mathematician Sir Isaac Newton. At the age of 55 Hardy returned to writing poetry and between 1903 and 1908, he created what some consider his most successful poems. The age of new science and technology ushered in by the turn of the century was inevitably reflected in the literature of the day, the new socialism was paraded in Morris's *News from Nowhere*, the young H. G. Wells wrote optimistically about *The First Men in the Moon* whilst the works of Kipling celebrated the glories of Empire. H. G. Wells was one of the world's most prominent literary personalities in the era between 1895 and 1920 and with Jules Verne, he was the inventor of science fiction. His science-fantasy novels are optimistic with their prophetic depictions of the triumphs of technology yet also pessimistic about the horrors of 20th century warfare. The English novelist, short-story writer, and poet Joseph Rudyard Kipling, was a literary giant in his own time, although the value of his works is now a source of considerable critical debate. He is most widely known for his works for children, especially *The Jungle Book* but his celebration of British Imperialism has attracted criticisms of jingoism.

After the Great War and the industrial unrest of the 1920s the London theatres were alive with the works of Noel Coward and Somerset Maugham, the social 'set' seemingly unaware of the impending doom of the Second World War. The foremost English poet of the day was Thomas Stearns Eliot, a major innovator in modern English poetry, famous above all for his revolutionary poem *The Waste Land*. Although born and educated for the most part in the US Eliot, with the outbreak of the First World War in 1914, decided to take up permanent residence in England and became a British subject in 1927. Eliot was not a prolific poet, but his small output soon gained respectful attention from readers of modern poetry on both sides of the Atlantic. His poems are an evocative expression of the Jazz Age. Later W.H. Auden came to be regarded by many as the most influential poet in English since Eliot. Auden emigrated to the United States in 1939 (he became an American citizen in 1946) where he influenced a new generation of poets by teaching, reading his poems and lecturing in colleges and universities throughout the United States and England. He returned to Oxford as an honorary fellow in 1972 and on his death in 1973 was generally thought to be the most important poet writing in English.

Shepherds Crag with Skiddaw beyond.

Canny Cummerlan

Yer buik-larn'd wise gentry that's seen monie counties,
  May preach and palaver, and brag as they will
O' mountains, lakes, valleys, woods, watters, and meadows,
  But canny auld Cummerlan caps them aw still:
It's true, we've nae palaces sheynin amang us,
  Nor marble tall towers to catch the weak eye;
But we've monie feyne cassels, where fit our brave fadders,
  When Cummerland cud onie county defy.

Whea that hes climb'd Skiddaw, has seen sec a prospec,
  Where fells frown owre fells, and in majesty vie?
Whea that hes seen Keswick, can count hawf its beauties,
  May e'en try to count hawf the stars i' the sky:
Theer's Ullswater, Bassenthwaite, Wastwater, Derwent,
  That thousands on thousands ha'e travell'd to view;
The langer they gaze, still the mair they may wonder,
  And ay, as they wonder, may fin summet new.

Robert Anderson (Published c. 1820)

Dover Beach

The sea is calm to-night.
The tide is full, the moon lies fair
Upon the straits; — on the French coast the light
Gleams and is gone; the cliffs of England stand,
Glimmering and vast, out in the tranquil bay.
Come to the window, sweet is the night-air!
Only, from the long line of spray
Where the sea meets the moon-blanch'd land,
Listen! you hear the grating roar
Of pebbles which the waves draw back, and fling,
At their return, up the high strand,
Begin, and cease, and then again begin,
With tremulous cadence slow, and bring
The eternal note of sadness in.

Sophocles long ago
Heard it on the Ægean, and it brought
Into his mind the turbid ebb and flow
Of human misery; we
Find also in the sound a thought,
Hearing it by this distant northern sea.

The Sea of Faith
Was once, too, at the full, and round earth's shore
Lay like the folds of a bright girdle furl'd.
But now I only hear
Its melancholy, long, withdrawing roar,
Retreating, to the breath
Of the night-wind, down the vast edges drear
And naked shingles of the world.

Matthew Arnold (1822-1888)

Not quite the White Cliffs of Dover, but very similar! These are the Seven Sisters near Eastbourne.

A Musical Instrument

WHAT was he doing, the great god Pan,
  Down in the reeds by the river ?
Spreading ruin and scattering ban,
Splashing and paddling with hoofs of a goat,
And breaking the golden lilies afloat
  With the dragon-fly on the river.

He tore out a reed, the great god Pan,
  From the deep cool bed of the river :
The limpid water turbidly ran,
And the broken lilies a-dying lay,
And the dragon-fly had fled away,
  Ere he brought it out of the river.

High on the shore sate the great god Pan,
  While turbidly flowed the river ;
And hacked and hewed as a great god can,
With his hard bleak steel at the patient reed,
Till there was not a sign of a leaf indeed
  To prove it fresh from the river.

He cut it short, did the great god Pan,
  (How tall it stood in the river !)
Then drew the pith, like the heart of a man,
Steadily from the outside ring,
And notched the poor dry empty thing
  In holes, as he sate by the river.

'This is the way,' laughed the great god Pan,
  Laughed while he sate by the river,)
'The only way, since gods began
To make sweet music, they could succeed.'
Then, dropping his mouth to a hole in the reed,
  He blew in power by the river.

Sweet, sweet, sweet, O Pan!
  Piercing sweet by the river!
Blinding sweet, O great god Pan!
The sun on the hill forgot to die,
And the lilies revived, and the dragon-fly
  Came back to dream on the river.

Yet half a beast is the great god Pan,
  To laugh as he sits by the river,
Making a poet out of a man :
The true gods sigh for the cost and pain, —
For the reed which grows nevermore again
  As a reed with the reeds in the river.

Ah, love, let us be true
To one another! for the world, which seems
To lie before us like a land of dreams,
So various, so beautiful, so new,
Hath really neither joy, nor love, nor light,
Nor certitude, nor peace, nor help for pain;
And we are here as on a darkling plain
Swept with confused alarms of struggle and
flight,
Where ignorant armies clash by night.

Elizabeth Barrett Browning (1806-1861)

Beech tree reflections.

The New Jerusalem

And did those feet in ancient time
Walk upon England's mountains green?
And was the holy Lamb of God
On England's pleasant pastures seen?

And did the Countenance Divine
Shine forth upon our clouded hills?
And was Jerusalem builded here
Among these dark Satanic mills?

Bring me my bow of burning gold:
Bring me my arrows of desire:
Bring me my spear: O clouds unfold!
Bring me my chariot of fire.

I will not cease from mental fight,
Nor shall my sword sleep in my hand
Till we have built Jerusalem
In England's green and pleasant land.

William Blake (1757-1827)

Hardknott Fort above Eskdale.

Poverty in East London — Spitalfields soup kitchen in 1867.

London

I wander thro' each charter'd street,
Near where the charter'd Thames does flow,
And mark in every face I meet
Marks of weakness, marks of woe.

In every cry of every Man,
In every Infant's cry of fear,
In every voice, in every ban,
The mind-forg'd manacles I hear.

How the Chimney-sweeper's cry
Every black'ning Church appalls;
And the hapless Soldier's sigh
Runs in blood down Palace walls.

But most thro' midnight streets I hear
How the youthful Harlot's curse
Blasts the new born Infant's tear,
And blights with plagues the Marriage hearse.

Devoke Water from Harter Fell.

The night is darkening round me

THE night is darkening round me,
    The wild winds coldly blow ;
But a tyrant spell has bound me,
    And I cannot, cannot go.

The giant trees are bending
    Their bare boughs weighed with snow ;
The storm is fast descending,
    And yet I cannot go.

Clouds beyond clouds above me,
    Wastes beyond wastes below ;
But nothing drear can move me :
    I will not, cannot go.

Emily Bronte (1818-1848)

Home Thoughts, From Abroad

Oh, to be in England
Now that April's there,
And whoever wakes in England
Sees, some morning, unaware,
That the lowest boughs and the brushwood sheaf
Round the elm-tree bole are in tiny leaf,
While the chaffinch sings on the orchard bough
In England — now!

And after April, when May follows,
And the whitethroat builds, and all the swallows!
Hark, where my blossomed pear-tree in the hedge
Leans to the field and scatters on the clover
Blossoms and dewdrops — at the bent spray's edge —
That's the wise thrush; he sings each song twice over,
Lest you should think he never could recapture
The first fine careless rapture!
And though the fields look rough with hoary dew,
All will be gay when noontide wakes anew
The buttercups, the little children's dower
— Far brighter than this gaudy melon-flower!

Robert Browning (1812-1889)

Bluebell — white sport.

She Walks in Beauty

She walks in beauty, like the night
  Of cloudless climes and starry skies;
And all that's best of dark and bright
  Meet in her aspect and her eyes:
Thus mellow'd to that tender light
  Which heaven to gaudy day denies.

One shade the more, one ray the less,
  Had half impair'd the nameless grace
Which waves in every raven tress,
  Or softly lightens o'er her face;
Where thoughts serenely sweet express
  How pure, how dear their dwelling-place.

And on that cheek, and o'er that brow,
  So soft, so calm, yet eloquent,
The smiles that win, the tints that glow,
  But tell of days in goodness spent,
A mind at peace with all below,
  A heart whose love is innocent!

George Gordon, Lord Byron (1788-1824)

Tarn Hows.

Loughrigg Tarn.

Jabberwocky

'Twas brillig, and the slithy toves
did gyre and gimble in the wabe.
All mimsy were the borogoves,
And the mome raths outgrabe.

'Beware the Jabberwock, my son!
The jaws that bite, the claws that catch!
Beware the Jubjub bird, and shun
the frumious Bandersnatch!'

He took his vorpal sword in hand:
Long time the maxome foe he sought —
So rested he by the Tumtum tree,
And stood a while in thought.

As in uffish thought he stood,
The Jabberwock, with eyes of flame,
Came whiffling through the tulgey wood,
And burbled as it came.

One, two! One, two! And through and through
The vorpal blade went snicker-snack.
He left it dead, and with its head
He went galumphing back.

'Has thou slain the Jabberwock?
Come to my arms, my beamish boy!
O frabjous day! Calloh! Callay!
He chortled in his joy.

'Twas brillig, and the slithy toves
Did gyre and gimble in the wabe:
All mimsy were the borogoves,
And the mome raths outgrabe.

Lewis Carroll
[Rev. Charles Dodgson]
(1832-1898)

Loughrigg Tarn.

September

The dark green Summer, with its massive hues,
Fades into Autumn's tincture manifold.
A gorgeous garniture of fire and gold
The high slope of the ferny hill indues.
The mists of morn in slumbering layers diffuse
O'er glimmering rock, smooth lake, and spiked array
Of hedge-row thorns a unity of grey.
All things appear their tangible form to lose
In ghostly vastness. But anon the gloom
Melts, as the Sun puts off his muddy veil;
And now the birds their twittering songs resume,
All Summer silent in the leafy dale.
In Spring they piped of love on every tree,
But now they sing the song of memory.

Hartley Coleridge (1796-1849)

Frost at Midnight

The frost performs its secret ministry,
Unhelped by any wind. The owlet's cry
Came loud _ and hark, again! loud as before.
The inmates of my cottage, all at rest,
Have left me to that solitude, which suits
Abstruser musings: save that at my side
My cradled infant slumbers peacefully.
'Tis calm indeed! so calm, that it disturbs
And vexes meditation with its strange
And extreme silentness. Sea, hill, and wood,
This populous village! Sea, and hill, and wood,
With all the numberless goings on of life,
Inaudible as dreams! the thin blue flame
Lies on my low burnt fire, and quivers not;
Only that film, which fluttered on the grate,
Still flutters there, the sole unquiet thing.
Methinks, its motion in this hush of nature
Gives it dim sympathies with me who live,
Making it a companionable form,
Whose puny flaps and freaks the idling Spirit
By its own moods interprets, every where
Echo or mirror seeking of itself,
And makes a toy of Thought.

But O! how oft,
How oft, at school, with most believing mind,
Presageful, have I gazed upon the bars,
To watch that fluttering stranger! and as oft
With unclosed lids, already had I dreamt
Of my sweet birth-place, and the old church-tower,
Whose bells, the poor man's only music, rang
From morn to evening, all the hot Fair-day,
So sweetly, that they stirred and haunted me
With a wild pleasure, falling on mine ear
Most like articulate sounds of things to come!
So gazed I, till the soothing things I dreamt
Lulled me to sleep, and sleep prolonged my dreams!
And so I brooded all the following morn,
Awed by the stern preceptor's face, mine eye
Fixed with mock study on my swimming book:
Save if the door half opened, and I snatched
A hasty glance, and still my heart leaped up,
For still I hoped to see the stranger's face,
Townsman, or aunt, or sister more beloved,
My play-mate when we both were clothed alike!

Dear Babe, that sleepest cradled by my side,
Whose gentle breathings, heard in this deep calm,
Fill up the interspersed vacancies
And momentary pauses of the thought!
My babe so beautiful! it thrills my heart
With tender gladness, thus to look at thee,
And think that thou shalt learn far other lore
And in far other scenes! For I was reared
In the great city, pent 'mid cloisters dim,
And saw nought lovely but the sky and stars.
But thou, my babe! shalt wander like a breeze
By lakes and sandy shores, beneath the crags
Of ancient mountain, and beneath the clouds,
Which image in their bulk both lakes and shores
And mountain crags: so shalt thou see and hear
The lovely shapes and sound intelligible
Of that eternal language, which thy God
Utters, who from eternity doth teach
Himself in all, and all things in himself.
Great universal Teacher! he shall mould
Thy spirit, and by giving make it ask.

Therefore all seasons shall be sweet to thee,
Whether the summer clothe the general earth
With greenness, or the redbreast sit and sing
Betwixt the tufts of snow on the bare branch
Of mossy apple-tree, while the nigh thatch
Smokes in the sun-thaw; whether the eve-drops fall
Heard only in the trances of the blast,
Or if the secret ministry of frost
Shall hang them up in silent icicles,
Quietly shining to the quiet Moon.

Samuel Taylor Coleridge (1772-1834)

Winter dusk by Loughrigg Tarn.

Kubla Khan

In Xanadu did Kubla Khan
A stately pleasure-dome decree:
Where Alph, the sacred river, ran
Through caverns measureless to man
  Down to a sunless sea.
So twice five miles of fertile ground
With walls and towers were girdled round:
And there were gardens bright with sinuous rills,
Where blossomed many an incense-bearing tree;
And here were forests ancient as the hills,
Enfolding sunny spots of greenery.

But oh! that deep romantic chasm which slanted
Down the green hill athwart a cedarn cover!
A savage place! as holy and enchanted
As e'er beneath a waning moon was haunted
By woman wailing for her demon-lover!
And from this chasm, with ceaseless turmoil seething,
As if this earth in fast thick pants were breathing,
A mighty fountain momently was forced:
Amid whose swift half-intermitted burst
Huge fragments vaulted like rebounding hail,
Or chaffy grain beneath the thresher's flail:
And 'mid these dancing rocks at once and ever
It flung up momently the sacred river.
Five miles meandering with a mazy motion
Through wood and dale the sacred river ran,
Then reached the caverns measureless to man,
And sank in tumult to a lifeless ocean:
And 'mid this tumult Kubla heard from far
Ancestral voices prophesying war!
  The shadow of the dome of pleasure
  Floated midway on the waves;
  Where was heard the mingled measure
  From the fountain and the caves.
It was a miracle of rare device,
A sunny pleasure-dome with caves of ice!
  A damsel with a dulcimer
  In a vision once I saw:
  It was an Abyssinian maid,
  And on her dulcimer she played,
  Singing of Mount Abora.
  Could I revive within me
  Her symphony and song,
  To such a deep delight 'twould win me,
  That with music loud and long,
  I would build that dome in air,
  That sunny dome! those caves of ice!
  And all who heard should see them there,
  And all should cry, Beware! Beware!
  His flashing eyes, his floating hair!
  Weave a circle round him thrice,
  And close your eyes with holy dread,
  For he on honey-dew hath fed,
  And drunk the milk of Paradise.

Samuel Taylor Coleridge (1772-1834)

A stately pleasure dome for the Prince Regent: Brighton Pavilion.

Daniel Defoe was the son of a butcher and led a fascinating career as a pamphleteer, secret agent and journalist before taking up novels in his 50s. Robinson Crusoe *was published in 1719,* Moll Flanders *in 1722. He is buried in Bunhill Fields, Finsbury.*

The True Born Englishman (exerpts)

Thus from a mixture of all kinds began,
That het'rogeneous thing, an Englishman:
In eager rapes, and furious lust begot,
Betwixt a painted Britain and a Scot.
Whose gend'ring off-spring quickly learn'd to bow,
And yoke their heifers to the Roman plough:
From whence a mongrel half-bred race there came,
With neither name, nor nation, speech nor fame.
In whose hot veins new mixtures quickly ran,
Infus'd betwixt a Saxon and a Dane.
While their rank daughters, to their parents just,
Receiv'd all nations with promiscuous lust.
This nauseous brood directly did contain
The well-extracted blood of Englishmen.

Which medly canton'd in a heptarchy,
A rhapsody of nations to supply,
Among themselves maintain'd eternal wars,
And still the ladies lov'd the conquerors.

The western Angles all the rest subdu'd;
A bloody nation, barbarous and rude:
Who by the tenure of the sword possest
One part of Britain, and subdu'd the rest
And as great things denominate the small,
The conqu'ring part gave title to the whole.
The Scot, Pict, Britain, Roman, Dane, submit,
And with the English-Saxon all unite:
And these the mixture have so close pursu'd,
The very name and memory's subdu'd:
No Roman now, no Britain does remain;
Wales strove to separate, but strove in vain:
The silent nations undistinguish'd fall,
And Englishman's the common name for all.
Fate jumbled them together, God knows how;
What e'er they were they're true-born English now.

The wonder which remains is at our pride,
To value that which all wise men deride.
For Englishmen to boast of generation,
Cancels their knowledge, and lampoons the nation.
A true-born Englishman's a contradiction,
In speech an irony, in fact a fiction.
A banter made to be a test of fools,
Which those that use it justly ridicules.
A metaphor invented to express
A man a-kin to all the universe.

For as the Scots, as learned men ha' said,
Throughout the world their wand'ring seed ha' spread;
So open-handed England, 'tis believ'd,
Has all the gleanings of the world receiv'd.

Some think of England 'twas our Saviour meant,
The Gospel should to all the world be sent:
Since, when the blessed sound did hither reach,
They to all nations might be said to preach.

'Tis well that virtue gives nobility,
How shall we else the want of birth and blood supply?
Since scarce one family is left alive,
Which does not from some foreigner derive.

Daniel Defoe (1660-1731)

With the initials of his monarch proudly emblazoned on his chest, this is a 'Beefeater' a member of the Yeoman Warders of the Tower of London. His blue costume is of Tudor origin and he is one of 40 ex-servicemen who assist visitors around the tower.

The Doubt of Future Foes

The doubt of future foes exiles my present joy,
And wit me warns to shun such snares as threaten mine annoy;
For falsehood now doth flow, and subjects' faith doth ebb,
Which should not be if reason ruled or wisdom weaved the web.
But clouds of joys untried do cloak aspiring minds,
Which turn to rain of late repent by changed course of winds.
The top of hope supposed the root upreared shall be,
And fruitless all their grafted guile, as shortly ye shall see.
The dazzled eyes with pride, which great ambition blinds,
Shall be unsealed by worthy wights whose foresight falsehood finds.
The daughter of debate that discord aye doth sow
Shall reap no gain where former rule still peace hath taught to know.
No foreign banished wight shall anchor in this port;
Our realm brooks not seditious sects, let them elsewhere resort.
My rusty sword through rest shall first his edge employ
To poll their tops that seek such change or gape for future joy.

Elizabeth I, Queen of England (1533-1603)

A Rememberance of Grasmere

O vale and lake, within your mountain-urn
Smiling so tranquilly, and set so deep!
Oft doth your dreamy loveliness return.
Colouring the tender shadows of my sleep
With light Elysian; for the hues that steep
Your shores in melting lustre, seem to float
On golden clouds from spirit-lands remote,
Isles of the blest; and in our memory keep
Their place with holiest harmonies. Fair scene,
Most loved by evening and her dewy star!
Oh! ne'er may man, with touch unhallowed jar
The perfect music of thy charm serene!
Still, still unchanged, may one sweet region wear
Smiles that subdue the soul to love, and tears, and prayer.

Felicia Dorothea Hemans (1793-1835)

Grasmere from Loughrigg.

The Hills

Now men there be that love the plain
  With yellow cornland dressed,
And others love the sleepy vales
  Where lazy cattle rest;
But some men love the ancient hills,
  And these have chosen best.

For in the hills a man may go
  For ever as he list
And see a net of distant worlds
  Where streams and valleys twist
A league below, and seem to hold
  The whole earth in his fist.

Or if he treads the dales beneath
  A new delight is his,
For every crest's a kingdom-edge
  Whose conqueror he is,
And every fell the frontier
  Of unguessed emperies.

And when the clouds are on the land
  In shelter he may lie,
And watch adown the misty glens
  The rain go marching by,
Along the silent flank of fells
  Whose heads are in the sky.

And in the hills are crystal tarns
  As deep as maidens' eyes,
About whose edge at middle-noon
  The heavy sunshine lies,
And deep therein the troll-folk dwell
  Can make men wondrous wise.

The gorse of spring is like a host
  Of warriors in gold,
And summer heather like a cloak
  Of purple on the wold,
While autumn's russet bracken is
  Monks' livery of old.

Our lord the sun knows every land,
  But most he loves the fells;
At morning break his earliest torch
  Upon their summit dwells,
At eve he lingers there to catch
  The sound of vesper bells.

The men who dwell among the hills
  Have eyes both strong and kind,
For as they go about their works
  In Heaven's sun and wind,
The spirit of the 'stablished hills
  Gives them the steadfast mind.

William Noel Hodgson (1893-1916)

Over Derwentwater toward Newlands Valley.

Prologue

spoken by Mr. Garrick at the opening of the theatre in Drury Lane, 1747

When Learning's triumph o'er her barb'rous foes
First rear'd the stage, immortal Shakespear rose;
Each change of many-colour'd life he drew,
Exhausted worlds, and then imagin'd new:
Existence saw him spurn her bounded reign,
And panting Time toil'd after him in vain:
His pow'rful strokes presiding Truth impress'd,
And unresisted Passion storm'd the breast.

Then Jonson came, instructed from the school,
To please in method, and invent by rule;
His studious patience, and laborious art,
By regular approach essay'd the heart;
Cold Approbation gave the ling'ring bays,
For those who durst not censure, scarce could praise.
A mortal born he met the general doom,
But left, like Egypt's kings, a lasting tomb.

The Wits of Charles found easier ways to fame,
Nor wish'd for Jonson's art, or Shakespear's flame,
Themselves they studied, as they felt, they writ,
Intrigue was plot, obscenity was wit.
Vice always found a sympathetic friend;
They pleas'd their age, and did not aim to mend.
Yet bards like these aspir'd to lasting praise,
And proudly hop'd to pimp in future days.
Their cause was gen'ral, their supports were strong,
Their slaves were willing, and their reign was long;
Till Shame regain'd the post that Sense betray'd,
And Virtue call'd Oblivion to her aid.

Then crush'd by rules, and weaken'd as refin'd,
For years the pow'r of tragedy declin'd;
From bard, to bard, the frigid caution crept,
Till Declamation roar'd, while Passion slept.
Yet still did Virtue deign the stage to tread,
Philosophy remain'd, though Nature fled.
But forc'd at length her ancient reign to quit,
She saw great Faustus lay the ghost of wit:
Exulting Folly hail'd the joyful day,
And pantomime, and song, confirm'd her sway.

But who the coming changes can presage,
And mark the future periods of the stage? —

Perhaps if skill could distant times explore,
New Behns, new Durfoys, yet remain in store.
Perhaps, where Lear has rav'd, and Hamlet died,
On flying cars new sorcerers may ride.
Perhaps, for who can guess th' effects of chance?
Here Hunt may box, or Mahomet may dance.

Hard is his lot, that here by Fortune plac'd,
Must watch the wild vicissitudes of taste;
With ev'ry meteor of caprice must play,
And chase the new-blown bubbles of the day.
Ah! let not censure term our fate our choice,
The stage but echoes back the public voice.
The drama's laws the drama's patrons give,
For we that live to please, must please to live.

Then prompt no more the follies you decry,
As tyrants doom their tools of guilt to die;
Tis yours this night to bid the reign commence
Of rescu'd Nature, and reviving Sense;
To chase the charms of Sound, the pomp of Show,
For useful Mirth, and salutary Woe;
Bid scenic Virtue form the rising age,
And Truth diffuse her radiance from the stage.

Samuel Johnson (1709-1784)

Robin Hood

No! those days are gone away
And their hours are old and gray,
And their minutes buried all
Under the down-trodden pall
Of the leaves of many years:
Many times have winter's shears,
Frozen North, and chilling East,
Sounded tempests to the feast
Of the forest's whispering fleeces,
Since men knew nor rent nor leases.

No, the bugle sounds no more,
And the twanging bow no more;
Silent is the ivory shrill
Past the heath and up the hill;
There is no mid-forest laugh,
Where lone Echo gives the half
To some wight, amaz'd to hear
Jesting, deep in forest drear.

On the fairest time of June
You may go, with sun or moon,
Or the seven stars to light you,
Or the polar ray to right you;
But you never may behold
Little John, or Robin bold;
Never one, of all the clan,
Thrumming on an empty can
Some old hunting ditty, while
He doth his green way beguile
To fair hostess Merriment,
Down beside the pasture Trent;
For he left the merry tale
Messenger for spicy ale.

Gone, the merry morris din;
Gone, the song of Gamelyn;
Gone, the tough-belted outlaw
Idling in the "grenè shawe";
All are gone away and past!
And if Robin should be cast
Sudden from his turfed grave,
And if Marian should have
Once again her forest days,
She would weep, and he would craze:
He would swear, for all his oaks,
Fall'n beneath the dockyard strokes,
Have rotted on the briny seas;
She would weep that her wild bees
Sang not to her — strange! that honey
Can't be got without hard money!

So it is: yet let us sing,
Honour to the old bow-string!
Honour to the bugle-horn!
Honour to the woods unshorn!
Honour to the Lincoln green!
Honour to the archer keen!
Honour to tight little John,
And the horse he rode upon!
Honour to bold Robin Hood,
Sleeping in the underwood!
Honour to maid Marian,
And to all the Sherwood-clan!
Though their days have hurried by
Let us two a burden try.

John Keats (1795-1821)

Furness Abbey.

Wastwater Screes

Written on the Banks of Wastwater During a Calm

Is this the lake, the cradle of the storms,
Where silence never tames the mountain-roar,
Where poets fear their self-created forms,
Or, sunk in trance severe, their God adore?
Is this the lake for ever dark and loud,
With wave and tempest, cataract and cloud?
Wondrous, O Nature, is thy sovereign power,
That gives to horror hours of peaceful mirth;
For here might beauty build her summer bower!
Lo! where yon rainbow spans the smiling earth,
And clothed in glory, through a silent shower
The mighty Sun comes forth, a god-like birth;
While, 'neath his loving eye the gentle Lake
Lies like a sleeping child too blest to wake!

Christopher North, pseudonym of
Professor John Wilson (1785-1854)

Field poppy

Anthem for Doomed Youth

What passing-bells for these who die as cattle?
        Only the monstrous anger of the guns.
        Only the stuttering rifles' rapid rattle
Can patter out their hasty orisons.
No mockeries for them; no prayers nor bells,
Nor any voice of mourning save the choirs, —
The shrill, demented choirs of wailing shells;
And bugles calling for them from sad shires.

What candles may be held to speed them all?
        Not in the hands of boys, but in their eyes
Shall shine the holy glimmers of goodbyes.
        The pallor of girls' brows shall be their pall;
Their flowers the tenderness of patient minds,
And each slow dusk a drawing-down of blinds.

Wilfred Owen (1893-1918)

Outward Bound

There's a waterfall I'm leaving
 Running down the rocks in foam,
There's a pool for which I'm grieving
 Near the water-ouzel's home;
And it's there that I'd be lying,
 With the heather close at hand,
And the curlews faintly crying
 'Mid the wastes of Cumberland.

While the midnight watch is winging
 Thoughts of other days arise,
I can hear the river singing
 Like the saints in Paradise;
I can see the water winking
 Like the merry eyes of Pan,
And the slow half-pounder sinking
 By the bridge's granite span.

Ah! to win them back and clamber
 Braced anew with winds I love,
From the river's stainless amber
 To the morning mist above,
See through cloud-rifts rent asunder,
 Like a painted scroll unfurled,
Ridge and hollow rolling under
 To the fringes of the world.

Now the weary guard are sleeping,
 Now the great propellers churn,
Now the harbour lights are creeping
 Into emptiness astern,
While the sentry wakes and watches
 Plunging triangles of light
Where the water leaps and catches
 At our escort in the night.
Great their happiness who, seeing
 Still with unbenighted eyes
Kin of theirs who gave them being,
 Sun and earth that made them wise,
Die and feel their embers quicken
 Year by year in summer time
When the cotton grasses thicken
 On the hills they used to climb.

Shall we also be as they be,
 Mingled with our mother clay,
Or return no more it may be?
 Who has knowledge, who shall say?
Yet we hope that from the bosom
 Of our shaggy father Pan,
When the earth breaks into blossom
 Richer from the dust of man,

Though the high gods smite and slay us,
 Though we come not whence we go,
As the host of Menelaus
 Came there many years ago;
Yet the self-same wind shall bear us
 From the same departing place
Out across the Gulf of Saros
 And the Peaks of Samothrace:

We shall pass in summer weather
 We shall come at eventide,
Where the fells stand up together
 And all quiet things abide;
Mixed with cloud and wind and river
 Sun distilled in dew and rain,
One with Cumberland for ever,
 We shall not go forth again.

Noel Oxland (1895-1915)

Derwentwater

The Nymph's Reply

If all the world and love were young,
And truth in every shepherd's tongue,
These pretty pleasures might me move
To live with thee and be thy love.

Time drives the flocks from field to fold,
When rivers rage and rocks grow cold,
And Philomel becometh dumb;
The rest complains of cares to come.

The flowers do fade, and wanton fields
To wayward winter reckoning yields;
A honey tongue, a heart of gall,
Is fancy's spring, but sorrow's fall.

Thy gowns, thy shoes, thy beds of roses,
Thy cap, thy kirtle, and thy posies
Soon break, soon wither, soon forgotten, —
In folly ripe, in reason rotten.

Thy belt of straw and ivy buds,
The coral clasps and amber studs,
All these in me no means can move
To come to thee and be thy love.

But could youth last and love still breed,
Had joys no date nor age no need,
Then these delights my mind might move
To live with thee and be thy love.

Sir Walter Raleigh (c. 1552-1618)

River Brawthey at Colwith Force.

High Sweden Bridge, Ambleside

Under the Greenwood Tree

excerpt from 'As You Like It"

Under the greenwood tree
Who loves to lie with me,
And turn his merry note
Unto the sweet bird's throat,
Come hither, come hither, come hither:
Here shall he see
No enemy
But winter and rough weather.

Who doth ambition shun,
And loves to live i' the sun,
Seeking the food he eats,
And pleas'd with what he gets,
Come hither, come hither, come hither:
Here shall he see
No enemy
But winter and rough weather.

William Shakespeare (1564-1616)

Shall I compare thee to a summer's day?

Shall I compare thee to a summer's day?
Thou art more lovely and more temperate.
Rough winds do shake the darling buds of May,
And summer's lease hath all too short a date.
Sometime too hot the eye of heaven shines,
And often is his gold complexion dimm'd;
And every fair from fair sometime declines,
By chance or nature's changing course untrimm'd;
But thy eternal summer shall not fade
Nor lose possession of that fair thou ow'st;
Nor shall Death brag thou wander'st in his shade,
When in eternal lines to time thou grow'st:
So long as men can breathe or eyes can see,
So long lives this, and this gives life to thee.

William Shakespeare (1564-1616)

Staveley-in-Cartmel.

'C'est magnifique mais ce n'est pas le guerre' — 'It's magnificent but it's not war,' said a French observer as Lord Cardigan led his Light Brigade toward the Russian guns at Balaclava in 1856.

Charge of the Light Brigade

Half a league, half a league,
  Half a league onward,
All in the valley of Death
  Rode the six hundred.
'Forward, the Light Brigade!
Charge for the guns!' he said:
Into the valley of Death
  Rode the six hundred.

'Forward, the Light Brigade!'
Was there a man dismay'd?
Not tho' the soldier knew
  Some one had blunder'd:
Their's not to make reply,
Their's not to reason why,
Their's but to do and die:
Into the valley of Death
  Rode the six hundred.

Cannon to right of them,
Cannon to left of them,
Cannon in front of them
  Volley'd and thunder'd;
Storm'd at with shot and shell,
Boldly they rode and well,
Into the jaws of Death,
Into the mouth of Hell
  Rode the six hundred.

Flash'd all their sabres bare,
Flash'd as they turn'd in air
Sabring the gunners there,
Charging an army, while
  All the world wonder'd:
Plunged in the battery-smoke
Right thro' the line they broke;
Cossack and Russian
Reel'd from the sabre-stroke
  Shatter'd and sunder'd.
Then they rode back, but not
  Not the six hundred.

Cannon to right of them,
Cannon to left of them,
Cannon behind them
  Volley'd and thunder'd;
Storm'd at with shot and shell,
While horse and hero fell,
They that had fought so well
Came thro' the jaws of Death,
Back from the mouth of Hell,
All that was left of them,
  Left of six hundred.

When can their glory fade?
O the wild charge they made!
  All the world wonder'd.
Honour the charge they made!
Honour the Light Brigade,
  Noble six hundred!

Alfred, Lord Tennyson (1809-1883)

Rule Britannia

When Britain first, at Heaven's command,
Arose from out the azure main;
This was the charter of the land,
And guardian angels sung this strain:
"Rule, Britannia, rule the waves;
Britons never will be slaves."

The nations, not so blest as thee,
Must, in their turns, to tyrants fall:
While thou shalt flourish great and free,
The dread and envy of them all.
"Rule, Britannia, rule the waves;
Britons never will be slaves."

Still more majestic shalt thou rise,
More dreadful, from each foreign stroke:
As the loud blast that tears the skies,
Serves but to root thy native oak.
"Rule, Britannia, rule the waves;
Britons never will be slaves."

Thee haughty tyrants ne'er shall tame:
All their attempts to bend thee down,
Will but arouse thy generous flame;
But work their woe, and thy renown.
"Rule, Britannia, rule the waves;
Britons never will be slaves."

To thee belongs the rural reign;
Thy cities shall with commerce shine:
All thine shall be the subject main,
And every shore it circles thine.
"Rule, Britannia, rule the waves;
Britons never will be slaves."

The Muses, still with freedom found,
Shall to thy happy coast repair:
Blest isle! with matchless beauty crown'd,
And manly hearts to guard the fair.
"Rule, Britannia, rule the waves;
Britons never will be slaves."

James Thomson (1700-1748)

Above: *Sir Francis Drake at Plymouth Hoe when he famously insisted on finishing his game of bowls before setting out to defeat the Spanish.*

Right: *The Royal Navy was the most powerful in the world in the Victorian era and on into the 20th century. Epitomising strength and technology is HMS* Warrior, *the first propeller-driven warship.*

Windermere from Loughrigg, early morning

From 'The Prelude'

A dreary moor
Was crossed, a bare ridge clomb, upon whose top
Standing alone, as from a rampart's edge,
I overlooked the bed of Windermere,
  Like a vast river, stretching in the sun.
  With exultation, at my feet I saw
Lake, islands, promontories, gleaming bays,
A universe of Nature's fairest forms
Proudly revealed with instantaneous burst,
Magnificent, and beautiful and gay.

William Wordsworth (1770-1850)

I Wandered Lonely as a Cloud

I wandered lonely as a cloud
  That floats on high o'er vales and hills,
When all at once I saw a crowd,
  A host, of golden daffodils;
Beside the lake, beneath the trees,
Fluttering and dancing in the breeze.

Continuous as the stars that shine
  And twinkle on the milky way,
They stretched in never-ending line
  Along the margin of a bay:
Ten thousand saw I at a glance,
Tossing their heads in sprightly dance.

The waves beside them danced; but they
  Out-did the sparkling waves in glee:
A poet could not but be gay,
  In such a jocund company:
I gazed _ and gazed _ but little thought
What wealth the show to me had bought:

For oft, when on my couch I lie
  In vacant or in pensive mood,
They flash upon that inward eye
  Which is the bliss of solitude;
And then my heart with pleasure fills,
And dances with the daffodils.

William Wordsworth (1770-1850)

Gowbarrow Park, Ullswater

22 Fine Art and Painters

At the beginning of the accession of the Tudors to the English throne profound changes were taking place in the land. The ideas of Renaissance, that flowering of art and literature which had begun in northern Italy over a century earlier, was spreading across Europe bringing it out of the Middle Ages. By the time Henry VIII acceded the throne his court was graced by scholars and artists, and the painter Hans Holbein whose portraits of the magnificent King were to adorn the country houses of his faithful subjects. Holbein was in the first rank of German artists and was one of the greatest portrait painters of the northern European Renaissance and in 1536 was named painter to the king. English art flourished more or less continuously for two centuries through the golden Elizabethan age, the Reformation and the 'Glorious Revolution' of William and Mary to the Hanoverians. During the Hanoverian reign English art entered a new golden age alongside the technical advances of the Industrial Revolution.

The early part of the Hanoverian reign saw the Italian artist Canaletto come to England to paint his pictures of Georgian London and was also the age when Thomas Gainsborough and Joshua Reynolds were at the height of their powers as painters. Gainsborough was one of the most accomplished English painters of the 18th century, excelling both in landscapes and portraits. Throughout his life Gainsborough painted and drew landscapes but he is probably better known for his portraits of prosperous English families which was better remunerated at the time with *The Blue Boy* his most celebrated work. In 1768, Gainsborough became a founding member of the Royal Academy of Arts in London and established a large portrait practice in rivalry with his great contemporary, Sir Joshua Reynolds. Between 1750 and 1752 a stay in Italy introduced Reynolds to the great works of the Renaissance and on his return to England he executed several portraits that brought him into prominence in London society. In 1768 he became the first president of the newly formed Royal Academy and in 1784 was appointed Painter-in-Ordinary to the king, George III.

This was also the time when Josiah Wedgwood, the most important figure in British ceramic history, was creating his works in Burslem, in the Midlands. His most famous productions were his copies of the Portland Vase, a Roman glass amphora with white relief decoration on a dark blue ground. Wedgwood's creamware, however, ensured the prosperity of his business and was always his main product. Its refinement and practicality made it the most desirable utilitarian pottery of the late 18th century, and it enjoyed a huge export trade. Wedgwood was permitted to name his creamware 'Queen's ware', after furnishing tableware to Queen Charlotte, the consort of George III. Working at the same time as Wedgwood, in the mid-18th century, Thomas Chippendale dominated English cabinet making to such an extent that the name Chippendale became synonymous with all English furniture designs of the 1740s through the 1760s. English romanticism found one of its most complete expressions in Chippendale's Gothic and Chinese designs and his eclecticism enabled him to make the transition to a classical style in the 1760s after the introduction of neoclassical interior decorations and furnishings by James Stuart and Robert Adam. Chippendale's influence was maintained by his son, Thomas (c. 1749-1822), who carried on the studio until the early 19th century.

In Gainsborough's many landscape drawings, discovered only after his death, John Constable, 'the father of modern landscape painting', found encouragement for his own studies of natural scenery.

He was the first major English artist to concentrate exclusively on the depiction of rural scenes and to paint such scenes on the scale usually reserved for recording important events in history. One of his most notable works, *The Hay Wain* is1.8m (6ft) wide. Devoting his life to painting a small portion of the English countryside, especially the area around the River Stour in East Anglia, he never founded a school, although he did exert a strong influence on the genre. The romantic bravura of Gainsborough's later work also anticipates the style of J. M. W. Turner who is often regarded as the greatest of all landscape painters and an artist of uniquely varied ability. Turner is well known for his scenes in which the fury of the elements underlines humanity's insignificance against their mighty powers. The well-known *Fighting Temeraire* was rivalled some years later by *Rain, Steam and Speed*. Constable and Turner did for painting very much what Wordsworth and Coleridge did for poetry namely to 'choose incidents from common life and present them to the mind in an unusual aspect'.

Turner's work was at first derided by the critics but the social reformer, artist and author John Ruskin taught the public to recognise the genius of the landscape painter. Towards the end of the 19th century Ruskin's advocacy of the Pre-Raphaelites encouraged a revolt against the conventional academic painting of the day. A coalition of British artists, united in their distaste for formal academic art and the neoclassical style dominating the art of the early part of the century, formed the Pre-Raphaelite movement. Founded in 1848, the principal members of the movement were Holman Hunt, John Everett Millais, and Dante Gabriel Rossetti. The group selected the name Pre-Raphaelite because of their belief that Raphael was the source of the academic tradition they abhorred and felt that art should return to the purer vision of Gothic and Early Renaissance. Hunt established his reputation when he painted *The Light of the World* which is one of the best-known Pre-Raphaelite pictures. In Millais's later years he turned his attention to a more sedate treatment of anecdotal and sentimental themes that appealed to average Victorian taste. Such subjects as *The Boyhood of Raleigh* proved to be great popular favourites, and the use in a soap advertisement of his picture of a small boy blowing soap bubbles created a sensation. The influence of the Pre-Raphaelite movement was particularly important to the development of Art Nouveau and the European symbolist movement.

Above Left: *Black Basalt is a fine-grained black stoneware body developed by Josiah Wedgwood I in around 1768. He said of it, 'the black is sterling and will last forever.' It is still in production today.*

Above: *White and pale blue Jasper snake-handled vase, sometimes referred to as the 'Venus' vase because of the visible bas-relief of Venus in her chariot drawn by a swan. The piece is dated around 1785.*

Left: *Group of Wedgwood bone china tea ware comprising teapot with parapet edge, covered sugar basin and cream jug.*

Art Nouveau refers to a style of architecture, of commercial and decorative art, and, to some extent, a style of painting and sculpture that was popular about 1900. Although the style was then thought of as modern and was given the title 'new art', it was adapted from older styles and art forms. Art Nouveau was a rich, voluptuous style that appealed to an enlightened elite, to personalities such as the actress Sarah Bernhardt and to the *nouveaux riches*, whose tastes, uninhibited by tradition, encouraged designers to stylistic excesses. Much was derived from the Gothic and rococo and from the arts of Java and Japan. The movement was also inspired by Celtic manuscripts and the drawings of William Blake. A favourite Art Nouveau theme was a nymph with flowers in her abundant streaming hair. Other favourites were peacocks, dragonflies, and moths worked into combs, brooches, and other adornments in brilliant enamels and gold filigree. The style's patrons grew bored with it, however, and it declined in fashion within a decade and was out of fashion before the First World War had begun. In the 1960s a reappraisal of the style began and Art Nouveau was incorporated in the rebellious psychedelic style of the time, on posters and on rock album covers, and finally became established as a significant style in the history of modern art.

A giant in modern art was the British abstract sculptor Henry Spencer Moore who was acclaimed as one of the great sculptors of the 20th century and is best known for his large, semi-abstract sculptures of the human figure. From the beginning of his artistic career he displayed a predilection for the sculpture of primitive and ancient peoples and was influenced by pre-Columbian Mexican sculpture with its primitive grandeur and simplicity. With his *Reclining Figure* he employed swelling shapes, undulating extensions, and rounded indentations that mirror natural forms, a theme which he continued to depict throughout his career. Apart from his sculptures, a series of drawings of Londoners huddled in tube stations during the Second World War air raids stand on their own as works of art poignantly expressing the impact of war on civilians. With his large sculptures Moore was perhaps the pre-eminent 20th century master of monumental sculpture and he continued to be creatively active into his eighties until his death in 1986.

Among modern artists the romantic tradition and the emphasis on line may be seen in the paintings of Francis Bacon, David Hockney, and Graham Sutherland and the late 20th century has seen the celebrated emergence of such individual artists as the Jewish-American-Briton R. B. Kitaj and the German-Jewish-Briton Lucian Freud, acclaimed as one of the world's greatest realist painters.

Left: *Sir Joshua Reynolds (1723-92) was born in what is now Plymouth and studied in Rome 1749-52. He became the first president of the Royal Academy in 1768. This is a set of windows of his in Oxford.*

Right: *The Arts and Crafts Movement of the late 19th century would influence its continental successor Art Nouveau.*

23 Music

English music has followed an often idiosyncratic course of development with fertile periods of native composition and performance alternating with long periods dominated by Continental musicians and influences. At other times musical development has been interrupted by political and religious upheavals, notably, the break between the Anglican and Roman churches in 1529, and the turmoil of the 17th century Civil War and Commonwealth period. The standard musical period labels (baroque, classical, and so on), which have evolved to distinguish historical stylistic qualities primarily in Italian, German, and French compositions, often prove less meaningful when applied to English music. Frequently more revealing are relationships between musical developments and contemporary British political, social, and artistic currents.

Composers of the Tudor era (1485-1603) produced much of the finest English sacred music and the heightened activity during the Elizabethan Renaissance produced a golden age of English instrumental music and secular song. William Byrd, Orlando Gibbons, and Thomas Morley are some Elizabethan composers who adapted the madrigal from Italian models to suit English tastes and Thomas Tallis left a legacy that gives testimony to his virtuosity as an organist. Songs for solo voice, such as those by John Dowland, rivalled any composed in Europe and instrumental music was not ignored; John Bull, Giles Farnaby and Francis Cutting all contributing scores for various ensembles. By the death of Elizabeth in 1603 and the accession to the throne of her cousin, James VI of Scotland, who became James I of England, the exuberance had begun to fade, and a more sombre note coloured Jacobean life and music. The Civil Wars (1642-1649) and the repressions of the Commonwealth (1649-1660) also severely disrupted English musical life.

During the artistically more open Restoration period that followed Italian techniques of baroque music, dominant in most of Europe, were slow to take hold in England. French music was more in favour, and Italian forms were fully mastered only by Henry

Left: *Edward Elgar (1857-1934) is considered one of the greatest English classical composers. His* Enigma Variations *(1899) and* The Dream of Gerontius *(1900) won him world-wide acclaim. He was knighted in 1904 and was appointed Master of the King's Musick in 1924, a position he held for 10 years.*

Right: *Most English music in the Middle Ages was inspired by the court and the church — particularly the great cathedrals. The Norman towers of Exeter cathedral date back to around 1112-50; most of the rest of the building was rebuilt between 1270 and 1370 and its vaulting boasts the longest unbroken line in the Gothic style anywhere. This, the west front of the cathedral, is weatherworn but still exhibits fine 14th century sculpture.*

Left: *Sir Paul McCartney was born in Liverpool in 1942 and will be remembered best for the success he had writing hit after hit with John Lennon for the Beatles. He was knighted in 1997.*

Right: *Noel Gallagher sums up 1990s' style in typical fashion. Oasis — the band he and his brother Liam formed — has been touted as the Beatles of the 1990s.*

Purcell (c. 1659-1695), the most eminent British composer of his time. In 1679 he was appointed organist of Westminster Abbey, and from 1682 onward he served as one of the organists of the Chapel Royal. Despite a creative career of less than 20 years he wrote music of the highest quality and originality for virtually every known genre. After Purcell, English music was dominated by Continental techniques and foreign musicians for almost 200 years. It is somewhat of a mystery why there was such a barren period in native composition relieved only for a short time by the work of George Frideric Handel. The oratorio, an extended dramatic work on a religious theme, had its roots in Rome and spread throughout Europe through the work of the German-English composer but it was in England, and in English, that he composed the most popular of all oratorios, the *Messiah* (1741). It was Handel's English oratorios, combining operatic elements with English choral traditions, that had a lasting impact on British and other music.

Throughout the Victorian rule of the 19th century the only English works to gain a wide following outside of Britain were the fourteen satirical operas of Gilbert and Sullivan but a revival in native English music began with the romantic orchestral works of Frederick Delius and Sir Edward Elgar. Though thoroughly schooled in German and French techniques, both Ralph Vaughn Williams and Gustav Holst sought inspiration in the traditions of English folk song and Tudor music. More recent British music has been characterised by a stylistic eclecticism and a special interest in theatrical genres. Benjamin Britten excelled at opera and other vocal genres. Michael Tippett, though most familiar in America for his orchestral works, has also contributed significantly to the renewal of British opera. Peter Maxwell Davies and Harrison Birtwistle have developed thoroughly contemporary but highly personal musical styles while drawing freely from English musical practices from the Middle Ages to the present day.

We mentioned earlier the relationship between musical developments and contemporary British political, social and artistic currents in the history of English music and perhaps this relationship is most apparent today in the world of popular music. In the 1950s a whole new youth culture exploded with the arrival of 'rock'n'roll'. A generation was coming to maturity with more money and freedom than ever before and they had their own music, clothes and style which for the most part excluded their parents — the first 'teenagers' were born. It was all ephemeral but it did worry certain areas of the establishment and concern was expressed in the House of Commons particularly about 'teddy boys'. In the 1960s, the Beatles and the Rolling Stones saw to it that England and the 'Swinging London' of the King's Road and Carnaby Street became famous the world over. Although Lennon and McCartney were brilliant pop composers, it was not the music that was startlingly different, rather the whole style and consciousness of the time. In 1968 John Lennon's *Revolution* and Mick Jagger's *Street Fighting Man* (written after the anti-Vietnam protest in Grosvenor Square), although somewhat ambivalent, represented a refusal to accept the established system. Barry Miles, the writer, biographer and founder of the *International Times* — the radical newspaper of the period — classifies the late 1960s as a unique era: 'In those days it meant something, in the sense that people would really wait with bated breath for the next Rolling Stones or Beatles album because these were art works of tremendous political importance'.

Some ten years later the King's Road was again at the hub of a new culture — the nihilism of Punk and the Sex Pistols. This short lived phenomena affected the attitudes of many contemporary pop musicians and traces of the legacy prevails today. A new Labour government came to power in May 1987 and set about wooing the younger generation by inviting some of the top pop stars of the day to Downing Street but history will tell us if the inherent rebelliousness of youth will reject the establishment (as did their predecessors) in today's 'Cool Britannia'.

PART 4: A TASTE OF ENGLAND

WHITBREAD FINE ALES
KINGS ARMS
CARTMEL
GOOD FOOD

24 Beers

To generations of Britons, beer means 'bitter' — hopped ale which is top-fermented beer with sign of fruitiness. Bitters show hop bitterness with colours ranging from light pale to dark copper and alcohol in the 3.5 to 4.5 range, and are manufactured in many breweries in England today. After the predations of the post-war years which saw so many small traditional companies subsumed within vast brewing empires, CAMRA — the Campaign for Real Ale — has done much to revive this ancient style of brewing. This brief survey gives but a taste of the beers and breweries available today in draught or bottled form. It is worth experimenting to find your favourites.

Previous Page: *Britain is famed for its pubs, and for the convivial atmosphere to be found inside. Here, possibly sleeping it all off!, a solitary figure outside the King's Arms in Cartmell, Lancashire.*

Left, Right and Below: *Traditional draught bitter has been manufactured on the site of Young's Ram Brewery in the London suburb of Wandsworth since at least 1581 — making the brewery the oldest site in Britain on which beer has been brewed continuously. The Young family bought the business in 1831 and have retained much of the old equipment — such as Victorian vessels where the beer ferments for a week, two 19th century steam engines and two brewing coppers, used for over 100 years to boil ale, stout and porter with hops. The company boasts London's last remaining cooperage, where wooden barrels used to be made and are still repaired, and its own stable of dray horses to deliver the beer — in the traditional manner as is evinced by the scenes of Young's brewery in the 19th century (***Right***). Young's runs full tours of its Ram Brewery and stables and is well worth a visit. Address: Young's Brewery, Ram Street, Wandsworth SW18 4JD. Telephone: 0181 875 7000.*

See how beer is made at Britain's oldest brewery
THE RAM BREWERY WANDSWORTH
EST. 1831
YOUNG'S

Above: *The Turk's Head in Exeter. Established in medieval times when Exeter was a thriving cathedral city, this ancient public house is where Charles Dickens observed and immortalised his 'Fat Boy', Mr Wardle's servant in* The Pickwick Papers.

Below: *Samples of the range of Young's bottled beers, including the Double Chocolate Stout, produced from three varieties of malt — including chocolate malt — as well as roasted barley, a special blend of sugars, and Fuggles and Goldings hops. Melted chocolate bars are added to the boil and chocolate essence is introduced after filtration.*

Brewery: Bass Brewers

Address: 137 High Street
Burton-on-Trent
Staffordshire
DE14 1JZ
England

Telephone: 01283 511000

Bass is one of the UK's big three brewers, producing a wide selection of beers ranging from Tennent's lagers to Draught Bass. Over the years Bass has merged with many brewers to form the huge combine it is today, from the big names—such as the other famous Burton brewery, Worthington, in the 1920s or the the merger with Charrington United Breweries—to the small, such as the Younger Brewery of Alloa, Scotland.

Emblazoned on the bottle of Bass's wonderful bitter is a red triangle, which announces another claim to fame: it was Britain's first registered trademark on its pale ale; the second was the red diamond on the front of Bass' No. 1, a barley wine.

Bass pale ales are directly descended from the original pales made for the colonial market. The draught Bass is made at Burton from a single barley malt, using Challenger and Northdown hops and two strains of yeast to give a complex taste and aroma. At 4.4% AbV, it may not be the strongest beer on the market, but there is no doubting its quality and taste, particularly if drunk in the British way (not too cold!).

In Birmingham, Cape Hill produce the best-known bottled Pale Ale: Worthington White Shield, 5.6% AbV—dry, hoppy and fruity with a slight smokiness, it is one of the few bottle-conditioned ales in Britain.

Brewery: Whitbread Beer Company

Address: Porter Tun House
Capability Green
Luton
Bedfordshire
LU1 3LS
England

Telephone: 0582 391166

Whitbread is one of Britain's largest brewery groups, with a number of famous brands under its wing. Its origins are respectably ancient: Samuel Whitbread, a small London brewer, made his name and fortune by switching production to porter. By 1760 he had built the famous Porter Tun Room in his Chiswell Street premises and vast vats to contain the maturing beer.

Now without a London plant (in 1992 when it wanted to celebrate its 250th anniversary the commemorative porter was brewed in Castle Eden, Co. Durham), Whitbread produces Mackeson, Gold Label, and the beer highlighted here — the, as the advertising slogan would have it, 'cream of Manchester'.

Boddingtons certainly is Mancunian — it's Manchester's oldest brewery, dating back to 1778. It is very close to the city center and was extensively damaged during the Second World War, undergoing a huge reconstruction and modernization program afterwards. The word 'creamy' also reflects its draft well — particularly in cans where the revolutionary 'widget' gives a very creamy drink. Boddingtons also makes produces a Mild—dark and medium sweet — and a Best Mild which is stronger. Its bottled beers include Boddington Light—a light dinner ale almost like a lager in character, a Strong Ale and, Boddington Nut Brown — a sweet brown ale — and Boddington Extra Stout.

Brewery: The Freedom Brewing Co Ltd

Address: The Coachworks
80 Parson's Green Lane
Fulham
London SW6 4HU
England

Telephone: 0171 731 7372

The Freedom Brewing Company, the UK's first and only lager microbrewery, may only have been founded in 1995 but the hand-crafted beer it produces, Freedom Premium Pilsener (5% AbV), is consistently rated the best bottled lager brewed in the UK.

Freedom is a magical combination of Bavarian yeast, Czech and American hops, and English malt. The centuries-old strain of yeast, brought by hand from the Spaten Brauerei, is bottom-fermenting. The hops used are a blend of Liberty hops from North West America — an aromatic variety which shares the prized characteristics of the renowned Hallertauer Hersbrücker and yet also enjoys a distinctively individual fragrance — and the world famous Saaz hops from the Czech Republic. The malted barley, Maris Otter from East Anglia, is floor-malted in the traditional manner and is justifiably acknowledged throughout the brewing world as one of the finest quality malts available today.

Using these outstanding ingredients, Freedom is brewed with ten days' chilled fermentation followed by four to six weeks' lagering at -2°C (which is unique in the UK), in accordance with the strict demands of the Reinheitsgebot (the German Purity Beer Law of 1516). To retain its distinctive contemporary taste Freedom is not pasteurized and the brewery prides itself on delivering to its clients immediately after filtration and bottling.

Brewery: Marston, Thompson, and Evershead

Address: Shobnall Road
Burton-upon-Trent
Staffordshire
England

Telephone: 01283 531131

John Marston built his brewery in Burton on Trent in 1834. It was the height of the pale ale revolution that saw lighter, hoppy beers replace dark porters and stouts in popularity, and the center of British brewing switch from London to Burton.

The small East Midlands town, famous for its beers since the early middle ages, has remarkable water in the wells and springs that dot the Trent Valley — rich in gypsum and magnesium salts that give a crisp sparkle to pale ales, intensify hop bitterness, and encourage a powerful fermentation.

Marston's today remains a potent link with the heyday of British brewing. It is still the only brewery in Burton — indeed, the only brewery in the world — using the 'union room" method of fermentation in a linked series of oak casks. It is this that gives Marston's Pedigree, the flagship brew, its complex and subtle characteristics.

Pedigree, a 4.5% AbV bitter, is the traditional quaffing ale, a golden pale ale, with a delicate balance of malt and a full but not astringent flavor, Pedigree has a dry hop aroma, but with a full range of all the complex flavors associated with Burton — dryness, drinkability, and just a hint of sulphur character. It is one of Marston's three main brands — the others are Marston's Bitter and Owd Rodger.

Brewery: Scottish and Newcastle Breweries

Address: Tyne Brewery
Gallowgate
Newcastle upon Tyne NE99 1RA
England

Telephone: 0191 232 5091

Newcastle Brown is the biggest-selling bottled ale within Britain, and is exported in bottles worldwide. It is a brown ale, a type originally produced as a rival for the paler ales which originated in and around the East Midlands of central England. It is brewed by one of the great breweries of northeastern England — Scottish and Newcastle Beweries, formed in 1960 when Newcastle Breweries merged with the McEwan's and Younger's from across the border in Scotland. The resulting brewing giant is one of the largest and most influential drinks groups in Britain.

First brewed by Colonel Porter in the 1920s, Newcastle Brown was launched in 1927. It is a blend of two beers specifically made for it — one dark brown, the other a pale amber — and a complex combination of four different kinds of hops. To this are added crystal malts and caramel. The end result is a very distinctive, dark browny-red, smooth, sweet, fairly strong (4.7% AbV) malty brew that gained instant popularity. Today, Newcastle Brown is a fundamental part of Tyneside's characteristic ambience — particularly since its logo has been emblazoned in sponsorship on the shirts of Premiership football team Newcastle United.

Brewery: Wychwood Brewery Ltd

Address: The Eagle Maltings
The Croftts
Witney
Oxfordshire
OX8 7AZ
England

Telephone: 01993 702574

Available since December 1995, Wychwood Brewery's Hobgoblin (AbV 5.5%) is described by the brewers as 'a powerful, full-bodied, copper-red, well balanced brew, with a moderate hoppy, bitterness'. It is splendidly packaged and marketed and shows how small independents can gain international sales.

The Wychwood Brewery is based in the Cotswolds, at Witney in Oxfordshire and uses traditional methods—English malt, hops, yeast, and water from the local Windrush river—to produce its range of ales which includes the interestingly ebullient "Dog's Bollocks," Old Devil, Black Wych Stout, Fiddler's Elbow and Wychwood Special.

The brewery takes its name from the ancient Wychwood forest that surrounded Witney in medieval times. Clinch and Co. had started the Eagle Brewery on the site in 1839 but beer was not brewed there following Courage's 1962 takeover. In 1983 Paddy Glenny started to brew there again and since then expansion has been substantial, thanks in part to Government legislation allowing pubs belonging to big breweries to guest ales. Starting out as just a two-man operation producing 10 barrels a week, Wychwood now produces 200 barrels a week and can now be enjoyed throughout Europe, North America, and Canada.

Above Right and Right: *Fuller's is another of London's breweries and the producers of two fine beers — London Pride and ESB — brewed at the Fuller Smith and Turner Griffin Brewery, Chiswick Lane South, London W4 2QB. These two photographs from the Fuller's archives show brewery employees with the tools of their trade and an early Foden steam wagon. It was wagons like this that heralded the end of the dray-horse era.*

PART 5: AN ENGLISH CHRONOLOGY

25 Chronology

300,000-8000 BC Palaeolithic or Old Stone Age
8000-2700 BC Mesolithic or Middle Stone Age
2700-1900 BC Neolithic or New Stone Age
c. 2500 BC-1600 BC Early and Middle Bronze Ages
c. 2200 BC-1300 BC Stonehenge built
2000 BC-1600 BC Avebury Stones erected
c. 2000 BC Immigration of Beaker Folk
c. 1600 BC-AD 43 Iron Age
c. 1000 BC First hill forts built
c. 800 BC Immigration of Celts
100 BC Immigration of Belgae
55 BC Julius Caesar's first expedition to Britain
50 BC Cassivellaunus, British chieftain

AD
43 Roman invasion
c. 50 Foundation of London
61 Rebellion of Iceni under Boudicca
70-84 Conquest of Wales and north
122 Hadrian's Wall begun
197 Barbarians overrun Hadrian's Wall
c. 208 Hadrian's wall rebuilt by Septimus Severus
306 Constantine the Great proclaimed Emperor at York
407 Constantine the Third proclaimed Emperor in Britian
409 Last Roman legions leave
c. 450 Contact between Rome and Britain severed
c. 450 Hengist and Horsa settle in Kent
c. 455 Hengist rebels against Vortigern
c. 470 Saxons settle in Susex
c. 495 Saxons settle in Wessex
c. 672 Rise of Mercia
757 Offa becomes King of Mercia
c. 793 First Viking raids on Britian
829 Northumbrians submit to Egbert, King of West Saxons
867 Northumbria falls to Danes
871 Accession of King Alfred
878 Alfred defeats Danes
886 Danelaw established in Northern England
973 Edgar acknowledged as their overlord by British princes
991 Danegeld first levied
1016 Cnut chosen as King
1042 Edward the Confessor becomes King
1066 Battle of Hastings
1066 William I crowned in Westminster Abbey
1071 Herweward the Wake holds Isle of Ely against William
1078-1088 Tower of London built

Previous Page: *London's North Bank showing the imposing St. Paul's Cathedral.*

Left: *Boudicca, or Boadicea, Queen of the Iceni, a statue near the Houses of Parliament. She died, legend has it, in 61 AD after taking poison following defeat by the Romans. Her grave is said to be under platform 10 of King's Cross station where the battle took place.*

Right: *William I (1027-1087), known as the 'Bastard' or 'Conqueror'. This statue is in Falaise, Normandy. He is buried at St. Stephen's church, Caen.*

Left: *Statue of Richard I (1157-99) 'Coeur de Lion', or 'Lionheart', outside the Houses of Parliament. The Plantagenet king is buried in Fontevrault Abbey, Anjou.*

Right: *Statue of Charles I (1600-49) in Westminster. The only English sovereign to be executed, Charles I's body is interred in St. George's chapel, Windsor castle.*

1086 Domesday survey
1087 Accession of William II
1100 Accession of Henry I
1135 Accession of Stephen
1139 Canonisation of Edward the Confessor
1139-1153 Civil war
1141 Stephen captured
1152 Henry of Anjou (Henry II) marries Eleanour of Aquitaine
1153 Henry of Anjou invades England
1154 Accession of Henry II
1162 Thomas à Becket Archbishop of Canterbury
1170 Becket murdered
1173 William the Lion, King of Scotland invades north of England; Becket canonised
1189 Accession of Richard I
1193 Richard I imprisoned in Germany
1195-1199 Richard I engaged in warfare in France
1199 Accession of King John
1209 King John excommunicated
1214 Battle of Bouvines, King Philip II Augustus of France defeats King John
1215 Civil war in England; King John obliged to sign the *Magna Carta*
1216 French army lands in Kent
1216 Accession of Henry III
1249 University College, Oxford founded
1259 Treaty of Paris between France and England
1264 Battle of Lewes: Henry III captured
1265 Battle of Evesham
1272 Accession of Edward I
1281 Peterhouse, Cambridge founded
1282-1283 Edward's conquest of Wales
1295 Meeting of Model Parliament
1296 Edward invades Scotland
1296 Edward I takes Stone of Scone to Westminster
1306 Rebellion of Robert Bruce
1307 Accession of Edward II
1314 Battle of Bannockburn
1321-1322 Civil War
1327 Accession of Edward III
1337 Start of Hundred Years War
1340 Battle of Sluys
1346 Battles of Crecy and Neville's Cross
1347 Calais captured
1348 Black Death
1356 Battle of Poitiers
1362 English language used for the opening of Parliament
1370 Black Prince sacks Limoges
1376 Death of the Black Prince
1377 Accession of Richard II

EDWARDVS VII
REX IMPERATOR

1381 Peasant's Revolt
1387-1400 Chaucer's *Canterbury Tales*
1399 Accession of Henry IV
1400 Rebellion of Owain Glyndwr
1413 Accession of Henry V
1415 Battle of Agincourt
1420 Henry V marries Catherine of Valois
1422 Accession of Henry VI
1440 Eton College founded
1445 Henry VI marries Margaret of Anjou
1453 End of the Hundred Years War
1455 Outbreak of the Wars of the Roses
1459 Defeat of the Duke of York
1461 Accession of Edward IV
1471 Edward IV defeats Earl of Warwick at Tewkesbury
1471 Death of Henry VI
1474 William Caxton prints first book in English
1483 Death of Edward IV. Accession of Richard III
1485 Battle of Bosworth Field
1485 Accession of Henry VII
1509 Accession of Henry VIII
1513 Battle of Flodden
1533 Henry VIII marries Anne Boleyn
1534 Act of Supremacy
1542 Battle of Solway
1547 Accession of Edward VI
1553 Accession of Mary
1558 Accession of Elizabeth I
1568 Mary Stuart arrives in England
1570 Royal Exchange opened
1570 Elizabeth excommunicated
1587 Mary Stuart executed
1588 Spanish Armada defeated
1600 East India Company founded
1603 Accession of James I (VI of Scotland)
1605 Gunpowder Plot
1609 Rebellion in Ireland
1611 James's First Parliament dissolved
1620 Pilgrim Fathers emigrate to New England
1624-1630 War with Spain
1625 Accession of Charles I
1626-1629 War with France
1629 Parliament dissolved by Charles I
1640 Long Parliament called
1642 Outbreak of Civil War
1642 Battle of Edgehill
1644 Battle of Marston Moor
1645 Battle of Naseby
1648 Battle of Preston
1649 Charles I executed

Left: *Edward VII (1841-1910) was the eldest son of Queen Victoria and was 59 when he came to the throne. He is buried in St. George's chapel, Windsor castle.*

Right: *George V (1865-1936) is also buried in St. George's chapel, Windsor castle, in a tomb designed by Lutyens. Created Prince of Wales in 1901, he succeeded his father to the throne in 1910.*

1649-1650 Cromwell conquers Ireland
1650-1652 Cromwell conquers Scotland
1651 Battle of Worcester
1652 First Anglo-Dutch war
1653 Cromwell becomes Lord Protector
1658 Richard Cromwell succeeds his father
1659 Richard Cromwell overthrown by army
1660 Restoration of the Monarchy: Accession of Charles II
1664-1665 Great Plague
1666 Great Fire of London
1667 Arrival of the Dutch in the Medway
1674 End of the War against the Dutch
1685 Accession of James II
1688 Glorious Revolution
1689 Accession of William III and Mary II
1694 Bank of England established
1701 War of Spanish Succession begins
1702 Accession of Anne
1704 Battle of Blenheim
1707 Union of England and Scotland
1710 St Paul's Cathedral completed

1714 Accession of George I
1715 Jacobite rebellion
1720 South Sea Bubble
1727 Accession of George II
1745 Jacobite rebellion of 'Bonny Prince Charlie'
1753 British Museum founded
1756 Seven Years War begins
1757 Battle of Plessey
1759 Quebec captured
1760 Accession of George III
1763 Peace of Paris to end Seven Years War
1768 Royal Academy founded with Sir Joshua Reynolds as its first President
1773 Boston Tea Party
1776 American Declaration of Independence
1780 Gordon Riots
1781 Surrender at Yorktown
1783 Americans win independence
1803 War with France
1805 Battle of Trafalgar
1815 Battle of Waterloo
1820 Accession of George IV
1824 National Gallery founded
1832 Great Reform Bill
1833 Slavery abolished in the British Empire
1837 Accession of Queen Victoria
1851 Great Exhibition
1854 Crimean War
1860 Barry's Houses of Parliament completed
1876 Queen Victoria becomes Empress of India
1880 First Boer War
1899 Second Boer War
1901 Accession of Edward VII
1914-1918 First World War
1916 Battles of Somme and Jutland
1917 Battle of Passchendaele
1919 Treaty of Versailles
1924 First Labour Government
1926 General Strike
1929 Votes for women over twenty-one
1939-1945 Second World War
1940 Battle of Britain
1940 Dunkirk evacuation
1942 Battle of El Alamein
1944 D-Day invasion of France
1945 Labour government under Atlee
1951 Festival of Britain
1956 Invasion of Suez
1973 Joined European Common Market
1982 Falklands War
1991 Gulf War

Right: *The Queen's arms.*

Left: *Much of the pagentry of London is tied in to the protection of the monarch and government.*